# Five Chekhov Plays

# Five Chekhov Plays

New Versions
by Libby Appel

*From Literal Translations
by Allison Horsley*

Commissioned by the Oregon Shakespeare Festival

Copyright of new translations © 2013 Libby Appel. All rights reserved. No part of this book may be used or reproduced in any manner whatsoever without permission except in case of brief quotations embodied in critical articles and reviews.

Caution: Professionals and amateurs are hereby warned that the plays in this volume are fully protected under the copyright laws of the United States of America, The British Empire, The Dominion of Canada, and are thereby subject to royalty arrangements. All performance rights, including professional, amateur, motion picture, recitation, lecturing, public reading, and radio and television broadcasting, and the rights of translation into foreign languages, are strictly reserved. Permission for performances and readings must be addressed to fivechekhovplays@gmail.com.

Cover photo by Jenny Graham courtesy of the Oregon Shakespeare Festival. Tasso Feldman as Konstantin Treplyov in Chekhov's *Seagull*. Directed by Libby Appel at the Oregon Shakespeare Festival in 2012.

Back cover photo by David Cooper Photography

Cover and interior design by C Book Services

Printed in the United States of America

15 16 17 18    10 9 8 7 6 5 4

ISBN: 978-0-615-87430-2

*Special thanks to Susan Whitmore, Michael Barakiva, Larissa Kokernot, Douglas Langworthy, Dr. Alexander Zaslavsky, Dr. Luc Beaudoin, and Lue Douthit.*

# Contents

Ivanov ✦ 1

Seagull ✦ 83

Uncle Vanya ✦ 157

Three Sisters ✦ 227

The Cherry Orchard ✦ 321

# *Translating Chekhov*

I discovered Anton Chekhov's plays at age 16 when an English teacher in my junior year of high school class assigned us *The Cherry Orchard* to read. It was a revelation for me from the first moment I picked it up. I still have difficulty understanding how a teenage girl could fall so madly in love with a play about loss, memory and grief, but fall in love I did. And this was the start of a life-long passion with all of Chekhov's works.

I studied all the biographies and critical discussions I could find about Chekhov's life and works, literally feeling his presence in my life. I developed a reputation for being the three sisters—all of them at one time. When I discovered that my penchant in the theater was for directing, I made it my business to direct all of the plays, several times, including a few of the one-act farces. I have been reading the stories all of my life and have taught Chekhov works in my acting and theater classes.

Thus it seemed a natural progression when I had the opportunity to link up with a literal Russian to English translator, Allison Horsley, and begin my journey as a translator/adaptor of Chekhov's plays. My first venture was *The Cherry Orchard*—which seems an obvious choice as it rests in my heart as my first love. Allison and I worked very harmoniously to produce the working draft which I then took into rehearsal and directed with a superb cast of actors at the Oregon Shakespeare Festival.

From that first translation, I felt compelled to continue with all the major plays. Fortunately, the new artistic director at Oregon Shakespeare Festival, Bill Rauch, agreed that something special was happening with these translations and he commissioned me and Allison to continue on with as many plays as we had the desire to do.

When there are so many translations available in American English, what makes our work so special? Well, I believe a lifetime of studying and interpreting and "living with" A.P. Chekhov has made his works an essential part of my being. I feel I understand the plays deep in my soul. I think these translations have a freshness of approach (I am a great believer in the idea that as the language changes in our lives, new translations need to be developed every few years) and they are a merging of Chekhov's late 19th and early 20th centuries' language with a contemporary 21st century idiom. Each play is undoubtedly Chekhov's but the translations put you into your own life at the present moment.

I feel that I have found that elegance and sparseness of language and the subtle yet profound, buried passions of the characters that is Chekhov's signature. The translations keep the Russian names as Chekhov wrote them. They also include some Russian words to give us the rich flavor of the period, place and time while retaining the truth of the characters in our own time.

The starting point for these translations is absolutely a labor of love.

–Libby Appel

# *The Variants*

A distinctive trademark of our new versions of Chekhov's plays is our inclusion of certain variants that have rarely been incorporated into American translations of Chekhov's work. Chekhov, like all Russian playwrights of the period, experienced government censorship of his manuscripts in which politically or socially controversial lines and ideas were required to be cut or changed. Additionally, amiable but forceful suggestions came from his collaborators and director at the Moscow Art Theatre, Konstantin Stanislavski. Perhaps Chekhov himself made some of the changes of his own volition, but we can never know just how much Chekhov approved of the changes in the text. Fortunately, these early cuts and additions were preserved and published in a Soviet-era Chekhov collection I used to create my literal translations. Libby then selected the variants she felt would be most compatible with our adaptations and included them in the text.

You will note that in *The Cherry Orchard* a whole scene has been added with Charlotta and Firs at the end of the 2nd act. Charlotta's monologue about her life has been moved from the first scene in that act to the scene with Firs. There are other lines added to *Uncle Vanya* and *Three Sisters*. In *Seagull* there are several changes including additions to Polina's speech about her husband in Act 2 and a scene between Polina and Dorn near the end of Act 4.

We believe these additional variants add richness to the characters and the plays. They have been used very judiciously as we wish to be true to Chekhov's intentions in every way possible. But we are sure that added to the American flow and rhetoric of the language, the variants make our translations completely unique.

–Allison Horsley

# *Ivanov*

## A Comedy in Four Acts

### (1887)

# CHARACTERS

**Nikolai Alekseyevich Ivanov,** a permanent member of the rural Committee for Peasant Affairs.

**Anna Petrovna,** his wife, née Sarra [Sarah] Abramson.

**Matvei Semyonovich Shabelsky,** a Count, his maternal uncle.

**Pavel Kirillych Lebedev,** chair of the zemstvo (county council).

**Zinaida Savishna,** his wife.

**Sasha,** the Lebedevs' daughter, 20 years old.

**Yevgenii Konstantinovich Lvov,** a local doctor.

**Marfa Yegorovna Babakina,** a young widow, landowner, daughter of a wealthy merchant.

**Dmitrii Nikitich Kosykh,** a tax man.

**Mikhail Mikhailovich Borkin,** a distant relative of IVANOV'S and steward of his estate.

**Avdotya Nazarovna,** an old woman.

**Yegorushka,** a boarder.

**First Guest.**
**Second Guest.**
**Third Guest.**
**Fourth Guest.**

**Pyotr,** Ivanov's footman.

**Gavrila,** the Lebedevs' footman.

**Guests of both genders, footmen.**

*The action takes place in one of the counties of the central region of Russia.*

# ACT I

*A garden on IVANOV's estate. On the left is the façade of the house with a terrace. One window is open. In front of the terrace is a wide semicircular area, from which there is a garden, and to the right are paths. On the right side are little garden divans and little tables. On one of the latter a lamp burns. Night is falling. At rise can be heard a piano and cello practicing a duet.*

*IVANOV sits at the table and reads a book. BORKIN in large boots, with a gun, appears in the depths of the garden; he is tipsy; seeing IVANOV, he goes to him on tiptoes and, coming up alongside him, takes aim at his face.*

IVANOV: *(Seeing BORKIN, shudders and leaps up)* Oh for God's sake. You scared me, Misha... I'm a mess these days, but you never stop with your stupid little jokes... *(He sits)* Oh sure, scaring me to death is your favorite sport...

BORKIN: *(He laughs)* I give up. *(Puts his hands in the air)* I did it. But I promise, no more, no more... *(He sits next to him and takes off his peaked cap)* It's hot. Take it from me, my darling, I covered eleven miles in about three hours... I'm exhausted. Put your hand on my heart. Feel how fast it's pounding.

IVANOV: *(Reading)* Later, please...

BORKIN: No, feel it. Feel it now. *(He takes IVANOV'S hand and puts it on his chest)* Hear it? Tu-tu-tu-tu-tu-tu. I must be having a heart attack. I'm going to die any minute. Will you be sorry if I die?

IVANOV: I'm reading... later...

BORKIN: No, seriously, will you be sorry if I die? Come on, Nikolai Alekseyevich, will you be sorry if I die?

IVANOV: Cut it out!

BORKIN: My darling, tell me: will you be sorry?

IVANOV: I am sorry that you stink of vodka. Disgusting!

BORKIN: *(He laughs)* Do I really stink? Shocking! Actually, not so shocking. In Plesniki I met a prosecutor, and we knocked back eight glasses. I know, I know — drinking is really bad for you. Don't you think — bad, bad, BAD. Bad?

IVANOV: Will you please stop it! I can't take any more of this…

BORKIN: Yes, yes… I did it. I give up. Take it easy, calm down… *(He stands and walks)* Amazing, you're not even allowed to say anything anymore… It's even forbidden to talk. *(He returns)* Oh, yes, I almost forgot… Eighty-two rubles please!…

IVANOV: What eighty-two rubles?

BORKIN: To pay the workmen tomorrow.

IVANOV: I don't have any money.

BORKIN: I am your most obedient servant. *(Bowing)* "I don't have any money." You do know the workmen have to be paid? Yes? Yes?

IVANOV: I don't know anything. I don't have any money. Wait until the first of the month, when I get paid.

BORKIN: It's so nice to talk with people like you. The workmen will come for their money tomorrow — not the first of the month!

IVANOV: So what am I supposed to do? Kill me… You are such an obnoxious pest. I'm trying to read…

BORKIN: Now tell me, do the workers need to be paid or not? I can't even talk to you!… *(He waves his hand)* You're all alike — to hell with "country gentlemen…" All your "scientific agriculture"… three thousand acres of land — and not a *kopek* in your pocket... a gorgeous bottle of wine, but no corkscrew... Okay, so I'll sell the *troika* tomorrow! Sure!... I sold the oats before they were ready, and tomorrow I'll sell the rye. *(He paces around the stage)* Do you think I won't? Dare me — I dare you — Dare me!

*The voice of SHABELSKY from the window: "It's impossible to play with you... your ear is worse than a stuffed pike and your touch is disgraceful."*

ANNA PETROVNA: *(Appearing at the open window)* Who said that just now? Is that you, Misha? Why are you stomping up and down like that?

BORKIN: Believe me, you'd be stomping too.

ANNA PETROVNA: Please, Misha, we need the hay on the croquet lawn.

BORKIN: *(Waves his hand)* Shut up, please.

ANNA PETROVNA: Why do you speak to me like that — it's not like you... If you want to attract women, don't get so angry and stop showing off. *(To her husband)* Nikolai, let's play in the hay!

IVANOV: Don't stand in the open window, Anyuta. It's not good for you. Go, please... *(He shouts)* Uncle, close the window!

*The window is closed.*

BORKIN: Don't forget, in two days the Lebedev interest payment is due.

IVANOV: I won't. Today I'll be at the Lebedevs and I'll ask him for more time... *(He looks at his watch)*

BORKIN: When are you going there?

IVANOV: Now.

BORKIN: *(Quickly)* Stop. Wait a minute! I almost forgot, today is Shurochka's birthday... Te-te-te-te... What a crazy head I have! I completely forgot. *(He bows)* I'm going, I'm going... *(He sings)* I'm going... I'll go for a swim, do something about this breath, take something for this hangover, and then — I'll be as fresh as a baby. My darling friend, Nikolai Alekseyevich, my *mamusya*, my angel, you're always cranky — honestly, honestly — you moan and groan — constantly in a *merlekhlundiya*. But God only knows how much trouble we could get into together — FUN! I'm ready for anything... Do you want me to marry Marfusha Babakina for you? Half the dowry is yours... hell, take all of it — all!

IVANOV: Shut up...

BORKIN: No, seriously, do you want me to marry Marfusha? Half the dowry... But why am I talking to you? You'll never get it, will you... *(He mocks)* "Shut up." You're a good man, yes, very intelligent, but you don't have any drive — no ambition. You're a lunatic, a cry-baby, but if you had a little *vzmakha*, in a year you'd be a millionaire. For example, if I had twenty-three hundred rubles right now, in two weeks I'd have twenty thousand. True? I know, I know, you think I'm just talking nonsense. Okay, give me twenty-three hundred rubles, and in a week I'll give you twenty thousand. Over there, Ovsyanov is selling a strip of land, right there, for twenty-three hundred rubles. Just buy that land, then we'll own both sides of the river. And if we own both sides, then, don't you get it, we'll be able to dam the river. Get it? We'll build a mill, and then we'll announce to everyone downstream of the dam, *kommen sie hier* — If you don't want the dam, then pay the price. Get it? The Zarev factory will give us five thousand, Korolkov three thousand, the monastery will give five thousand...

IVANOV: Misha, it's a con game... If you don't want to fight with me, then shut up.

BORKIN: *(He takes a seat at the table)* Of course!... I knew it!... You won't do anything, and you tie my hands...

SHABELSKY: *(Entering with DR. LVOV from the house)* Doctors — the same as lawyers, and the only difference between you is lawyers steal, and doctors steal and murder... Present company excepted, of course. *(He takes a seat on the little divan)* Charlatans, con men... Maybe, somewhere in Utopia you can find an exception to that rule, but... I've shelled out over twenty thousand for treatments and I've never met one doctor who wasn't a complete swindler.

BORKIN: *(To IVANOV)* Sure, you won't budge an inch and you tie my hands. That's why we're always broke...

SHABELSKY: Present company excepted of course... Maybe there are exceptions here or there, but... *(He yawns)*

IVANOV: *(Closes the book)* Yes, doctor?

LVOV: *(Looking around in the window)* As I said this morning, she needs to go to the Crimea immediately. *(He enters)*

SHABELSKY: *(Bursts out laughing)* To the Crimea! Why aren't we doctors, Misha? It's that simple... Camille or Ophelia has a tickle in her throat or coughs out of boredom, the course of action: Get a young doctor, take a trip to the Crimea, in Crimea meet a young Crimean...

IVANOV: *(To the COUNT)* Akh, stop blabbering! *(To LVOV)* To go to the Crimea, we need money. Even if I could find some, she would definitely refuse to go...

LVOV: Yes, she would.

   Pause.

BORKIN: Listen, doctor, is Anna Petrovna really so sick, she has to go to the Crimea?

LVOV: *(Looking around to the window)* Yes, it's tuberculosis...

BORKIN: Psssss!... Not good... I've seen it myself — she won't last long.

LVOV: Please speak quietly. They can hear you...

*Pause.*

BORKIN: *(Sighing)* Life is like a flower, splendidly growing in a field; along comes a goat, eats it and — no more flower...

SHABELSKY: Nonsense, nonsense, and nonsense!... *(He yawns)* Nonsense and robbery.

*Pause.*

BORKIN: And I, gentlemen, am always telling Nikolai Alekseyevich he has to make money. I gave him a brilliant idea, but as usual, he won't listen to a word I say. Just look at him: the picture of melancholy — sad, irritable, depressed, unbearably sad, sad, sad.

SHABELSKY: *(He stands and stretches)* You've got an answer for everyone, don't you — everyone but me... Alright, tell me something, smart guy. Go ahead...

BORKIN: *(He stands)* I'm going for a swim. Farewell, gentlemen... *(To the COUNT)* You might think there are always a million ways to go... but if I were you, I'd have twenty thousand in a week. *(He starts to leave)*

SHABELSKY: *(Goes after him)* Oh sure, how? Come on, tell me...

BORKIN: There's nothing to tell. It's very simple... *(He returns)* Nikolai Alekseyevich, give me a ruble!

*IVANOV silently gives him a ruble.*

Merci! *(To the COUNT)* You still have a fistful of aces in your hand.

SHABELSKY: *(Going after him)* Yes, and?

BORKIN:  If I were you, I'd have twenty thousand in a week — maybe more. *(He exits with the COUNT)*

IVANOV:  *(After a pause)* Losers — with nothing to say, who never stop talking — they all exhaust me, make me sick, Doctor. I know I get so irritated, angry, nasty — so petty. I don't even know who I am these days. I walk around with a terrible headache, I never sleep, I hear ringing in my ears… Where can I go? Nowhere… I'm stuck… Positively stuck…

LVOV:  Nikolai Alekseyevich, I need to talk with you — seriously.

IVANOV:  Talk.

LVOV:  It's about Anna Petrovna. *(He sits)* She refuses to go to the Crimea, but she would if you went with her.

IVANOV:  *(Thinking)* For us to go, we'd need money. And I can't get a leave of absence. This year I've already taken a lot of time…

LVOV:  Even if this is true, you must hear me out. The most important treatment for tuberculosis is absolute peace, but your wife doesn't have a moment of peace. She's always upset because you ignore her. Please forgive me, but I'm very disturbed and I have to speak frankly. Your behavior is killing her.

  *Pause.*

Nikolai Alekseyevich, I want to think better of you!…

IVANOV:  True… true… true… Yes, probably, I'm awfully guilty, but I'm so confused these days, I'm exhausted all the time and I do nothing — I can barely move. I don't understand anyone — I don't understand me! *(He looks in the window)* They can hear us, let's go, let's go for a walk.

  *They stand.*

I'd love to tell you everything, dear Doctor — but there's so much going on inside me, I couldn't finish until tomorrow.

*They walk.*

Anyuta is a splendid, special woman… For my sake she sacrificed her faith, deserted her father and mother, left behind her family fortune, and if I wanted a hundred other sacrifices, she would gladly make them, without batting an eye. Well sir, as you can see, I'm in no way splendid or special, and I have never sacrificed anything. Sorry, this is too long a story… The whole point is, dear Doctor — *(he thinks)* to make a long story short, I married for love… for passion, and I swore I'd love her eternally… Well, five years later, she still loves me, but I… *(He spreads his hands in a gesture of hopelessness)* You're saying to me now that she will die soon, but I don't feel love, or pity. I just feel empty, tired. I know this sounds horrible — probably… In truth I don't understand what is happening to me…

*He exits.*

*SHABELSKY and ANNA PETROVNA enter.*

SHABELSKY: *(He laughs loudly)* Honest to God, Borkin is not a con man, he's a genius! They ought to build a monument to him. All by himself he has a million disgusting professions: shyster, quack, and moneygrubber. *(He takes a seat on the lower step of the terrace)* He has no education, but he's brilliant. Can you imagine how much he would steal if he had any college degrees, any culture? He says he'll get me twenty thousand in a week. He says I have an ace up my sleeve, I'm a Count! Any rich woman would give you everything so long as she could be a Countess. *(He laughs loudly)*

*ANNA PETROVNA opens the window and looks down.*

He says, "You want me to fix you up with Marfusha?" *Qui est ce que c'est* Marfusha? Ah yes, it's Marfusha Balabakina… Babakakina… she's the one who looks like a washer woman.

ANNA PETROVNA: Count?

SHABELSKY: Yes?

ANNA PETROVNA *laughs.*

*(In a Yiddish accent)* What's so funny, dollink.

ANNA PETROVNA: I'm trying to remember that funny story you told us at lunch. The one about the horse thief... How does it go?

SHABELSKY: Why does a baptized Jew and a gelded horse cost the same?

ANNA PETROVNA: *(She laughs)* You can't tell a joke without being cruel. You are such a wicked man. *(Seriously)* I mean it, Count, you are truly wicked. It's really hard to live with you, you make me depressed. You're always complaining and your friends are terrible scoundrels. Honestly, Count, have you ever spoken well of someone else?

SHABELSKY: Am I being interrogated?

ANNA PETROVNA: We have lived under the same roof for five years, and I have never heard you say anything nice about anyone — you always make fun of everybody. What's so bad about other people? Do you really think you're better than everyone?

SHABELSKY: I don't think that at all. I'm just a bad as everyone else — we're all bastards. *Mauvais ton.* I'm just as hard on myself. Who am I? What am I? Once I was rich, free, even happy, but now... I'm a parasite, a hanger-on, a nobody. I'm an idiot, a clown. I think I'm better than everyone else, but nobody takes that seriously. When I laugh at people, they smile and nod their heads, "the old guy is off his rocker." But most of the time, no one even listens to me...

ANNA PETROVNA: *(Quietly)* He's howling again...

SHABELSKY: Who's howling?

ANNA PETROVNA: The owl. Every night he's howling.

SHABELSKY: So let him howl. Things can't get any worse around here. *(He stretches)* Ekh, my sweet Sarra, if I could just win the lottery — a hundred or two hundred thousand, I would really show you something. I'd be out of here in a flash. I'd just walk away from all of you — from your charity — and never set foot here again until the end of the world itself...

ANNA PETROVNA: And if you won, what would you do?

SHABELSKY: *(Thinking)* First of all, I'd go to Moscow and listen to gypsy music all night. Then... then I'd go to Paris. I'd rent an apartment, go to a Russian church...

ANNA PETROVNA: And what else?

SHABELSKY: I would sit at my wife's grave for hours and hours and think. Oh, I'd like to sit at her grave until I keeled over. My wife is buried in Paris...

*Pause.*

ANNA PETROVNA: This is really boring. Shall we play another duet?

SHABELSKY: Good. Get the sheet music out.

*ANNA PETROVNA exits.*

IVANOV: *(Appearing on the path with LVOV)* Even though you finished your degree a year ago, you're still cheerful, optimistic. But I'm thirty five. I have the right to tell you a thing or two. Don't marry a Jew or a neurotic or even an educated woman. Go for something else — an ordinary, plain woman — no drama. Of course, you are in charge of making your own life. The greyer the background, the better. My friend, don't go tilting at windmills, don't beat your head against the wall... And God keep you from government bureaucracies, "scientific agriculture" and fervent political passion... Just find yourself a little space and live a quiet life — believe me, it's nicer, healthier and more honest. Now, don't ask how tiresome my life is — completely finished! Don't ask how many mistakes I've made, how many injustices I've suffered, how ridiculous it all is... *(Seeing the COUNT, annoyed)* Everywhere I go, there you are, Uncle — underfoot... Can't I have a moment to myself?

SHABELSKY: *(In a weepy voice)* Oh for God's sake, there's no place for me! *(He leaps up and walks into the house)*

IVANOV: *(Shouting after him)* Yes, yes, I'm to blame, yes. *(To LVOV)* Oh, why did I offend him? No, I must be crazy. I've got to stop this —

LVOV: *(Worrying)* Nikolai Aleskeyevich, I've listened to you carefully... pardon me, I must speak candidly. Everything you say, every undertone in your voice, is so filled with heartless egotism — so callous... someone you supposedly love is dying because of your callousness, her days are literally numbered, and you... you walk around giving advice, acting like you know everything... I'm not good at expressing myself, but... but... I dislike you intensely!

IVANOV: Maybe, maybe... From your point of view, it probably all seems so clear... but, but... maybe I am to blame... *(He listens)* Ah, I think they've brought the horses. I'll go get dressed... *(He goes toward the house and comes to a stop)* I know you don't like me, Doctor — you hardly conceal the fact. And your frankness does you honor... *(He exits into the house)*

LVOV: *(Alone)* Damn him! And once again, my temper got in the way. I couldn't tell him what I needed to. I can't seem to stay patient with him. I start to say a word and I get all choked up with fury — my tongue gets stuck in my mouth. I detest this hypocrite, this snobbish swindler, with all my soul... He just walks away from me... and from his unhappy wife. All she needs is for him to be in the room. She actually can't breathe without him. She begs him to stay home, be with her — but he... he cannot... Yes, he claims he's "stifled" at home — he feels "suffocated" if he spends one night there. He thinks he'll blow his brains out from depression. Oh, poor man... he needs his freedom, so that he can do everything his own way! Oh, I know why you go to the Lebedev's every night! I know!

SHABELSKY: *(Entering with IVANOV and with ANNA PETROVNA from the house)* Honestly, *Nicolas*, this is inhuman! You get to go out every night, and we're left here alone. We go to sleep every night at eight o'clock because there's nothing else to do. It's a disgrace — it's not living at all! Why is it that you get to leave, but we cannot? Why?

ANNA PETROVNA: Count, leave him alone! Let him go, let him...

IVANOV: *(To his wife)* And where do you think a sick person should go? You are ill and you cannot be out of doors after sunset... Ask the doctor here. You're not a child, Anyuta, you must see reason... *(To the COUNT)* And why are you in such a hurry to go?

SHABELSKY: I would go meet the devil in hell, sit in the teeth of a crocodile instead of staying here every night. I'm bored! I've grown dull from boredom! Everyone is sick to death of me. You make me stay at home, so she won't be bored alone, but all I do is worry her to death, torment her to death!

ANNA PETROVNA: Leave him alone, Count, leave him alone! Let him go if he'll be happier there.

IVANOV: Anya, what are you saying? You know, I don't go there for fun! I need to talk about the promissory note.

ANNA PETROVNA: I don't understand, why are you trying to justify it? Just go! Who's keeping you here?

IVANOV: Ladies and gentlemen, let's not make each other crazy! Is it really necessary!?

SHABELSKY: *(In a weepy voice)* Nicolas, my dear, well, I beg you, take me with you! I'll take a look at the con men and the idiots and maybe — just maybe — I'll have a good time. You know I haven't seen anybody since Easter!

IVANOV: *(Irritatedly)* Fine, let's go! I'm sick of all of you!

SHABELSKY: Really? *Merci, merci*... *(He happily takes him under the arm and leads him to the side)* Can I wear your straw hat?

IVANOV: You can — only quickly, please!

*The COUNT runs to the house.*

I'm sick of all of you! But, oh no, what am I saying? Anya, I'm being so rude to you. I was never like this before. Well, *do svidanya*, Anya, I'll be back by one.

ANNA PETROVNA: Kolya, my sweet, stay home!

IVANOV: *(Agitated)* My little darling, my dear one, I beg you, don't keep me from going out this evening. I know I'm not being fair, but allow me to do this. I feel so excruciatingly heavy! When it gets dark outside, my depression sets in and weighs heavy on my soul. So terrible! Don't ask me why — honestly, I don't know. I swear to God, I don't know! Depression sets in here, and when I go to the Lebedev's, it's even worse; I come home and I'm more depressed. It's like that all night long. I'm in despair!

ANNA PETROVNA: Kolya... Please stay! We'll sit and talk as we used to... We'll eat dinner together, we'll read... Mr. Grumbler and I can play many duets for you... *(She embraces him)* Stay!

*Pause.*

I don't understand you. This has been going on for a whole year already. Why have you changed?

IVANOV: I don't know, I don't know...

ANNA PETROVNA: And why don't you want me to come with you in the evening?

IVANOV: You are forcing me to say this — it's cruel, I know, but it's better to finally say it... When this depression gets to me, I... I don't love you. I have to run away from you. The truth is, I need to get out of here.

ANNA PETROVNA: Depression? I understand, I understand… Do you know what, Kolya? Try, like you used to, try to sing, to smile, even to be a little angry… Stay, we'll laugh, drink brandy, and we'll get rid of your depression in one minute. Do you want me to sing? Or we'll sit in your office, in the dark, just like we used to, and you can tell me about your depression… Your eyes are so full of suffering! I will look into them and weep, and it'll all be better for us both… *(She laughs and weeps)* Oh, Kolya, why? Flowers bloom again every spring, but joy — no? Yes? Well, go, go…

IVANOV: Pray for me, Anya! *(He goes, comes to a stop and thinks)* No, I can't! *(He exits)*

ANNA PETROVNA: Go… *(She takes a seat at the table)*

LVOV: *(He paces)* Anna Petrovna, take this as a rule: as soon as the clock strikes six o'clock, you must go indoors and not come out again until morning. Evening dampness is harmful to you.

ANNA PETROVNA: Yes sir.

LVOV: "Yes sir!" I'm speaking seriously.

ANNA PETROVNA: But I don't want to be serious. *(She coughs)*

LVOV: See, you're coughing already…

SHABELSKY: *(Enters from the house in a hat and coat)* Where's Nikolai? Did they bring the horses? *(He quickly goes and kisses ANNA PETROVNA's hand)* Good night, my precious! *(He makes a face, and says in a Yiddish accent)* Oy gevalt! Please to forgive! *(He quickly exits)*

LVOV: Clown!

*Pause; the far-off sounds of an accordion can be heard.*

ANNA PETROVNA: Excruciating boredom!... The coachman and the cook give a ball, but I... I — like Cinderella... abandoned... Yevgenii Konstantinovich, why are you pacing? Come here, sit!

LVOV: I cannot sit.

*Pause.*

ANNA PETROVNA: In the kitchen they are playing *cheezhic*. *(She sings)* "*Cheezhic, cheezhic*, fly down here. Are you drinking too much beer?"

*Pause.*

Doctor, are your parents still alive?

LVOV: My father is dead, but I still have my mother.

ANNA PETROVNA: Are you bored with your mother?

LVOV: I don't have time to be bored.

ANNA PETROVNA: *(She laughs)* Flowers bloom every spring, but joy — no. Who said that? I wish I could remember... Maybe Nikolai said it. *(Listening)* The owl is howling again!

LVOV: Well let it howl.

ANNA PETROVNA: I'm beginning to think, doctor, that I got short-changed in this life. So many people, who are just like me, are happy and they don't have to pay for their happiness. But I have paid everything, absolutely everything!... And how dearly I pay! Why should I have to pay such exorbitant interest?... My friend, you are so attentive to me, much too attentive. You're afraid to tell me the truth. Don't you think I know what is wrong with me? I know it all too well. But I'm being boring. *(In a Yiddish accent)* Please to forgive! You have funny stories to tell?

LVOV: No. None.

ANNA PETROVNA: But Nikolai has. I'm starting to be astonished by how unfair life is. Why do people return love with lies? Tell me: how long will my father and mother hate me? They live thirty miles from here, and I can still feel their hatred — night and day. And how am I supposed to understand Nikolai's misery? He tells me he doesn't love me every evening, when the depression sets in. I understand this, even accept it, but is it possible that he has stopped loving me completely? Of course, I don't think that's possible — but what if — No, no, I can't think about that. *(She sings)* "Cheezhic, cheezhic, where have you been?..." *(She shudders)* What dreadful thoughts I have!... You, Doctor, you're not a family man, and there are many things you can't understand…

LVOV: You are astonished… *(He takes a seat beside her)* No, I… I am astonished by you! Well, tell me, explain how it is that you — intelligent, honest, almost a saint — can allow yourself to be so disgustingly deceived and dragged into this hornet's nest? Why are you here? What do you have in common with this cold, heartless — but let's leave your husband out of it — what are you doing in a place like this? Oh, my God!… That eternally grumbling, crazy Count, that repulsive scoundrel, swindler of swindlers, Borkin, with his ugly body… Tell me, what are you doing here? How did you find yourself here?

ANNA PETROVNA: *(She laughs)* That is exactly the same way he used to talk… Word for word… But his eyes were bigger, and, as he began to talk about something passionately, they burned like coals… Yes, talk, talk!

LVOV: *(He stands and waves his hand)* What am I supposed to say? Go inside…

ANNA PETROVNA: You tell me that Nikolai is this way or that way. How would you know? Is it possible to know a person in six months? You'd have to be a pretty remarkable doctor! I'm just sorry that you didn't know him two or three years ago. Now he is depressed, sullen, he doesn't do anything, but before… He was so charming, fascinating… I fell in love with him at first sight. *(She laughs)* At the first glance, I was captivated — PFFT! He said, let's go… I cut myself off from everything and everyone, and I left…

*Pause.*

But now it's not the same… Now he goes to the Lebedevs', in order to have fun with other women, and I… sit in the garden and listen, as the owl howls…

*The WATCHMAN taps.*

Doctor, do you have any brothers?

LVOV: No.

*ANNA PETROVNA sobs.*

What's happening? Why are you…?

ANNA PETROVNA: *(She stands)* I can't be here, Doctor, I'm going over there…

LVOV: Where?

ANNA PETROVNA: There, where he is… I'm going… Please order the horses to be harnessed… *(She goes toward the house)*

LVOV: You are forbidden to go…

ANNA PETROVNA: Leave me alone, it's none of your business… I'm going… Tell them to bring me the horses… *(She runs into the house)*

LVOV: No, I absolutely refuse to work under these conditions! It's not enough they don't pay me a *kopek*, but I let my feelings get involved!… No, I refuse! Enough!… *(He goes into the house)*

CURTAIN

# ACT II

*A hall in the home of the Lebedevs; straight ahead is the exit to the garden; to the right and to the left are doors. Antique, expensive furniture. A chandelier, candelabras and pictures — all of this is under dust covers.*

*ZINAIDA SAVISHNA sits on the sofa. On both sides of her are old lady-guests in arm-chairs; on side chairs are the young people. In the middle, near the exit to the garden, they play cards; among those playing: KOSYKH, AVDOTYA NAZAROVNA and YEGORUSHKA. GAVRILA stands at the right door. The guests circulate from the garden through the right door and back in continuous action. BABAKINA exits from the right door and heads toward ZINAIDA SAVISHNA.*

ZINAIDA SAVISHNA: *(Joyfully)* Sweetie pie, Marfa Yegorovna…

BABAKINA: Hello, Zinaida Savishna! I am so pleased to congratulate you on your daughter's birthday…

*They kiss.*

God bless…

ZINAIDA SAVISHNA: Thank you, sweetie pie, I'm so happy… how's your health?

BABAKINA: Thank you. *(She takes a seat next to her on the sofa)* Hello, my young friends!

*The guests stand bow.*

1ST GUEST: *(Laughs)* Young friends… are you really that old?

BABAKINA: *(Sighing)* What are we to do about these youngsters?

1ST GUEST: *(Deferentially laughing)* Excuse me, but are you serious? You may be a widow, but you can run rings around any girl I know.

*GAVRILA serves BABAKINA tea.*

ZINAIDA SAVISHNA: *(To GAVRILA)* What are you doing? Bring some jam. Gooseberry, maybe…

BABAKINA: Don't trouble yourself, I'm very grateful…

*Pause.*

1st GUEST: Did you come by way of Mushkino, Marfa Yegorovna?

BABAKINA: No, through Zaimische. The road is better there.

1ST GUEST: Yes it is, ma'am.

KOSYKH: Two spades.

YEGORUSHKA: Pass.

AVDOTYA NAZAROVNA: Pass.

2ND GUEST: Pass.

BABAKINA: Lottery tickets, darling Zinaida Savishna, went up again. Can you imagine — the first draw already cost two hundred seventy, but the second almost two hundred fifty… It's never been so high…

ZINAIDA SAVISHNA: *(She sighs)* Lucky for someone who's got a lot of tickets…

BABAKINA: Don't even think about it — it's so expensive and there's practically no chance of winning. The insurance alone will be the end of you.

ZINAIDA SAVISHNA: That's as may be, but all the same, my sweet, one must have hope… *(She sighs)* Our Gracious Lord is good to us…

3ʳᴰ GUEST: If you ask me, *Mesdames,* it doesn't pay to have high investments these days. Interest-bearing securities yield very low dividends, and to put a lot of money into circulation is extraordinarily dangerous. I understand, *mesdames*, that it's harder to decide for a person who has a great deal of capital, but, *mesdames*…

BABAKINA: *(She sighs)* So true!

*1ˢᵀ GUEST yawns.*

Can you possibly be yawning in front of the ladies?

FIRST GUEST: *Pardon, mesdames*, an accident…

*ZINAIDA SAVISHNA stands and exits through the right door; long silence.*

YEGORUSHKA: Two diamonds.

AVDOTYA NAZAROVNA: Pass.

2ᴺᴰ GUEST: Pass.

KOSYKH: Pass.

BABAKINA: *(From the side)* For heaven's sake, I could just die from boredom…

*ZINAIDA SAVISHNA and LEBEDEV enter.*

ZINAIDA SAVISHNA: *(Quietly)* Why were you sitting in there alone? What a prima donna! Spend some time with your guests! *(She takes a seat in her former place)*

LEBEDEV: *(He yawns)* Ahk, forgive us our sins! *(Seeing BABAKINA)* Ah, here's our little delicious dumpling… Sweetheart! *(He greets her)* How's my precious girl?

BABAKINA: I'm very grateful to you.

LEBEDEV: Well, thank God!... Thank God! *(He takes a seat in an armchair)* Ah, yes... Gavrila!

*GAVRILA serves him a shot of vodka and a glass of water; he tosses back the vodka and drinks the water.*

1<sup>ST</sup> GUEST: To your good health!

LEBEDEV: To my good health indeed!... Well, so far I haven't died, so thanks for that. *(To his wife)* Zyuzyushka, where's our birthday girl?

KOSYKH: *(Whiny)* Tell me, for God's sake: why didn't we get those last tricks? *(He leaps up)* How could we lose them? I had the ace of spades and —

AVDOTYA NAZAROVNA: *(She leaps up angrily)* If you, old boy, don't know how to play, then don't join us. What right do you have to lead someone else's suit? So you are left with your worthless ace!

*Both suddenly rush away from the table.*

KOSYKH: *(In a weepy voice)* Permit me, ladies and gentlemen... I had the ace, king, queen and eight of diamonds, the ace of spades and one, if you noticed, one little heart, but God knows why, she couldn't get a small slam!... I called no trump...

AVDOTYA NAZAROVNA: *(Interrupting)* I was the one who called no trump! You said two no trump...

KOSYKH: This is an outrage!... Permit me... you had... I had... you had... *(To LEBEDEV)* You be the judge, Pavel Kirillych... I had the ace, king, queen, and eight of diamonds...

LEBEDEV: *(He plugs his ears)* Leave me alone, please... leave me alone...

AVDOTYA NAZAROVNA: *(She shouts)* I was the one who said no trump!

KOSYKH: *(Savagely)* Let me be damned in hell if I ever play with that barracuda again! *(He quickly exits into the garden)*

2ND GUEST *goes after him,* YEGORUSHKA *remains at the table.*

AVDOTYA NAZAROVNA: Oof!... I'm burning up... because of him! Barracuda!... You're the barracuda!...

BABAKINA: Calm down, dear heart... you are too angry...

AVDOTYA NAZAROVNA: *(Seeing BABAKINA, clasps her hands)* Oh, my beauty!... You're here, but I was so angry I didn't see you... My dear sweet... *(She kisses her on the shoulder and takes a seat next to her)* This makes me so happy! Let's have a look at you, you gorgeous girl. Poo, poo, poo. *(Over left shoulder)*

LEBEDEV: Well, she's good and ready. Let's find her a new bridegroom...

AVDOTYA NAZAROVNA: I'll find one! I won't go to my grave, sinner that I am, until she and Sanichka are married...! I won't lie in my grave... *(Deep sigh)* Only, how can we find the right kind of bridegroom around here these days? There they sit, the eligible bachelors, they sit there like wet noodles.

3RD GUEST: An unfortunate thing to say. If you ask me, if men, *mesdames*, if young men remain single, it's the fault of society, not the men themselves.

LEBEDEV: Well, well!... Enough philosophy!... I hate it!...

SASHA: *(She enters and goes to her father)* It's so beautiful outside, but you, ladies and gentlemen, sit in this stuffy room.

ZINAIDA SAVISHNA: Sashenka, Marfa Yegorovna is here, don't you see?

SASHA: Oh, I'm sorry... *(She goes to BABAKINA and greets her)*

BABAKINA: You've become so stuck-up, Sanichka, so stuck-up, you haven't been over to see me even once. *(They kiss)* Happy Birthday, darling...

SASHA: Thank you. *(She takes a seat next to her father)*

LEBEDEV: Yes, Avdotya Nazarovna, it's hard to find good bridegrooms these days. Not just bridegrooms — you can't find a decent man anywhere. Young men today, no offense meant, are, God bless them, spoiled... They can't dance, or talk, or even drink the right way!

AVDOTYA NAZAROVNA: Oh, trust me, they know how to drink, alright...

LEBEDEV: It's no great trick to drink — a horse can drink... No, you have to drink the right way. In my day, you studied all day long — it was so, all day long you struggled — but as soon as it turned dark, you headed straight for the bright lights, to spin like a top until the break of day... And you would dance, and entertain the young ladies, and that took *finesse*. *(He flicks himself on the neck)* It went on and on — non-stop blabbering; you would tell lies, until you couldn't open your mouth anymore. But today... *(He waves his hand)* I don't understand... Neither here nor there... In our entire county there's only one decent young guy, and he's married *(He sighs)* and, I hear he's started to go crazy.

BABAKINA: Who do you mean?

LEBEDEV: Nikolasha Ivanov.

BABAKINA: Yes, he's a good man *(Grimaces)*, just unlucky...

ZINAIDA SAVISHNA: So true, so true, darling, but how could he be happy! *(She sighs)* He made such a mistake, poor man... He married his Yid — and he counted on her father and mother giving her a pile of gold, but it turned out the complete opposite... From the moment she converted, the parents didn't want to know her, they cursed her... So he didn't get a *kopek*. Now he's sorry, but it's too late...

SASHA:  Mama, that's not true.

BABAKINA:  *(Heatedly)* Shurochka, what's not true? Everyone knows about it. Indeed if there hadn't been the promise of money, why would he marry a Yid? Aren't there enough pretty Russian girls? He made a mistake, darling, he made a mistake... *(Animatedly)* And good God, doesn't she get it from him now! It's hilarious. He arrives home from somewhere and immediately says to her: "Your father and mother cheated me! Get out of here!" But where can she go? Her parents won't take her back. I suppose she could become a housemaid, but she's not even trained for that... Nowadays he mocks her all the time. If the Count didn't intervene, she'd be dead by now.

AVDOTYA NAZAROVNA:  And I hear he puts her in the cellar and says — "eat garlic, you so-and-so"... She eats it and eats it, until she can't stand it anymore, and she stinks up the whole house.

*Laughter.*

SASHA:  Papa, you know they're telling lies!

LEBEDEV:  So what? If it makes them feel good to talk nonsense, let them. *(He shouts)* Gavrila!

*GAVRILA serves him vodka and water.*

ZINAIDA SAVISHNA:  So that's how he got ruined, poor man. His business completely collapsed, darling... If Borkin didn't look after the farm, then he and his Jew girl would have nothing. *(She sighs)* And darling, we certainly have suffered because of him!... Such suffering, as only God sees! Would you believe, my dear, he has owed us nine thousand for the past three years.

BABAKINA:  *(With horror)* Nine thousand!...

ZINAIDA SAVISHNA: Yes… my dear Pashenka loaned it to him. Poor darling, he doesn't understand who you can lend to and who you can't. I'm not even talking about the principal—God be with him, if he'd just pay the interest on time!

SASHA: *(Impassioned)* Mama, you never stop talking about this!

ZINAIDA SAVISHNA: What's it to you? Why are you standing up for him?

SASHA: *(Rises)* How can you have the heart to talk like that about someone who has never done you any harm? Tell me, what did he do to you?

3rd GUEST: Aleksandra Pavlovna, permit me to say two words! I respect Nikolay Alekseyich and have always considered it an honor to know him, but, *entre nous*, he strikes me as a scoundrel.

SASHA: Then I congratulate you.

3RD GUEST: To show you what I mean — and it was passed along to me *(Sotto voce)* by Borkin — two years ago, at the time of the cattle epidemic, he bought some cattle, insured them…

ZINAIDA SAVISHNA: Yes, yes, yes! I remember that. I heard about it too.

3RD GUEST: He insured them, then he infected them with the disease and then he collected the insurance money.

SASHA: Akh, what nonsense! Nonsense! No one was buying and infecting cattle! Borkin himself made up that scheme and he boasted to everyone about it. When Ivanov found out about it, Borkin begged his forgiveness for two weeks. Ivanov is only guilty of being soft because he didn't have the heart to fire Borkin. He is only guilty of trusting people too much! Everything he had has been stolen because of his generosity and his *naivete*.

LEBEDEV: Shura, you firebrand! That's enough!

SASHA: Why do they talk such nonsense? Akh, it's so boring, so boring! Ivanov, Ivanov, Ivanov — can't anyone talk about anything else? *(She goes to the door and turns back)* I am amazed! *(To the young people)* I am positively amazed by your patience, ladies and gentlemen! Aren't you bored out of your minds by all this? The air in this room is stifling — congealed by boredom. Talk about something else, amuse the young ladies, get going! Well, if you can't think of any subjects besides Ivanov, then at least laugh, sing, dance, or…

LEBEDEV: *(He laughs)* Give it to them, give it to them good!

SASHA: Do me a favor, will you — if you don't want to dance, to laugh, to sing, if all of that is boring, then I beg you, I implore you, for once in your life, for curiosity, just to surprise me a little or make me laugh, summon all your strength and try to come up with something witty, brilliant, even rude or vulgar, just so long as it's funny and new! Or for once in your lives do something small, hardly noticeable, but maybe resembling a heroic deed, just so that for once in their lives the young ladies, seeing you, can say: "Ah!" Listen, you know you want to be liked but why don't you try and make an effort to be liked? Akh, gentlemen! You're all wrong, all wrong, all wrong… One look at you, and flies die and lamps begin to smoke. It's wrong, all wrong… A thousand times I've said this to you and I'll never stop saying it, you're wrong, wrong, wrong!…

SHABELSKY: *(Entering with IVANOV from the right door)* Who's making so much noise in here? Is that you, Shurochka? *(He laughs loudly and squeezes her hand)* Happy Birthday, my angel, may God grant you a long life and the luck not to be born again…

ZINAIDA SAVISHNA: *(Joyfully)* Nikolai Alekseyevich, Count!

LEBEDEV: What? What? Who's here? — the Count! *(He goes to meet him)*

SHABELSKY: *(Seeing ZINAIDA SAVISHNA and BABAKINA, he holds out his hands)* Two money machines on one sofa!... It's nice to see you! *(He greets them; to ZINAIDA SAVISHNA)* Hello, Zyuzyushka! *(To BABAKINA)* Hello, little pompom!...

ZINAIDA SAVISHNA: I'm so pleased. You rarely grace us with your presence, Count. *(She shouts)* Gavrila, tea! Sit, please! *(She rises, exits out the right door and immediately returns; she seems extremely preoccupied)*

*SASHA sits. IVANOV silently greets everyone.*

LEBEDEV: *(To SHABELSKY)* Where did you come from? What "ill wind" brought you to us? I'll be damned, this is a surprise. *(He kisses him)* Count, you know you are an old scamp! Respectable people don't do what you do! *(He leads him by the hand downstage)* Why don't we ever see you? Are you angry with us?

SHABELSKY: And how am I supposed to get here? On a broomstick? I don't have my own horses, and Nikolai never takes me with him. He orders me to stay home with Sarra, so she won't be bored. Send me your horses, and I'll be here...

LEBEDEV: *(He waves his hand)* Yes, yes!... Zyuzyushka would sooner snap in two than lend the horses. You are so sweet, so dear to me — dearer to me than my family! You and I are all that's left from the old days. In you I see all my sufferings and my lost youth... All kidding aside, I'm starting to cry... *(He kisses the COUNT)*

SHABELSKY: Let me go, let me go! You stink like a brewery...

LEBEDEV: Sweetheart, you can't imagine how lonely I am without my old friends! I'm ready to hang myself from boredom... *(Quietly)* Zyuzyushka is so stingy and so greedy, she's driven away all the decent people around here, and what's left? Only the dregs — Dudkins and Budkins... Well, let's have some tea...

*GAVRILA serves the COUNT tea.*

ZINAIDA SAVISHNA: *(Anxiously to GAVRILA)* Why are you serving it like that? Bring some sort of jam. Gooseberry, maybe...

SHABELSKY: *(He laughs loudly; to IVANOV)* What was I telling you? *(To LEBEDEV)* I made a big bet with him that when we arrived, Zyuzyushka would pull out the gooseberry jam...

ZINAIDA SAVISHNA: You are such a smart-aleck, Count... *(She sits)*

LEBEDEV: We boiled twenty barrels of it, so what else would we do with it?

SHABELSKY: *(Sitting near the table)* You are really piling it up, aren't you, Zyuzyushka? What are you worth these days? A million, huh?

ZINAIDA SAVISHNA: *(With a sigh)* Yes, it might look from the outside like we're so much richer than anybody else, but where does the money come from? It's all blah blah blah...

SHABELSKY: Well, sure, sure!... We know! We know how tough it is for poor you... *(To LEBEDEV)* Pasha, tell me the truth: have you got a million?

LEBEDEV: Honest to God, I don't know. Ask Zyuzyushka...

SHABELSKY: *(To BABAKINA)* And this plump little dumpling will soon have a little million! Honestly, she gets prettier and fatter by the day, by the hour! That's what happens when you've got a lot of cash...

BABAKINA: Thanks very much, your Highness, but I'm not crazy about being teased.

SHABELSKY: My sweet money machine, I can't help it. My mouth insists on spewing garbage when my soul is crying out to shut up... I love you and Zyuzyushka to death... *(Happily)* Delightful!... Ecstatic!... That's how I see you...

ZINAIDA SAVISHNA: You never stop — always the same. *(To YEGORUSHKA)* Yegorushka, put out those candles! If you're not playing, why are they still burning?

*YEGORUSHKA shudders; he puts out the candles and sits.*

*(To IVANOV)* Nikolai Alekseyevich, how's your wife's health?

IVANOV: Bad. Today the doctor said she definitely has tuberculosis…

ZINAIDA SAVISHNA: Really? What a pity!… *(Sigh)* We all love her so…

SHABELSKY: Nonsense, utter nonsense!… It's not tuberculosis, the doctor is a quack. Doctor Hippocrates likes to hang around her, so he made up tuberculosis. It's a good thing her husband isn't jealous. *(IVANOV makes an impatient gesture)* As far as Sarra is concerned, I don't believe a word she says either. In my whole life I've never trusted doctors, lawyers, or women. Nonsense, nonsense — absolute nonsense.

LEBEDEV: *(To SHABELSKY)* You are quite a character, Matvei!… You talk like you hate everybody — and you never shut up about it — non-stop motor mouth… You are a man like any other man, but you talk our heads off — it's as if you have a non-stop machine in your mouth. My God!…

SHABELSKY: What do you want me to do, hug and kiss all the swindlers and scoundrels?

LEBEDEV: And where do you see swindlers and scoundrels here?

SHABELSKY: Present company excepted, of course… but…

LEBEDEV: Uh huh, but… it's all an act…

SHABELSKY: An act — just as well you don't have anything to say about anything.

LEBEDEV: Something to say? I sit around and wait for death. That's what I have to say. We, my brother, don't have time to think up things to say. So that's that! *(He shouts)* Gavrila!

SHABELSKY: You've already Gavrila-ed it up plenty tonight. Look how red your nose is!

LEBEDEV: *(He drinks)* Never mind, dear heart… I'm not getting married today…

ZINAIDA SAVISHNA: It's been a long time since we've seen Doctor Lvov. He's completely forgotten us.

SASHA: Ooh, I can't stand him. Fancies himself "integrity personified." He can't get a drink of water or smoke a cigarette without showing off his rare integrity. He walks and talks like an ordinary human, but on his forehead is written: I am an honest man! It's boring to have him around.

SHABELSKY: Narrow-minded prig! *(He mocks)* "Here's to honest labor!" he shouts every minute. He thinks he's a second Dobrolyubov. Everyone is a scoundrel. Only his views are astonishing and profound. If a *muzhik* has some money and lives like a human being, that means he stole and swindled to get there. If I go around in a velvet jacket, and have a butler to dress me — I must be a thief and a slave driver. Yes, he's honest, so honest — just bursting with integrity. Nothing is good enough for him. I'm even a little afraid of him… Honest to God… Any minute he could turn on me, and from his elevated sense of duty he could pop me in the eye and call me a criminal.

IVANOV: He is a little exhausting, but all the same I like him — he is very sincere.

SHABELSKY: Sincere! He comes up to me last night and from out of nowhere, he says: "You, Count, disgust me!" Thanks a lot! And let me tell you, he doesn't simply say it, his voice trembles, and his eyes burn, and his knees shake… to hell with that "sincerity!" Well, if he finds me disgusting, that's his right… I actually agree, but does he have to say it to my face? Maybe I'm a worthless person, but can't he show a little respect to my gray beard? Third-rate, ruthless sincerity!

LEBEDEV: Now come on… you were young once — you get it.

SHABELSKY: Yes, I was young and stupid. I made fun of bastards and conmen, but I never in my life called a thief a thief to his face, and in the home of a hanged man did I talk about a noose? I was brought up to be civil. But this fool of a doctor of yours feels he has a special privilege from on high — in the name of principle — to give me a good beating in public.

LEBEDEV: Young people are all difficult. I had an uncle who was a Hegelian… and at every party, he would bring everyone together, stand up on a chair and say: "You are all ignoramuses! You are the very heart of the devil! When the new life dawns…" Blah, blah, blah. He would go on and on, lecturing us…

SASHA: What did the guests say?

LEBEDEV: Nothing… They just sat there and drank. Once, though, I challenged him to a duel… my own uncle. It was because of Francis Bacon. God help me, I remember, I sat — that's right, just where Matvei is now, and my uncle was standing there with the late Gerasim Nilych, roughly where Nikolasha is… Well sir, Gerasim Nilych asks me a question…

*BORKIN enters, dressed like a dandy, with a package in his hands, bobbing up and down and singing. A murmur of approval.*

YOUNG LADIES: *(Together)* Mikhail Mikhailovich!...

LEBEDEV: *Michel Michelich!* Is it really you?

SHABELSKY: Now the party can begin!

BORKIN: Yes, here I am! *(He runs up to SASHA)* Precious *signorina*, please allow me the liberty to congratulate the universe for the birth of such a marvelous flower — you... I can't help myself, I'm going to take the liberty to present you with these firecrackers, which I made myself. May they brighten this night, as you brighten the darkness of our world. *(He bows theatrically)*

SASHA: Thank you...

LEBEDEV: *(He laughs loudly, to IVANOV)* Why don't you get rid of this Judas?

BORKIN: *(To LEBEDEV)* Pavel Kirillych! *(To IVANOV)* My boss... *(He sings)* Nicolas-voila, ho-hee-ho! *(He goes around to everyone)* Most honorable Zinaida Savishna... Divine Marfa Yegorovna... Most ancient Avdotya Nazarovna... Your Highness Count...

SHABELSKY: *(He laughs loudly)* The life of the party... He's barely set foot in here, and it's already more fun. Did you notice that?

BORKIN: Oof, I'm exhausted... I think I've greeted everyone. Well, what's new, ladies and gentlemen? Anything special I should know? *(Lively, to ZINAIDA SAVISHNA)* Akh, listen, *Mamasha*... Just now as I was coming here... *(To GAVRILA)* Gavryusha, bring me some tea, only forget the gooseberry jam! *(To ZINAIDA SAVISHNA)* On my way over here, I saw some peasants stripping the bark off the willow trees by your river. Why don't you make some money from that?

LEBEDEV: *(To IVANOV)* Why don't you fire this Judas?

ZINAIDA SAVISHNA: *(Startled)* You know that's true, it never entered my mind!...

BORKIN: *(He does arm exercises)* I can't sit still... *Mamasha*, I'm feeling lucky — Marfa Yegorovna, I'm excited! *(He sings)* "I am before you again..."

ZINAIDA SAVISHNA: You get something started, or we'll all be bored.

BORKIN: Ladies and gentlemen, why are you all so depressed? They sit there with such long faces… Let's play something. What do you say? Forfeits, Hangman, Catch, dancing, firecrackers?…

YOUNG LADIES: *(They clap their hands)* Firecrackers, firecrackers! *(They run to the garden)*

SASHA: *(To IVANOV)* Why are you so low today?

IVANOV: I have a headache, Shurochka, and besides, I'm depressed…

SASHA: Come into the drawing room.

*They go to the door; everyone exits to the garden, except ZINAIDA SAVISHNA and LEBEDEV.*

ZINAIDA SAVISHNA: That's what I love — this young man is here for less than a minute, and already everyone starts having fun. *(She turns out the big lamp)* As long as they're all in the garden, no reason to keep all the candles burning. *(She damps the candles)*

LEBEDEV: *(Walking behind her)* Zyuzyushka, we need to give the guests something to eat…

ZINAIDA SAVISHNA: Look at all these candles… it's not for nothing people think we're rich. *(She damps them out)*

LEBEDEV: *(Walking behind her)* Zyuzyushka, really, give people something to eat… I'm sure the youngsters are probably hungry, poor things… Zyuzyushka…

ZINAIDA SAVISHNA: The Count didn't finish his drink. The sugar was just wasted. *(She walks to the left door)*

LEBEDEV: Phooey!… *(He exits to the garden)*

SASHA: *(Entering with IVANOV from the right door)* Everyone's in the garden.

IVANOV: So that's the way it is, Shurochka. I used to work all the time, and thought even more, and I never got tired; now I don't do anything, I never think at all, and I'm exhausted body and soul. My conscience troubles me all the time, I feel profoundly guilty, but I fail to understand what exactly I'm guilty of. Yes, my wife's illness, I'm broke, the perpetual squabbling in my house, the gossip, all the talk, talk, talk, stupid Borkin... My home has become loathsome to me, it's torture to live there. I'll tell you honestly, Shurochka, even my wife's company — and she loves me — has become hateful to me. You're my only friend, promise you won't be angry with me. I've come here to be amused, but I'm bored once I get to your house. Forgive me, I'll leave quietly...

SASHA: Nikolai Alekseyevich, I understand you. You feel lonely. You need someone around you who loves you and understands you. Only love can bring you back to life.

IVANOV: Good God, Shurochka! All I need is for an old dog like me to get involved in a new romance! God save me from that! No, my clever girl, it's not about romance. I swear to God, I will gladly put up with everything — the depression, the neuroses, the financial disaster — yes I'll lose my wife, and get old before my time — all the loneliness — but I won't put up with, will not endure, making a fool of myself. It's killing me that I, a healthy, strong man, have turned into Hamlet... God knows what... There are some wretched men who are flattered when they're called Hamlets, but for me it's — a disgrace! It gets me angry and makes me ashamed at the same time — I am suffering...

SASHA: *(Joking, on the verge of tears)* Nikolai Alekseyevich, let's run away to America.

IVANOV: I'm too lazy to walk through that door, and you talk about America... *(They go to the exit to the garden)* Really, Shura, how can you go on living here? When I look at the people around you, I get scared to death — who are you going to marry? Our only hope is that some dashing lieutenant will be passing through or some brilliant student will snatch you up and carry you away...

*ZINAIDA SAVISHNA enters from the left door with a jar of jam.*

IVANOV: Pardon me, Shurochka, I'll be right there…

*SASHA exits to the garden.*

Zinaida Savishna, may I ask you something…

ZINAIDA SAVISHNA: What do you want, Nikolai Alekseyevich?

IVANOV: *(In thought)* The problem is… the day after tomorrow my loan is due. I would be extremely obliged to you if you could grant me an extension or let me add the interest to the principal. I have absolutely no money right now…

ZINAIDA SAVISHNA: *(Frightened)* Nikolai Alekseyevich, how is that possible? How can I operate like that? No, don't even think of such a thing, for God's sake. Please do not torment a wretched woman like me…

IVANOV: Please pardon me, pardon me… *(He exits to the garden)*

ZINAIDA SAVISHNA: Psssh, poor guy — he really got me scared… I'm trembling… trembling… *(She exits to the right door)*

KOSYKH: *(Enters from the left door and walks across the stage)* I've got diamonds: an ace, king, queen, the ace of spades and one… one little heart, and she, the devil take her, she couldn't make a small slam! *(He exits to the right door)*

AVDOTYA NAZAROVNA: *(Exiting from the garden with the 1st GUEST)* I could just tear her to pieces, the cheapskate!… just tear her to pieces! It's no joke, I've been sitting here since five o'clock, and she's not given us a rotten herring!… What a house!… What hospitality!…

1ST GUEST: I'm so bored I could bang my head against the wall! God forgive me. I'm about to start baying at the moon like a wolf from boredom and hunger. Watch out, I may start gnawing on you…

AVDOTYA NAZAROVNA: Go ahead — tear her to pieces, the old witch.

1ST GUEST: One more for the road — then I'm off! Don't fix me up with any girls! How the hell can I think about love, if I haven't eaten since lunch?

AVDOTYA NAZAROVNA: Come on, let's look around for something…

1ST GUEST: Shh!… Be very quiet! I spy some schnapps in the dining room — on the buffet. We'll sneak it out of there… Shh!…

*They exit to the left door.*

*ANNA PETROVNA and LVOV enter from the right door.*

ANNA PETROVNA: It's fine, it's fine. They'll be happy to see us. There's no one here. They must be in the garden.

LVOV: The real question is, why did you bring me here, to these vultures? This isn't a place for you and me! Decent people don't belong here!

ANNA PETROVNA: Listen, Doctor Decent! It's discourteous to escort a woman to a party and talk the whole way here about your decency. It may be you're truly honest, but it's so boring to hear about it. It's best not to talk about your own virtues so much with women. My Nikolai, when he was single, sang songs and told fabulous lies to women — but everyone knew how honest he was.

LVOV: Akh, don't talk to me about your Nikolai, I understand him all too well!

ANNA PETROVNA: You're a good person, but you don't understand anything. Let's go into the garden. He never said stuff like — "I am so honest! I can't stand being here, I'm choking! Vultures! Owls! Crocodiles!" He left the animal kingdom in peace, and when he was very irritated, the only thing I heard from him was, "Akh, how awful I was today!" or "Anyuta, I feel sorry for so-and-so" — but you…

*They exit.*

1ˢᵗ GUEST: *(Entering from the left door)* It's not in the dining room, so, it must be somewhere in the pantry. We need to get it out of Yegorushka. Let's go through the parlor.

AVDOTYA NAZAROVNA: I'll tear her to pieces!...

*They exit through the right door.*

*BABAKINA and BORKIN run in from the garden with laughter; behind them SHABELSKY, laughing and rubbing his hands.*

BABAKINA: It's so tedious! *(She laughs loudly)* Everyone is walking around or sitting as stiff as boards! Every bone in my body is paralyzed with tedium. *(She jumps up)* I've got to get up and move!

*BORKIN takes her by the waist and kisses her cheek.*

SHABELSKY: *(He laughs loudly and snaps his fingers)* The hell with it! *(He wheezes)* Or something like that...

BABAKINA: Let go, let go of me, you naughty man — or God knows what the Count will think! Leave me alone!

BORKIN: Angel of my soul, carbuncle of my heart!... *(He kisses her)* Lend me two thousand three hundred *rubles*!...

BABAKINA: No-no-no... Take anything else you want, but no money — I'm very fond of you... No, no, no!... Akh, let go of me!...

SHABELSKY: *(He minces nearby)* Little pompom... she has her good points...

BORKIN: *(Seriously)* Well enough! Let's talk business. Let's talk like regular businessmen. Tell me the truth, without fancy dancing... Listen! *(He points to the COUNT)* This man needs money — a minimum annual income of three thousand. You need a husband. Do you want to be a Countess?

SHABELSKY: *(He laughs loudly)* Wonderful cynic!

BORKIN: Do you want to be a Countess? Yes or no?

BABAKINA: *(Agitatedly)* You are making this up, Misha, honestly... And this isn't a business deal... If the Count would like to... he can and... I don't know, this is all so sudden...

BORKIN: Let's face it! This *is* a business matter... Yes or no?

SHABELSKY: *(Laughing and rubbing his hands)* This is silly... I should do this myself... So? My little pompom... *(He kisses BABAKINA on the cheek)* Charming!... Little cucumber!...

BABAKINA: Stop, stop, you're scaring me to death... Go away, go away!... No, don't leave!...

BORKIN: Well, hurry up! Yes or no? We don't have time...

BABAKINA: Count, how about it? Come visit me for two or three days... My home is very cheerful — not like here... Come tomorrow. *(To BORKIN)* Oh no — no, you were joking, weren't you?

BORKIN: *(Angrily)* Who would joke in such serious matters?

BABAKINA: Hold it, hold it!... Akh, I feel faint! I feel faint! A Countess... I feel faint!... I'm falling...

> *BORKIN and the Count take her under the arms with laughter and, kissing her cheeks, exit through the right door.*
>
> *IVANOV and SASHA run in from the garden.*

IVANOV: *(In despair he grabs himself by the head)* What are you saying, Shurochka? — don't say it... it's not necessary!...

SASHA: *(With passion)* I'm so in love with you... I can't live without you — my life would be meaningless — no happiness, no joy! You are everything to me...

IVANOV: Why, why? My God, I don't understand... Shurochka, you don't have to...

SASHA: In my childhood I looked up to you — you were my only joy. I loved you and I loved your soul, and now... I love you, Nikolai Alekseyevich... I would go to the ends of the earth with you. I'd even go to the grave with you — only, for God's sake, we must leave soon — or I'll suffocate here.

IVANOV: *(He breaks into happy laughter)* Is this really happening? Can I really start all over again? Really, Shurochka?... My happiness! *(He draws her to him)* My youth, my freshness...

> ANNA PETROVNA *enters from the garden and, seeing her husband and* SASHA, *comes to a stop rooted to the ground.*

To live? Yes? To start all over again?

> A kiss. After the kiss IVANOV and SASHA look around and see ANNA PETROVNA.

*(In horror)* Sarra!

CURTAIN

# ACT III

*IVANOV's study. A writing desk, on which lie disordered papers, books, government papers, knick-knacks, revolvers; near the papers is a lamp, a decanter with vodka, a plate with herring, bits of bread and cucumbers. On the walls are land maps, pictures, rifles, pistols, farming hooks, whips, etc. — Midday.*

*SHABELSKY and LEBEDEV sit on the sides of the writing desk. BORKIN is in the middle of the room astride a chair. PYOTR stands by the door.*

LEBEDEV: In France politics are clear and definite. Frenchmen know what they want. They want to demolish the Krauts and that's it. But in Germany, brother, it's just the opposite. The Germans have a lot more fish to fry besides France.

SHABELSKY: Nonsense!... In my opinion, the Germans are cowards and the French are cowards... They are busy giving each other the finger, only they keep their fingers in their pockets. Believe me, their animus is strictly limited to fingers. They won't be fighting so soon.

BORKIN: And I say, why fight? What do we need all this defense spending? What should we do? Get all the dogs in the country, inject them with rabies, and let them loose in enemy territory. They would all go mad in a month.

LEBEDEV: *(He laughs)* See, his head may be small, but it's filled with brilliant ideas.

SHABELSKY: Brilliant!

LEBEDEV: God help you, you make me laugh, *Michel Michelich*! *(He stops laughing)* How does it go, gentlemen, don't get so caught up with war that you forget about your vodka. *Repetatur*! *(He pours three glasses)* Na zdorovye.

*They drink and eat a bite.*

The herring, mother of God, is the snack of all snacks.

SHABELSKY: No, the cucumber is better… The intelligentsia have been pondering that question all over the world and no one has come up with a better snack than the salted cucumber. *(To PYOTR)* Pyotr, let's have some more cucumbers and get the cook to make us *pirozhki* with onions. They have to be hot.

*PYOTR exits.*

LEBEDEV: Caviar is also good with vodka. Only how should it be served? You've got to… Take a quarter pound of caviar, half a green onion, olive oil, mix it all together and, you know, what you have… oh, and top it off with a little lemon… Unbelievable! The smell alone will drive you crazy.

BORKIN: It's also good to eat fried smelts with vodka. Only you have to know how to fry it. You need to clean it, then roll it in crushed bread crumbs and fry it until it's crisp so it'll be crunchy… cru-cru-cru…

SHABELSKY: Babakina served good snacks yesterday — white mushrooms. Mmmm…

LEBEDEV: And how… mmmm…

SHABELSKY: They were specially prepared. You know, with onions, and bay leaves, and all kinds of spices. The smell from the frying pan was… ecstasy!

LEBEDEV: How about it? *Repetatur*, gentlemen!

*They drink up.*

To our health… *(He looks at his watch)* I can't sit around waiting for Nikolasha. It's time for me to go. At Babakina's you get mushrooms, but at our house — no mushrooms — no anything! And why, may I ask, are you going to Marfutka's?

SHABELSKY: *(Nods at BORKIN)* Blame him! He wants me to marry her…

LEBEDEV: To marry?… How old are you?

SHABELSKY: Sixty two.

LEBEDEV: Absolutely the age to get married. And Marfutka is just the right mate for you.

BORKIN: It's not about Marfutka — it's Marfutka's moolah.

LEBEDEV: Ah, I see, you're after Marfutka's money… Anything else you want? You want to discover America too?

BORKIN: Yes, and once he gets married he'll be so rich and sitting pretty in America and you'll be sorry…

SHABELSKY: For heaven's sake, he's serious. This genius is convinced I'll listen to him and marry…

BORKIN: Are *you* serious? You're no longer convinced?

SHABELSKY: You have really lost your mind… When did I look convinced? Psss….

BORKIN: Ah, I see, thank you… I'm very thankful to you! So this means you're going to let me down? One minute you're getting married, the next, you're not… Who the hell can figure you out… But I already gave my word. So you're not getting married?

SHABELSKY: *(Shrugs his shoulders)* He's serious… Astonishing man!

BORKIN: *(Angered)* In that case, why did you upset an honorable woman? She desperately wants to be a Countess, she doesn't sleep, doesn't eat… Is this a joke to you? Honestly?

SHABELSKY: *(Snaps his fingers)* Okay, what if I did the dirty deed? Huh? Out of spite! I'll do it. I give you my word… Maybe it'll be fun!

*Enter LVOV.*

LEBEDEV: Doctor Hippocrates, your very humble… "Doctor, old friend, save me, I'm scared to death of dying…"

LVOV: Nikolai Alekseyevich hasn't arrived yet?

LEBEDEV: Of course not, I've been waiting for him more than an hour.

*LVOV impatiently strides around the stage.*

Dear heart, well, how is Anna Petrovna doing?

LVOV: Bad.

LEBEDEV: *(Sigh)* Can I go pay my respects?

LVOV: No, please, don't go. She's sleeping…

*Pause.*

LEBEDEV: Dear heart… *(He takes a deep breath)* On Shurochka's birthday, when she fainted at our house, I saw her face and right then I understood she's going to die soon, poor thing. I can't understand how this happened to her. I ran in, I see: she's pale, lying on the floor, and she's crying. Nikolasha, also pale as a ghost, is on his knees. Shurochka and I walked around in a daze all week after that.

SHABELSKY: *(To LVOV)* Tell me, most respected one, Prince of Science, when was it discovered that when a woman has a respiratory disease, she should be visited by a young doctor every day? That is some discovery! Brilliant! Is it personalized medicine?

*LVOV is about to answer, but makes a contemptuous gesture and exits.*

If looks could kill…

LEBEDEV: Couldn't you hold your tongue! Why did you offend him?

SHABELSKY: *(Irritatedly)* Why is he lying? "Tuberculosis. There's no hope. She will die…" He's lying! I cannot endure this!

LEBEDEV: Why do you think he's lying?

SHABELSKY: *(He rises and walks)* I cannot believe that a living person suddenly, for no reason at all, drops dead. Let's stop this conversation!

KOSYKH: *(Running in, out of breath)* Is Nikolai Alekseyevich home? Hello! *(He quickly shakes hands with everyone)* Home?

BORKIN: He's not here.

KOSYKH: *(He takes a seat and leaps up)* In that case, farewell! *(He drinks a glass of vodka and grabs a snack)* I'll go… Business… I'm so worn out… I can barely stand up…

LEBEDEV: Look what the wind brought in! Where from?

KOSYKH: From Barabanov's. We played bridge and just finished… I lost all my money… That Barabanov plays like an idiot! *(In a weepy voice)* Listen: I'm holding hearts the whole time… *(He appeals to BORKIN, who runs away from him)* He plays diamonds, I play hearts again, he diamonds… Well, there I am without a trick. *(To LEBEDEV)* We play four clubs. I have the ace, queen and a few small clubs, ace, ten, three of spades…

LEBEDEV: *(Plugs his ears)* Spare me, spare me, for the love of Christ, spare me!

KOSYKH: *(To the COUNT)* Do you get it? The ace, queen of clubs, plus the ace, ten, three of spades…

SHABELSKY: *(Pushes him with his hands)* Stop, I don't want to hear it!

KOSYKH: And incredibly the ace of spades is trumped in the first...

SHABELSKY: *(He grabs the revolver from the table)* Get out! I will shoot you!...

KOSYKH: *(He waves his hand)* What the hell... Can't I even talk to anybody? It's like living in Australia: everyone is so far from everyone else — no common interests... Alright, I have to go... it's time. *(He grabs his service cap)* Time is money... *(He gives his hand to LEBEDEV)* I pass!

*Laughter.*

*KOSYKH exits and in the doorway collides with AVDOTYA NAZAROVNA.*

AVDOTYA NAZAROVNA: *(Cries out)* What the hell, you almost knocked me over!

ALL: A-ha!... Miss Forever Present...

AVDOTYA NAZAROVNA: Ah, here you are, I've been looking all over. My heroes! *(She greets them)*

LEBEDEV: What are you doing here?

AVDOTYA NAZAROVNA: Business, dear friend! *(To the COUNT)* The business concerns you, your Highness. *(She bows)* She ordered me to bow and ask after your health... And she ordered me, my little dolly, to say if you don't come tonight, then she'll cry her little eyes out. So, she says, the honey bunny, take him aside and secretly whisper. What's such a secret? Everyone here is a friend. We're not stealing anything — this is about love — mutual love. I never touch the stuff, but maybe just this once I'll have a little drink.

LEBEDEV: And I'll drink with you. *(He pours)* You old crow, you never change. I've known you for thirty years…

AVDOTYA NAZAROVNA: I've lost count of the years… I've buried two husbands, I would have gladly married again, but who wants to marry a woman without a dowry. I've had about eight children… *(She takes the glass)* Well, God grant, we're making a good bargain. God grant we can finish it! They'll live happily ever after, and we'll look on them and rejoice! May they live in harmony… *(She drinks)* Strong vodka!

SHABELSKY: *(Laughing, to LEBEDEV)* Do they seriously think I would… How crazy!... Astonishing! *(He stands)* What do you think, Pasha, should I do this — this dirty deed? Out of spite?... Then they'll really say the old dog has some… what do you think Pasha? Really…

LEBEDEV: Stop talking nonsense, Count. It's our job, Brother, to think about dying, and we passed on Marfutka and her piles of cash long ago… Our time has passed.

SHABELSKY: No, I'll do it! Word of honor, I'll do it!

*Enter IVANOV and LVOV.*

LVOV: Would you spare me five minutes.

LEBEDEV: Nikolasha! *(He goes to meet IVANOV and kisses him)* Hello, my dear friend… I've been waiting for you a whole hour already.

AVDOTYA NAZAROVNA: *(She bows)* Hello, old boy!

IVANOV: *(With bitterness)* Gentlemen, once again you've turned my study into a tavern! I've asked you a thousand times not to do this… *(He goes up to the table)* Look — here you spilled vodka on this paper… crumbs… cucumbers… Disgusting!

LEBEDEV: Guilty, Nikolasha, guilty… Forgive us, dear friend. We must talk about very important business…

BORKIN: Yes, me too.

LVOV: Nikolai Alekseyevich, can I talk with you?

IVANOV: *(Indicates LEBEDEV)* He needs me. Can you wait till later... *(To LEBEDEV)* What do you want?

LEBEDEV: Gentlemen, I'd like to speak confidentially. I beg...

*The COUNT exits with AVDOTYA NAZAROVNA, behind them BORKIN, then LVOV.*

IVANOV: Pasha, you can help yourself to a drink. Take as much as you want — that's your problem — but I beg you not to drink with my uncle. He never used to drink in my house. It will kill him.

LEBEDEV: *(Frightened)* My darling, I didn't know... I didn't even pay attention...

IVANOV: God forbid he should die, believe me, you'd notice... What do you need?

*Pause.*

LEBEDEV: Well you see, my old friend... I don't know how to say this without sounding cruel... Nikolasha, I'm ashamed, I'm blushing, I'm tripping over my tongue... My dear friend, try to understand my position, try to see that I'm a man wholly dependent... a slave really... Forgive me...

IVANOV: What are you talking about?

LEBEDEV: My wife sent me.... Be so kind, be a friend, pay her the interest! You must believe me, she trampled me, she tore me into little pieces, tied me into knots, tormented me — Get her off my back for God's sake.

IVANOV: Pasha, you know, I don't have any money.

LEBEDEV: I know, I know, but what can I do? She won't wait. If she sues you for the money, how will Shurochka and I ever look you in the eye again?

IVANOV: I'm really ashamed, Pasha, I wish I could vanish into thin air, but... but how can I pay it? One idea: wait until autumn, when I'll sell the wheat.

LEBEDEV: *(He shouts)* She won't wait!

*Pause.*

IVANOV: I appreciate your position, but mine is even worse. *(He walks and thinks)* And I can't think of anything... There's nothing left to sell...

LEBEDEV: You could go to Milbakh, ask him for it. You know he owes you sixteen thousand.

*IVANOV hopelessly waves his hand.*

This is how it is, Nikolasha... I know you'll be angry, but... humor an old drunk! As a friend... See me as a friend... We were both students once, progressives... Community leaders... We both studied at Moscow University... *Alma mater...* *(He pulls out a piece of paper)* I have a little secret — no one knows in my house. Borrow the money from me... *(He pulls out money and puts it on the table)* Forget your pride and look on me as your friend... I would take it from you, honest to God...

*Pause.*

Here it is, on the table: eleven hundred. Go to her today and give it to her yourself. Here you are. Just say, "Zinaida Savishna, choke on it!" Only, look, don't tell her you got it from me. God forbid! Or I'll catch it from Miss Gooseberry Jam! *(He scrutinizes IVANOV's face)* Alright, alright, you don't have to do it! *(Quickly he takes the money from the table and puts it away in his pocket)* You don't have to! I was joking... Forgive me, for Christ's sake!

*Pause.*

Are you feeling sad?

*IVANOV waves his hand.*

Yes, this business! *(He sighs)* It's the sad time for you. A man is just like a samovar. It normally sits, nice and cool on the shelf, but now and then someone puts coal in it: psh... psh! It's a terrible comparison, but you know what I mean... *(He sighs)* Misfortune strengthens the soul. I don't pity you, Nikolasha, you will pull through this bad time and come out all the stronger — Yes, these are the times that try a man's soul. But what really gets me is what people are like... Do you know where all this gossip comes from? So many rumors are going around the county, brother, and I hate to say it but the Assistant Public Prosecutor is coming to see you. You're "a murderer, a blood-sucker, a robber, a traitor..."

IVANOV: It's all nonsense. Listen, my head is killing me.

LEBEDEV: You think too much!

IVANOV: I never think about anything.

LEBEDEV: Nikolasha, just lighten up and come visit us. Shurochka loves you, she understands and appreciates you. Nikolasha, she's a good, honest person. I don't know where she gets it from — certainly not from her mother or father — must be some stranger... I look at her sometimes and can't believe such a fat drunken lout like me could have such a treasure. Come over, talk to her about interesting things and — have a good time. She's a loyal, sincere person...

*Pause.*

IVANOV: Pasha, darling, leave me alone...

LEBEDEV: I understand, I understand... *(He hurriedly looks at his watch)* I understand. *(He kisses IVANOV) Do svidanya.* I'm late for a school dedication... *(He goes to the door and stops)* She's so intelligent...

Yesterday Shurochka and I were gossiping, *(He laughs)* and she blurted this out: "Papochka, fireflies," she says, "glow at night just so that they can be seen easier and eaten by night birds, and good people exist so they can be food for slander and gossip." Can you believe that? Genius! George Sand!...

IVANOV: Pasha! *(He stops him)* What's wrong with me?

LEBEDEV: To tell you the truth I wanted to ask you that myself — but I was shy. I don't know, brother! On the one hand, I can see that you are overwhelmed with misfortunes, on the other hand, I know, that you are strong enough to... to conquer all these troubles. Maybe there's more to it, Nikolasha — I don't know.

IVANOV: I don't know either. It seems to me... but no!

*Pause.*

What I wanted to say, maybe you remember my workman, Semyon? Once, when we were threshing, he was showing off his strength to the girls. He lifted two huge loads of rye and broke his back. He died. It seems to me I've been lifting too much and I'm breaking my back. High school, university, then agriculture school, projects... I thought I was different than everyone else, I didn't marry like everyone else, I was passionate, I took risks — with my own money, as you well know. I was happy and miserable at the same time. I loaded all that on my back, and I broke. At twenty we're all heroes, we take on everything, everything is possible, but at thirty we're all worn out, not fit for anything. So how do you explain such exhaustion? But maybe that's not it... No, not it!... Bless you, Pasha, I'm terrible company.

LEBEDEV: *(Suddenly)* You know what? You need a change of scenery!

IVANOV: Don't be stupid, Pasha. Go!

LEBEDEV: Yes, it's stupid. Now I get it, it's stupid. I'm going, I'm going!... *(He exits)*

IVANOV: *(Alone)* I'm such a pathetic, worthless person. I've got to be pretty pathetic for such a drunk like Pasha to love and respect me. My God! How I hate myself! How deeply I hate my voice, my walk, my hands, my clothes, my thoughts. This is crazy, isn't it? A year ago I was healthy and strong, full of life, indefatigable, impassioned. I worked hard with these hands, I spoke so well that even an idiot was moved to tears. I cried when something was sad, got angry when I encountered evil. I felt inspired and enjoyed the beauty and poetry of quiet nights when I'd sit working at my desk all night long, or just amuse myself with my own thoughts. I believed in the future, as if I was looking in the eyes of my own mother… But now, oh, my God! I'm so tired. I can't believe how lazy I am every day. Nothing works — my brain, my hands, or my feet. The estate is going to hell, the forest screams under the ax. *(He weeps)* Even my land looks at me like its an orphan. I'm waiting for nothing, I pity nothing, my soul trembles at the thought of tomorrow… And Sarra? I vowed eternal love, saw nothing but happiness, promised her a glorious future. She believed me. But during these whole five years I can see how the light is dying in her — how all her hopes and sacrifices have come to nothing. God knows, she's never given me so much as a questioning glance — not a word of reproach. So why have I stopped loving her… How? Why? I don't understand. Here she is suffering, she's dying, and I, like the lowest coward in the world, run away from her pale face, her sunken chest, her imploring eyes… It's shameful, shameful!

*Pause.*

And of course Sasha, a child really, is also affected by my misery. She tells me she loves me, me — an old man, and when she says it, I become intoxicated, I forget about everything else in the world, I'm enchanted, and I shout: "New life! Good fortune!" But the next day it's totally different, I believe in good fortune as much as I believe in fairy dust. What's wrong with me? Into what abyss am I falling? Why am I so weak? Why am I so nervous? It only takes my sick wife to get me going, or a servant who makes a mistake, or the sound of a rifle misfiring for me to become rude and ugly. I don't even know who I am anymore…

*Pause.*

I don't understand, I don't understand, I don't understand! Just put a bullet in my head!...

LVOV: *(Enters)* I need to talk with you, Nikolai Alekseyevich!

IVANOV: I don't think I can bear to talk right now, Doctor.

LVOV: Will you be so good as to hear me out?

IVANOV: I hear you out every day and frankly, I don't understand — what exactly do you want from me?

LVOV: I think I speak clearly and frankly, and only someone without a heart can possibly misunderstand me…

IVANOV: What, my wife is near death — I know. I am irretrievably guilty — I also know. You are an honest, direct man — yes, I know that too! What more do you need to say?

LVOV: Human cruelty makes me so angry… Your wife is dying. She has a father and mother whom she loves and would want to see before her death. They know all too well she will die soon and that she still loves them. But their cruelty makes them blind. They still curse her! You, the man for whom she has sacrificed everything — her faith, her family — you, without a shred of conscience, you go riding off to those Lebedevs every day!

IVANOV: Akh, I haven't been there in two weeks…

LVOV: *(Not listening to him)* With people like you, one must speak directly, no beating around the bush — if you don't want to listen to me, then don't listen! I am accustomed to calling things by their real name… you need her to die in order for you to take your next steps — so be it — but can't you wait? Let her die in her own time before you damage her any further with your undisguised cynicism. Would the Lebedevs and Sasha — with her dowry — run away from you so fast? Not now, maybe in a year or two, you, incredible hypocrite that you are, you, will have plenty of time to turn the head of that girl and seize her dowry… Why are you in such a hurry? Why do you need your wife to die now — not in a month, not in a year?...

IVANOV: This is torture... Doctor Lvov, are you such a terrible doctor that you can't see a man struggling to restrain himself? I'm controlling everything in me to keep from responding to your insults.

LVOV: Enough, who do you think you're fooling? I can see right through you.

IVANOV: You think you are so smart — you understand everything about me! Yes? I married Anna to get her large dowry... They didn't give me the dowry, I made a mistake and now I'm trying to kill her so that I can marry another woman and get an even bigger dowry... Yes? What a simplistic view of life you have... a man is so simple and uncomplicated? No, Doctor, we're all much too complex to be judged so easily by one impression. I don't understand you, you don't understand me — hell, we don't even understand our own selves. Is it possible to be a wonderful doctor — and at the same time know nothing about people? Don't be so sure of yourself about this.

LVOV: Yes, and in contrast, you think you are so deep, and I am so stupid that I can't distinguish duplicity from integrity?

IVANOV: Evidently, we'll never understand each other... I am asking one last time — and please answer me this time without more of your sermons — what exactly do you need from me? What are you getting at? *(Irritatedly)* And with whom do I have the honor of speaking: with my public prosecutor or with my wife's physician?

LVOV: I am a physician, and as a physician, I demand that you change your behavior... It is killing Anna Petrovna!

IVANOV: What do you want me to do? What? If you understand me better than I understand myself, then please tell me: what should I do?

LVOV: At least, don't flaunt your new love affair.

IVANOV: Ah, my God! Don't you even hear yourself? *(He drinks water)* Leave me alone. Yes, I am a thousand times guilty. I will answer before God, but no one has authorized you to torment me every day...

LVOV: And who has authorized you to insult and obscure the truth? You have exhausted and poisoned my soul. Before I came to this county, I knew there were people who were stupid, crazy, emotional, but I never believed there were people who were actual criminals, and knowingly, by their own will, did evil to others... I respected and loved people, but now that I have met you, I see...

IVANOV: I've heard enough!

LVOV: Oh, have you heard enough? *(Seeing SASHA entering; she is in a riding habit)* Of course. Yes, I hope we have well understood one another! *(He shrugs his shoulders and exits)*

IVANOV: *(Frightened)* Shura, is that you?

SASHA: Yes. Hi. You didn't expect me? Where have you been lately?

IVANOV: Shura, for God's sake, this is reckless! My wife will take this badly.

SASHA: She won't see me. I came in the back way. I am leaving soon. I'm worried: are you all right? Why haven't you come to see us for so long?

IVANOV: My wife is already upset — she's dying — she doesn't need you coming here. Shura, Shura, it is so thoughtless and cruel!

SASHA: What was I supposed to do? You haven't been to see us in two weeks. You didn't answer my letters. I was in torment. I was so worried that you were gravely ill, I haven't gotten any sleep. I'm leaving immediately... Just tell me: are you healthy?

IVANOV: Of course not! I make myself crazy, everyone else makes me crazy — I have no idea how to handle it all. But now you come here! This is absolutely crazy! Shura, you have no idea how guilty I feel, how guilty…

SASHA: You can't seem to stop saying dreadful, wretched things! You're guilty? Yes? Guilty? Of what?

IVANOV: I don't know, I don't know…

SASHA: That's not an answer. Every sinner knows why he feels guilty. Are you a thief? A murderer?

IVANOV: It's not funny!

SASHA: Guilty, because you fell out of love with your wife? Maybe, but a man can't master his own feelings, you didn't want to fall out of love with her. You're guilty because she saw us kissing? I know you didn't want her to see…

IVANOV: *(Interrupting)* Etcetera, etcetera… I fell in love, I fell out of love, I'm not the master of my own feelings — it's all tripe and it doesn't help…

SASHA: I get so exhausted talking to you. *(She looks at a picture)* What a lovely painting! Is that dog from real life?

IVANOV: From real life. This entire romance of ours — is pure fiction! "He loses heart and trips on firm ground. She shows up, cheerful, full of heart, strong, to help him." Yes, yes, it's beautiful and it only happens in romance novels — but in real life…

SASHA: And in real life it's the same.

IVANOV: You have no subtlety! All my moaning should inspire pure terror in you. But no, you think I'm a second Hamlet. The truth is my neuroses are a joke — nothing more! You should laugh your head off, but instead you cry "help!" You think you can save me. Akh, I hate myself today! But I have a feeling something is going to change inside me today… Or I'll crack…

SASHA: That's exactly what you need to do — crack something open… or scream out loud. You're angry with me, I did something stupid, I came here. Well, scream at me, stamp your feet. Well? Get angry…

*Pause.*

Well?

IVANOV: You're funny.

SASHA: Excellent! We seem to be smiling! Would you be so kind as to smile one more time!

IVANOV: *(He laughs)* I see: when you begin to knock some sense into me, you get this look on your face and your eyes get so big, like you are looking at something extraordinary. Wait, you have something on your shoulder. *(He wipes the lint from her shoulder)* We men are babies in your arms. You women look like you're so innocent — everything you do seems sweet and naïve, but you're not so innocent, believe me. If only everyone was like you. If a man is healthy, strong and happy, you don't pay him any attention, but as soon as he goes downhill and starts moaning about it, you throw yourself into his arms. Do you think it's worse to be the wife of a brave, courageous man than to be the nurse to an unlucky crybaby?

SASHA: Worse!

IVANOV: Why? *(He guffaws)* This will be news to Darwin! You'll be the death of the human race. Because of your kindness, soon there'll only be moaners and groaners and neurotics on this earth!

SASHA: You men don't get it, do you? Any girl is sooner attracted to a failure than a lucky man, because we women need to support our men… Do you understand? Support! Men are always busy with business and so love is put on the back burner. To have a talk with his wife, to take a walk with her in the garden, to spend some pleasant time, to shed tears on her little grave — that's it! But with women — love is our life! I love you — that means that I dream about how I'll cure you from your sadness, how I'll do anything for you… you're on the top of the mountain and I'm climbing up; you're in a hole at the bottom and I'm climbing down. I would be most happy when I am re-copying your papers all night long, or standing guard to make sure no one woke you, or walking sixty miles with you on foot. I remember, three years ago, at harvest-time, you came to our house completely covered in dust, sunburned, worn out, and you asked for something to drink. I brought you a glass of water, but you had already collapsed on the sofa and you were sleeping like the dead. You slept at our house for twelve hours and all that time I stood at the door, kept watch to make sure no one disturbed you. And I loved it! The more the work, the better the love. Don't you see, the more miserable you are, the more alive my love is.

IVANOV: Miserable love… Hm… That's just ridiculous, romantic trash! I don't know — *(He shrugs his shoulders)* God only knows! *(Cheerfully)* Shura, honest to God, I'm a respectable man! Judge for yourself, I've always loved to philosophize, but I've never in my life said: "women are spoiled" or "women will lead you down the garden path". Honestly, I've been thankful for women — just thankful! My little girl, you're so, so funny! And I, I'm a fool, a dolt! I disturb good Christian people by moaning and groaning all day long. Boo-oo! Hoo-oo! *(Quickly walking away)* Go, Sasha! We are forgetting ourselves…

SASHA: Yes, it's time to go. *Do svidanya.* I'm afraid your dutiful doctor will have already told Anna Petrovna that I'm here. Listen to me: go sit with your wife — sit, sit, sit… If necessary, sit there for a year. Ten years — sit there for ten years. Do your duty. Grieve, and beg her forgiveness, and weep — everything you have to do. But most importantly, don't forget your work.

IVANOV: I can't stop feeling as if I've eaten too many mushrooms. Again!

SASHA: Well, God bless you! Don't even think about me! Scribble me a line or two every couple weeks — I'd be happy for that. And I'll answer you…

*BORKIN peeks in the door.*

BORKIN: Nikolai Alekseyevich, may I come in? *(Seeing SASHA)* I'm sorry, I didn't see you… *(He enters) Bonjour!* *(He bows)*

SASHA: *(Embarrassed)* How do you do…

BORKIN: You have put on a little weight — prettier.

SASHA: *(To IVANOV)* So I'll go, Nikolai Alekseyevich… I'll go. *(She exits)*

BORKIN: Lovely vision! I arrived for prose, but stumbled onto poetry… *(He sings)* "You appeared, like a little bird to light…"

*IVANOV anxiously paces.*

*(He takes a seat)* And there is something about her, *Nicolas* — unique…. True? Something special… fantastic… *(He sighs)* In essence, the richest, most eligible girl in the entire county. Unfortunately, her mother is such a meanie, that no one wants to have anything to do with her. When she dies, Shurochka gets everything, but until then she'll give her a dowry of ten thousand and an ironing board, and still order you to bow down on your knees to her. *(He rummages in his pockets)* Want a smoke *de-los-makhoros*? *(He extends a cigar case)* They're great… a really good smoke.

IVANOV: *(Walks up to BORKIN, choking with anger)* Get the hell out of my house! This very minute!

*BORKIN starts to rise and drops his cigar.*

Out — this very minute!

BORKIN: *Nicolas,* what's going on? Why are you angry?

IVANOV: Why? And where did you get those cigars? Don't you think I know where you take the old man every day — and why!

BORKIN: *(He shrugs his shoulders)* So what?

IVANOV: You're such a good-for-nothing! All your dreadful schemes that you impose on everyone in the neighborhood — and I get blamed for them. We have nothing in common, and I ask you to leave my home this very minute! *(He quickly paces)*

BORKIN: I know you're feeling out of sorts so I'm not angry with you. Insult me all you want… *(He picks up the cigar)* But it's time to stop this sad little boy routine. You're not a kid…

IVANOV: What did I just say? *(Trembling)* Do you hear me?

*Enter ANNA PETROVNA.*

BORKIN: Well, here's Anna Petrovna… I'll go. *(He exits)*

*IVANOV stops near the table and stands, hanging his head.*

ANNA PETROVNA: *(After a pause)* Why did she come here just now?

*Pause.*

I'm asking you: why did she come here?

IVANOV: Please don't ask me, Anyuta…

*Pause.*

I am profoundly guilty. Think up whatever punishment you want, I will bear everything, but… don't ask… I don't have the strength to answer.

ANNA PETROVNA: *(Angrily)* Why was she here?

*Pause.*

You are really something! Now I understand you. Finally I see, what kind of person you are. Dishonorable, disgraceful... Do you remember when you lied to me, when you told me you loved me... I believed you and I gave up my father, my mother, my religion and I married you... You lied to me about truth, about kindness, about your own hopes and desires, and I believed every word...

IVANOV: Anyuta, I never lied to you...

ANNA PETROVNA: I lived with you for five years. It was so terrible for me to renounce my faith, but I loved you and I never abandoned you even for one minute... You were my hero... And what? All of that time you were deceiving me in the most disgraceful way...

IVANOV: Anyuta, that's not true. I have made many mistakes, yes, but I have never lied to you! In that you cannot reproach me...

ANNA PETROVNA: Now everything is clear... You married me for my money. Yes, that's what you thought...

IVANOV: Oh, good lord! Anyuta, I can't live through this... *(He weeps)*

ANNA PETROVNA: Be quiet! When you saw there was no money, you began a new conquest... Now I understand everything. *(She weeps)* You never loved me and never were true to me... Never!...

IVANOV: Libby, that's a lie!... You can say anything you want, but don't insult me with a lie...

ANNA PETROVNA: Dishonorable man... You owe Lebedev money, and now, in order to get out of the debt, you want to turn his daughter's head, to deceive her the same way you did me. True?

IVANOV: *(Choking)* Be quiet, for the love of God! I won't answer for myself... I'm choking with anger, and I... I could say something I'll regret...

ANNA PETROVNA: You've always deceived me outrageously, and not just me alone… All dishonorable tricks you blamed on Borkin, but now I know — whose they were…

IVANOV: Sarra, be quiet, go, or something awful will come out… *(He shouts)* Be quiet, Jew!

ANNA PETROVNA: I cannot be quiet… You have deceived me far too long.

IVANOV: So you won't be quiet? *(He struggles with himself)* For the love of God…

ANNA PETROVNA: Now go and deceive Miss Lebedev…

IVANOV: You are dying — do you know that? The doctor told me you will die soon…

ANNA PETROVNA: *(She sits, with a weak voice)* When did he tell you that?

*Pause.*

IVANOV: *(Clutching his head)* I'm so terrible — so terrible… *(He sobs)*

CURTAIN

# ACT IV

*One year has passed.*

*One of the sitting rooms in the LEBEDEV home. In the front is an arch, separating the sitting-room from the hall. To the right and left, doors. Antique bronze, family portraits. Festive decorations. An upright piano, on it a violin, nearby a cello. Continuously during the act guests stroll, dressed in evening clothes.*

LVOV: *(He enters, looks at his watch)* Five o'clock. The benediction should have started… There'll be the blessing and then the ceremony. Behold, a celebration of virtue and truth! He didn't succeed in robbing Sarra, but he plagued the life out of her till she died, and now he has found someone else. With this one he'll play the lover until he has robbed her, and when he's taken everything, they'll bury her next to poor Sarra. The same old greedy story…

*Pause.*

Landing in seventh heaven, he'll be in seventh heaven until he's a hundred and then die with a peaceful conscience. No, I must expose him! When I tear away your damned mask, everyone will recognize you — they will see the hungry wolf you are, you will be shot and sent to such a terrible hell from which even the devil couldn't save you! I am an honest man, my duty is to intervene in your life and open everyone's eyes. I will fulfill my responsibility and tomorrow you'll be kicked out of this damned county! *(He ponders)* How? It'll never work to just tell the Lebedevs — Challenge him to a duel? Make some gossip? My God, I'm as excited as a child. I've completely lost the ability to rationally examine the pros and cons of the situation. What should I do? A duel?

KOSYKH: *(He enters, joyfully to LVOV)* Yesterday I made a small slam with clubs, but I could have made a grand slam. Once again Barabanov gummed up the works! We start playing. I bid, no trump. He passes. Two clubs. He passes again. I bid two diamonds… three clubs… and imagine, can you imagine: I make a slam, but he never plays his ace. Show it, you bastard! If I knew about the ace, I could have had a no trump grand slam…

LVOV: Pardon me, I don't play cards. Therefore I have no idea what you're talking about. Is the benediction soon?

KOSYKH: It should be. Zyuzyushka will turn the tide. She is screaming and complaining about the dowry.

LVOV: Not about her daughter?

KOSYKH: No, the dowry. And it's such a pity. He's getting married so that he won't have to pay his debt. You can't sue your own son-in-law over an unpaid debt.

BABAKINA: *(Dressed up pretentiously, walks past LVOV and KOSYKH; the latter bursts out laughing; she looks around)* Idiot!

   *KOSYKH touches her waist with his finger and laughs.*

Muzhik! *(She exits)*

KOSYKH: *(He guffaws)* The old girl has gone completely nuts. Until she started climbing up the social ladder to get to become Her Highness — she was a nobody, but now I can't get near her. *(He mocks)* Muzhik!

LVOV: *(Anxious)* Listen, tell me candidly: what do you think of Ivanov?

KOSYKH: Not much. He plays cards like he had two left hands. Last year during Lent, listen to what happened: we sit down to play — the Count, Borkin, and me — I deal…

LVOV: *(Interrupting)* Is he a good person?

KOSYKH: Him? A rotter! He's a real swindler! He and the Count — two of a kind. They get the scent for some dirty work and off they go. He tried to get the Jew's fortune — couldn't do it, and now he's on the move to open up Zyuzyushka. I bet anything, if in a year he ruins Zyuzyushka, he and the Count will take all the cash and live happily ever after. Doctor, why are you so pale today? You don't look like yourself.

LVOV: Nothing. I drank too much yesterday.

LEBEDEV: *(Entering with SASHA)* Let's talk here. *(To LVOV and KOSYKH)* Buzz off, Zulus. Go see the pretty girls in the other room. We need to talk in private.

KOSYKH: *(Passing by SASHA, enthusiastically snaps his fingers)* Snap! Queen of hearts!

LEBEDEV: Go, troglodyte, go!

*LVOV and KOSYKH exit.*

Sit, Shurochka, sit... *(He takes a seat and looks around)* Listen carefully and respectfully. Here's the thing — your mother ordered me to tell you this — do you understand? I am not speaking for myself, your mother ordered me...

SASHA: Papa, get to the point!

LEBEDEV: A dowry of fifteen thousand is all set for you. Here... Don't say another word — hold it — be quiet! That's the beginning, I've got more to say. A dowry of fifteen thousand is set for you, but, taking into account that Nikolai Alekseyevich owes your mother nine thousand, we'll have to subtract that from your dowry... Well, sweetie, later... perhaps...

SASHA: Why are you talking to me about this?

LEBEDEV: Your Mother ordered me to!

SASHA: Leave me alone! If you respected me, or yourself even a little, you would never talk to me about this. I don't need your dowry! I didn't ask for it before and I don't now.

LEBEDEV: What are you yelling at me for? Gogol has two rats who sniff each other out, and then they go away. But you, Miss Emancipated Lady, you don't sniff, you just attack me.

SASHA: Leave me alone. I'm not interested in your money talk.

LEBEDEV: *(Flaring up)* Phooey! Women! I'll either stick a knife in myself or kill someone else! All day long you yell, yell, yell and she nags, nags and pinches pennies. And here sits Miss Emancipated Lady, damn her, who cannot understand one word her father says. Not interested? Too delicate for your emancipated ears? Five minutes ago, *(He indicates the door)* I was being drawn and quartered. She cannot understand! My head is splitting... well ladies, you are... *(He goes to the door and comes to a stop)* I'm not happy about this, not happy at all...

SASHA: Why aren't you happy?

LEBEDEV: I'm unhappy about everything!

SASHA: What is everything?

LEBEDEV: So I'm supposed to sit here and give a recital of everything I'm unhappy about? I'm not happy about anything! I don't like this marriage of yours! *(He goes to SASHA affectionately)* Forgive me, Shurochka, maybe your wedding is a good thing —honorable, and high principled, but there's something wrong about it — wrong, it's not like other weddings. You — you are young, fresh, pure as glass, beautiful, and he — a widower, he's broken down, worn out. And I don't understand him, God bless him. *(He kisses his daughter)* Shurochka, forgive me, but something is unclean here. Already people are talking. They are saying the minute Sarra died, he turned to you... *(Quickly)* Listen, don't listen to me — I'm like an old lady, gossiping... Don't listen to me. Just listen to yourself.

SASHA: Papa, I myself feel something isn't right... Not right, not right, not right. If only you knew how painful it is for me! It's unbearable! It's hard for me to tell you this... Papa, tell me what to do — tell me sweet Papa —

LEBEDEV: What's wrong? What?

SASHA: This is the worst thing that has ever happened to me! *(She looks around)* In truth, I don't understand him, I'll never understand him. For the entire time I've been his fiancée, he hasn't smiled once, not once has he looked me straight in the eye. There are the eternal complaints, the repentance for something he feels he's to blame… shivering, trembling… I'm exhausted. There are even moments when it seems to me, I… I don't love him as much as I should. When he comes to talk with me, I get bored. What does this mean, *Papochka*? I'm scared to death!

LEBEDEV: My little darling, my only baby, listen to your old father. Break this off!

SASHA: *(Frightened)* What are you saying? How can you say that?

LEBEDEV: It's true, Shurochka. There'll be a scandal, the whole county will be burning with gossip, but you know it's better to live through a scandal than to destroy your whole life.

SASHA: Don't speak, don't speak, Papa! I don't want to listen. Sometimes you have to struggle with your dark thoughts. He's a good, unlucky, misunderstood man; I will love him, understand him. I will get him back on his feet. I will carry out my mission. Yes, I have decided!

LEBEDEV: This isn't a mission, it's craziness.

SASHA: Enough. I said things to you that I didn't even want to say to myself. Don't tell anyone. We'll forget about this.

LEBEDEV: Either I don't understand anything or I've gotten stupid in my old age, or all of you are much smarter than me, and I'm the only one who doesn't get it — nothing…

SHABELSKY: *(Entering)* The hell with all of them, that includes me. It's disgraceful!

LEBEDEV: What's with you?

SHABELSKY: No, seriously, I've got to do something so vile and foul that everyone will be furious at me, including me. And I'll do it. Honest to God! I already told Borkin that today he can announce me as a bridegroom. *(He laughs)* Everyone is so low, and I'll be lowest of all.

LEBEDEV: I'm sick of you. Listen, Matvei, keep talking like that and they'll cart you off to the loony bin.

SHABELSKY: What's so terrible about the loony bin? In fact, be so kind as to throw me in there now. Please, please. Everyone's a scoundrel, small, insignificant, third-rate — and I'm the most repulsive of all. I don't believe a single word I say…

LEBEDEV: You know what, brother? Put a cork in your mouth before you breathe on people. Or better yet, take your hat and go home. There's a wedding going on here. Everyone's having a good time except you — caw, caw, caw, like a crow. Yes it's true…

*SHABELSKY drops his head on the piano and sobs.*

Dear old friend… Matvei!… Count!… What's going on? Matyusha, my own… my angel… Did I offend you? Well, forgive me, old dog… Forgive an old drunkard… Drink some water…

SHABELSKY: I don't need it. *(He lifts his head)*

LEBEDEV: Why are you crying?

SHABELSKY: It's nothing, so…

LEBEDEV: No, Matyusha, don't lie… what is it? Why are you crying? Tell me…

SHABELSKY: I looked at that cello and… and I remembered the little Jew…

LEBEDEV: What? *Now* you're thinking about her? God bless her but now is not the time to remember her...

SHABELSKY: I played duets with her... marvelous woman!

   *SASHA sobs.*

LEBEDEV: Now what? That's enough! Lord, they're both slobbering, but I... I... At least get out of here, the guests will see!

SHABELSKY: Pasha, when the sun shines, it's cheerful even in the cemetery. When there's hope, then even old age can be good. But I have no hope, not one!

LEBEDEV: Yes, I know, I know things aren't too good for you right now... You have no children, no money, no job... Well, what can you do! *(To SASHA)* And what do we do with you?

SHABELSKY: Pasha, give me some money. We'll settle up in the other world. I'll go to Paris, sit by my wife's grave. I've given away so much all my life — my whole fortune — so I have the right to ask. And I'm asking you as a friend...

LEBEDEV: *(Confused)* My darling, I don't have a *kopek*! But, yes, alright... fine... good... I'm not promising anything, mind you but... excellent, excellent! *(Aside)* They've completely worn me out!

BABAKINA: *(She enters)* Where's my cavalier? Count, how dare you leave me alone? Ooh, you naughty boy! *(She hits the COUNT with her fan on the arm)*

SHABELSKY: *(Disgustedly)* Leave me in peace! I hate you!

BABAKINA: *(Struck dumb)* What?... Huh?

SHABELSKY: Step aside!

BABAKINA: *(She sinks into an armchair)* Akh! *(She cries)*

ZINAIDA SAVISHNA: *(She enters, crying)* Finally, the groom has arrived... It's time to go to the church... *(She sobs)*

SASHA: *(Imploringly)* Mama!

LEBEDEV: Now everyone is screeching! A quartet! That's enough! Everybody shut up! Matvei!... Marfa Yegorovna!... You know I'll start crying myself... *(He cries)* Oh Lord!

ZINAIDA SAVISHNA: *(To Sasha)* Fine, fine, don't ever consider your Mama. Go do what you want — I give you my blessing...

*Enter IVANOV; he is in a tail-coat and gloves.*

LEBEDEV: This is the last straw! What's wrong?

SASHA: What are you doing here?

IVANOV: It's all my fault. Gentlemen, permit me to talk with Sasha in private.

LEBEDEV: This isn't right — you're not supposed see the bride before the wedding! It's time for all of us to go to the church!

IVANOV: Pasha, I beg you...

*LEBEDEV shrugs his shoulders; he, ZINAIDA SAVISHNA, the COUNT, and BABAKINA exit.*

SASHA: *(Sternly)* What do you want?

IVANOV: I'm choking with anger, but I can speak calmly. Listen. Just now I dressed for the wedding and I looked at myself in the mirror — and at my beard... grey hairs. Shura, is this necessary? Before it's too late, let's call off this farce. You are young, pure, you have your whole life ahead of you but I...

SASHA: I've heard this a thousand times already and I'm sick of it. Let's go to the church, let's not keep everyone waiting.

IVANOV: I'm going home now, and you announce to everyone there won't be a wedding. Announce anything you like. It's time to come to our senses. I played Hamlet, and you played a high-minded, lofty heroine — and now it's enough.

SASHA: *(Flaring up)* What are you saying? I'm not even listening.

IVANOV: But I must speak and I will speak.

SASHA: Why are you here? Your whining is turning into a farce.

IVANOV: No, I'm not whining now! Farce? Yes, I'm a clown. And if I could, I'd be a thousand times funnier and make the whole world laugh hysterically at me! I looked at myself in the mirror — and it was like a shot burst in my head. I laughed at myself and I almost died of shame. *(He laughs)* Melancholy! Unrelenting sadness! Endless grief — the only thing I left out is writing poetry. To whine, to moan about my destiny, to make everyone around me miserable, to know I have no energy or life left in me, that I'm old, that my day has come and gone, that I'm a coward and I'm up to my eyeballs in this vile depression, to know when the sun shines brightly, even the ants carry their burden and are happy. No, no thank you, I'm having none of it! To see, how everyone thinks I'm a charlatan, everyone hates me — and — worst of all — I have to listen to your reverential sighs and watch as you turn me into the Messiah and wait for the second coming… No, thank God, I still have my pride and my conscience! I laughed at myself all the way here and for the first time I could hear the birds laughing at me, and the trees laughing…

SASHA: You're not angry — you're insane!

IVANOV: Do you think so? No, I'm not insane. Now I finally see things in their true light, and my thoughts are as pure as your conscience. We love one another, but we can't get married! I myself can be as furious as

I want and I can mope all day long, but I don't have the right to destroy others! With all my whining I poisoned my wife in the last year of her life. Since you've become my fiancée, you have forgotten how to laugh, you've aged five years. Your father, who is certain about everything in life, since I've been around he has stopped understanding anything. If I visit with people, go hunting with friends — anywhere I go — I bore everyone to death with my depression and my dissatisfaction. Wait, don't interrupt me! I know I'm being harsh, but forgive me, my anger is choking me and I can't help myself. I never used to lie, never railed against my fate, but since I've become a whiny grumbler I can't stop saying awful things about life — I can't stop complaining and everyone near me is poisoned with my opinions and they too bemoan their fate. Just listen to me — it's as if I'm doing life a favor by living! To hell with me!

SASHA: Stop… I can hear you say that you are tired of complaining — you are ready to begin a new life!… That's wonderful!…

IVANOV: I don't see anything wonderful here. What new life? I am irrevocably ruined! It's time for both of us to understand this. New life!

SASHA: Nikolai, pull yourself together! Why do you see yourself as ruined? So cynical! No, I don't want to listen… Let's go to the church!

IVANOV: Ruined — destroyed!

SASHA: Don't shout, the guests will hear you!

IVANOV: If a fairly smart, educated, healthy person, for no apparent reason, begins to bemoan his fate and goes downhill, then he's already lost, and there's no escape for him! How do I escape? How? I can't drink — I get a headache from wine; I can't start writing poetry — I don't know how. I can't praise my laziness or my weaknesses as lofty — I can't. Laziness is laziness, weakness is weakness — I have no other names for it. I'm ruined, destroyed — and there's no other way to say it! *(He looks around)* They might come in any minute. Listen, if you love me, then help me. Call off the wedding right now — Quickly…

SASHA: Akh, Nikolai, if only you knew how much you've worn me out! You've tormented my soul! Good, kind, intelligent man, you must realize how impossible this is for me. Every day it gets more difficult — I wanted a living love, but this is hell!

IVANOV: When you become my wife, it will be even more difficult. So give me up! Please understand: it's not love that speaks to you, it's stubbornness. You made up your mind to save me, to rescue me. It made you feel good about yourself, that you were doing something heroic. But now you're ready to step back and let go. Don't you see it?

SASHA: How crazy! You think I can give you up? How will I give you up? You don't have a mother, or sister, or even any friends… You're worn out, little by little you're losing your estate, people are saying terrible things about you everywhere…

IVANOV: I was so stupid in coming here. I should have done what I first wanted to do…

*Enter LEBEDEV.*

SASHA: *(She runs to meet her father)* Papa, for God's sake, he ran in here like a crazy person, and he's tormenting me! He's demanding that I give him up. He says he doesn't want to destroy me. Tell him I don't want his generosity! I know what I'm doing.

LEBEDEV: I don't understand this… What generosity?

IVANOV: The wedding is called off!

SASHA: No, Papa, tell him the wedding will go on!

LEBEDEV: Hold on, hold on a minute… Why do you want to call it off?

IVANOV: I already told her, but she doesn't want to understand.

LEBEDEV: No, not to her, explain it to me — yes, explain it to me, so that I can understand! Akh, Nikolai Alekseyevich! God be your judge!

You have made such a mess in our lives. It feels like I'm looking at a funhouse mirror. I look in it and I can't see anything... I just see distortion and horror... Well, what am I to do with you? Challenge you to a duel?

IVANOV: No, not necessary. All you need to do is be a rational human being and to understand Russian.

SASHA: *(Paces in agitation)* This is horrible, horrible! He's such a baby!

LEBEDEV: I'm supposed to shrug my shoulders and just listen to you? You listen, Nikolai! According to you it's all in your head — all a matter of psychology — but according to me it's scandal and misery. Listen to this old man one last time! Here's what I say to you: calm down! Look on things simply, like everybody else! Everything is simple in this world. The ceiling is white, boots are black, sugar is sweet. You love Sasha, she loves you. If you love her — stay; if you don't love her — go — no hard feelings. You see, it's so simple! You're both healthy, intelligent, moral, well-fed, thank God, and have clothes on your backs... What more do you need? Money? It means nothing! Happiness isn't money... Of course, I understand... your estate is mortgaged, there's no money to pay the interest, but I — yes, I understand... Sadly her mother, God be with her — she won't give any money — well the hell with that. Shura tells me she doesn't care about a dowry. She's spouting her principles, Schopenhauer or something... Nonsense... I have ten thousand in the bank... *(He looks around)* It's a secret — no one knows about it...it was your Grandmother's... Now it's for both of you... Take the money — one condition — give Matvei two thousand...

*In the hall guests are gathering.*

IVANOV: Don't say another word, Pasha. I'm going to follow my own conscience.

SASHA: And I'm following my conscience. You can talk all you want, but I won't change my mind. Papa, let's get to the church! I'll call Mama... *(She exits)*

LEBEDEV: I don't understand anything...

IVANOV: Listen, my poor friend... I'm not going to try to get you to understand me — either sane or crazy. I won't bore you with all the details. I'll just say I was young, passionate, sincere, not stupid; I loved, hated and saw the world differently than everyone else. I worked and had unlimited aspirations. I battled with windmills, I beat my head against the wall. I never understood my own strength, never understood life's burdens, so I overloaded myself, and just about broke my back. I thought I'd always be young and I used myself up. I drank and I worked and I was passionate — no limits on anything. Do you think I could have done it differently? There were so few of us and there was so much to do! So much! And now it all comes back in my face! I overdid it! Then at thirty years of age, I was finished. I was old, I was lying around the house in my bathrobe — lying around exhausted, broken, without love, without God, without any purpose in my life. I'm standing in the middle of a crowd and I can't figure out where I am or who I am or why I'm living at all. And to me it now seems, that love — all that nonsense, those kisses and caresses — it's all sickly sweet. Work is meaningless. Music and passionate speeches are vulgar and trite. And I bring this sadness with me everywhere — disinterested boredom, discontent, a disgust for life... I've destroyed everything, irrevocably! Before you stands a man, who, at thirty-five, is tired, disillusioned, crushed by his own insignificance. He is burning with shame, mocking his own weakness... Oh, my pride is killing me, my fury is strangling me! *(Staggering)* Oh my God, look how tired I am. I can't even walk straight... I'm too weak. Where's Matvei? He needs to take me home.

VOICE IN THE HALL: The best man has arrived!

SHABELSKY: *(Entering)* Here I am in a borrowed, shabby, threadbare tailcoat... without gloves... and everyone is giving me dirty looks and making nasty jokes... Disgusting, small-minded people!

BORKIN: *(Quickly enters with a bouquet; he is in tails, with a best-man's flower)* Oof! Where is he? *(To IVANOV)* They've been waiting for you in the church for a long time, but you're here, philosophizing for a change… What a clown! Don't you know — you come with me, you don't arrive with the bride! I will go back for the bride. My God, you don't even get this? What a jackass!

LVOV: *(He enters, to IVANOV)* Ah, you're here? *(Loudly)* Nikolai Alekseyevich Ivanov, I want to publicly declare — You are a scoundrel!

IVANOV: *(Coldly)* I most humbly thank you.

*General embarrassment.*

BORKIN: *(To LVOV)* How dare you insult him, sir! I challenge you to a duel!

LVOV: Sir, I not only consider it too degrading to fight with you, but I can't even speak to you! *(To IVANOV)* You, sir, can take satisfaction when it suits you.

SHABELSKY: Sir, I will fight with you!

SASHA: *(To LVOV)* Why? Why are you insulting him? Excuse me, gentlemen, let him tell me: why?

LVOV: Aleksandra Pavlovna, I certainly didn't insult him for no reason. I am here as an honest man in order to open your eyes and ask you hear me out.

SASHA: What do you have to tell us? You're an honest man? Everyone in the world knows that! I'd rather have you tell me honestly, do you understand yourself or not? You come here now as an honest man and throw terrible insults at him — which nearly killed me by the way. Earlier, when you were shadowing him, and choking the life out of him, you did it in the name of honesty — as if you were doing your duty. You meddled in his private life, said spiteful things about him and judged him for everything he did. Then you sent poisonous anonymous letters to me and all our friends. And all of this once again in the name of honesty. You were too honest, doctor, to spare his sick wife from your suspicions and give her any peace.

So whatever kind of violence, whatever brutal meanness you do, it will always appear to you as if you are an unusually honest and advanced man!

IVANOV: *(Laughing)* This isn't a wedding, it's a session of Congress! Bravo, bravo!...

SASHA: *(To LVOV)* Now do you understand yourself? Dumb, heartless people! *(She takes IVANOV by the hand)* Let's leave here, Nikolai! Father, let's go!

IVANOV: Where can we go? Stop! I'm going to finish everything! I'm finally awake again — I'm back! *(He takes out a revolver)*

SASHA: *(She cries out)* Nikolai, for God's sake!

IVANOV: I've been going downhill for so long. Now it's time to find my honor! Move away! Thank you, Sasha!

SASHA: *(She cries)* Nikolai, for God's sake! Stop him! Don't let him go!

IVANOV: Leave me alone! *(He runs offstage and shoots himself)*

    CURTAIN.

# *Seagull*

## A Comedy in Four Acts

(1896)

## CHARACTERS

**Irina Nikolayevna Arkadina**, by marriage Treplyova, an actress.

**Konstantin Gavrilovich Treplyov (Kostya)**, her son.

**Pyotr Nikolayevich Sorin**, her brother.

**Nina Mikhailovna Zarechnaya**, the daughter of a wealthy landowner.

**Ilya Afanasyevich Shamrayev**, a retired lieutenant, Sorin's farm manager.

**Polina Andreyevna**, his wife.

**Marya Ilyinichna (Masha)**, his daughter.

**Boris Alekseyevich Trigorin**, a fiction writer.

**Yevgenii Sergeyevich Dorn**, a doctor.

**Semyon Semyonovich Medvedenko**, a schoolteacher.

**Yakov**, a worker.

**A Cook.**

**A Housemaid.**

> *The action takes place on Sorin's country estate.*
> *Between the third and fourth acts two years pass.*

# ACT 1

*A grassy portion of SORIN's country home. A broad path, leading to a lake, with a stage hurriedly thrown up for an amateur performance, so the lake is not completely visible. To the left and right of the stage are shrubs. A few chairs, a little table.*

*The sun has just set. On the stage behind the lowered curtain are YAKOV and other workers; a cough and a tapping are heard. MASHA and MEDVEDENKO enter left, returning from a stroll.*

MEDVEDENKO: Why are you always in black?

MASHA: I am in mourning for my life. I'm unhappy.

MEDVEDENKO: Why? *(In thought)* I don't understand... You're healthy, your father does well enough. Life is a lot harder for me than for you. I make a total of 23 *rubles* a month, not counting all the deductions, and I don't wear black. *(They sit)*

MASHA: It's not about money. Even a poor man can be happy.

MEDVEDENKO: Oh sure, that's the theory, but here's how it really works: It's my mother, and my two sisters and my little brother, and me — all on 23 *rubles*. Do we need to eat and drink? Do we need tea and sugar? How about tobacco? There's no getting away from it.

MASHA: *(Looking around at the stage)* It's about to start.

MEDVEDENKO: Yes. The play is written by Konstantin Gavrilovich, and Nina Mikhailovna will be acting. They are in love, and today their souls will merge in their desire to create a single artistic vision. But my soul and yours don't meet anywhere. I love you, I cannot sit still at home because I'm so upset. Every day I walk four miles here and four back and I meet with nothing but indifference from you. I understand it. I have nothing to offer, my family is huge. Who would want to marry such a person?

MASHA: Stop it! *(She takes snuff)* I'm touched by your love but I can't return it, that's all. *(She extends the snuff-box to him)* Want some?

MEDVEDENKO: No thanks...

*Pause.*

MASHA: It's stifling. I bet there'll be a storm tonight. All you ever talk about is money. According to you, there's nothing worse than being poor, but in my opinion, it's a thousand times better to be a poor beggar than... Oh, you wouldn't understand...

*SORIN and TREPLYOV enter from the right.*

SORIN: *(Leaning on his walking-stick)* One is not oneself in the country, my dear, and that's understandable — but I will never get used to it here. Yesterday I went to sleep at ten and woke up at nine this morning feeling like my brain was stuck to my skull — so strange. *(He laughs)* And after lunch I fell asleep again, and now I am completely *razbit*. It's like constantly living in a nightmare, as it were...

TREPLYOV: You really should live in town. *(Seeing MASHA and MEDVEDENKO)* Ladies and gentlemen, we will let you know when we're starting, but right now you're not allowed to be here. Leave, please.

SORIN: *(To MASHA)* Marya Ilyinichna, be so kind as to ask your papa to unchain the dog, otherwise it will howl all night. My sister didn't sleep again last night.

MASHA: Talk to him yourself, I won't do it. Leave me alone, please. *(To MEDVEDENKO)* Let's go!

MEDVEDENKO: *(To TREPLYOV)* Don't forget to tell us when it's starting. *(Both exit)*

SORIN: I can hear it now, the dog will howl all night long. In truth, I have never lived the way I wanted in the country. We used to come here for a month's vacation, to rest, as it were, but once we arrived, it was so intolerable, we wanted to leave after the very first day. *(He laughs)* Leaving here was always the best part… Well… now that I'm retired, there is no place else to go. One keeps living whether one wants to or not.

YAKOV: *(To TREPLYOV)* Konstantin Gavrilovich, we're going for a swim.

TREPLYOV: Fine, only be back and ready to go in ten minutes. *(He looks at his watch)* It will start soon.

YAKOV: Sounds good. *(He exits)*

TREPLYOV: *(Casting a glance to the stage)* Now this is a theater! A curtain, downstage, upstage, and beyond that, total emptiness. No scenery of any kind. The scenery is the lake and the horizon. The curtain will go up at 8:30 sharp, when the moon is rising.

SORIN: Splendid.

TREPLYOV: If Nina doesn't get here soon, then, of course, the whole effect will be ruined. Oh God, she's already late. Her father and stepmother stand guard over her, and getting away from them is like escaping from prison. *(He adjusts his uncle's tie)* Your hair and beard are such a mess. I think you need a haircut, or something…

SORIN: *(Combing his beard)* The tragedy of my life. When I was young, I always looked like a drunkard, as it were. Women never liked me. *(Sitting)* Why is my sister so out of sorts?

TREPLYOV: Why? She's bored. She's jealous. She hates me, hates my play, hates this show, because her famous author might take a liking to Nina. She doesn't even know my play, but already she hates it.

SORIN: *(He laughs)* You're making that up…

TREPLYOV: No, she's already upset that it will be Nina's triumph on this little stage and not hers. *(Looking at his watch)* Quite a character—my mother. Undoubtedly talented, intelligent, she'll collapse weeping over a book, she recites all of Nekrasov by heart, she nurses the sick like an angel; but try to praise Duse in front of her! Ohoho no! You can only praise her, you have to rave about her, cry in rapture over her astounding performance in "*La dame aux camellias*," but here, in the country, she can't get any of that, so she's bored and edgy, and we are all her enemies, it's all our fault. And on top of that, she's superstitious, afraid of three candles, the number thirteen. She's a miser. She has seventy thousand in a bank in Odessa — I know that for a fact. But ask her for a loan, and she'll start to cry.

SORIN: You are imagining that your mother won't like your play, and you are already worried, as it were. Calm down, your mother adores you.

TREPLYOV: *(Plucking petals from a flower)* She loves me — she loves me not, loves me — loves me not, loves me — loves me not. *(He laughs)* See, my mother doesn't love me. So true! She wants to live, love, wear bright, beautiful clothes, but I'm twenty-five years old, and a continual reminder she's not young anymore. When I'm not around, she's only thirty-two, but when I am, she's forty-three, and for that she hates me. She also knows that I do not accept her theatre. She loves "the theatre." She thinks she's dedicated to serving humanity, to her sacred art, but in my opinion, contemporary theatre — is banal, meaningless tripe. When the curtain goes up and artificial lights suddenly go on, in a room with three walls, these great talents, these priestesses of sacred art show us "reality": how people eat, drink, make love, walk, sport their fashionable clothes. And from these vulgar, trivial scenes and dialogue they mightily endeavor to extort a moral — an important moral, something useful for living one's life — but in a thousand variations they always bring me the same old moral, the same trite idea — and then I run and run, like Maupassant ran from the Eiffel Tower, which crushed his brain with its vulgarity.

SORIN: Where would we be without the theater!

TREPLYOV: What we need are new forms. We need new forms and if we can't have them then give us nothing. *(He looks at his watch)* I love my mother, love her very much; but she smokes, drinks, lives openly with that author of hers, her name is always in the newspapers — and I can't stand it anymore. I know it's probably my ego speaking now, but I hate that she's a famous actress, and I think if she were just an ordinary woman I would be much happier. Uncle, could the situation be any worse? She's always surrounded by celebrities, artists and writers and I'm the only nobody in the room — and these celebrities only talk to me because I am her son. Who am I? What am I? I was expelled from the university in my third year under the "most questionable of circumstances". Here I am with no talent whatsoever, not a *kopek* to my name, and according to my passport I am forever classified as a "Kiev Provincial". My father, as you know, also never escaped being a "Kiev Provincial", even though he was a successful actor. And on the rare occasion when all the celebrities, the artists and writers in her living room condescend to turn their kind attention on me, I can feel them measuring my nothingness — I know what they are thinking and I feel humiliated.

SORIN: By the way, please tell me the gossip about this celebrated author of hers. He's hard to figure out. He's always so quiet.

TREPLYOV: Our celebrated author is actually intelligent, unpretentious, a little bit, you know, melancholy. He's very decent, really. He's not even forty, but he's already a star and he's as self-satisfied as a cat who swallowed the cream. These days he drinks a lot of beer and makes love to old women. As for his writing... what's there to say... He's clever, talented... but... after Tolstoy or Zola you don't want to read Trigorin.

SORIN: Ah, my boy, I love the *literati*. When I was young I passionately wanted two things: I wanted to marry and I wanted to become an author, but I didn't manage either one. Yes. I think it would be lovely to even be a minor author, as it were.

TREPLYOV: *(Listening)* I hear someone... *(He embraces his uncle)* I cannot live without her... Even the sound of her footsteps makes my heart tremble… I am desperately happy. *(Quickly he goes to meet NINA ZARECHNAYA, who enters)* Enchantress, my dream…

NINA: *(Agitatedly)* I'm not late… please tell me I'm not late…

TREPLYOV: *(Kissing her hands)* No, no, no…

NINA: I've been worrying all day. I was afraid my father wouldn't let me go… But he just went out with my stepmother. The sky is red, the moon is starting to rise, and I rode like a madman to get here. *(She laughs)* I'm so excited. *(She firmly presses SORIN's hand)*

SORIN: *(He laughs)* We haven't been crying, have we… No, no!

NINA: You're right… I'm completely out of breath. I have to leave in half an hour. We've got to hurry. Please don't make me be late. My father doesn't know I'm here.

TREPLYOV: Actually, it's time to begin. I'd better go get everyone.

SORIN: I'll go. This minute, as it were. *(He goes to the right and sings)* "To France two grenadiers…" *(He glances around)* Once when I began to sing, a friend, a public prosecutor said to me: "Your Excellency, you have a strong voice"… Then he thought for a moment and added: "But… an unpleasant one." *(He laughs and exits)*

NINA: My father and his wife don't want me to come here. They think this is "Bohemia"… they're afraid I'll become an actress… But I'm drawn here to this lake, like a seagull… My heart is so full of you. *(She glances around)*

TREPLYOV: We are alone.

NINA: I think someone is coming…

TREPLYOV: No one.

*They kiss.*

NINA: What kind of tree is that?

TREPLYOV: Elm.

NINA: Why is it so dark?

TREPLYOV: It's evening, everything looks dark. Don't leave early, I beg you.

NINA: Impossible.

TREPLYOV: What if I go to your house, Nina? I'll stand in the garden and look up at your window all night.

NINA: Impossible. The watchman will see you. And Trezor isn't used to you and he'll bark.

TREPLYOV: I love you.

NINA: Shh…

TREPLYOV: *(Hearing steps)* Who's there? Is that you, Yakov?

YAKOV: *(Behind the stage)* Yup.

TREPLYOV: Take your places. It's time. Is the moon rising?

YAKOV: Yup.

TREPLYOV: Have you got the methylated spirits? The sulphur? When the red eyes appear, it should smell like sulphur. *(To Nina)* Go, everything is ready. Are you nervous?

NINA: Yes, very. Your mother — No, I'm not afraid of her but there's Trigorin… I'm embarrassed, terrified to act in front of him. He's such an important writer… Is he young?

TREPLYOV: Yes.

NINA: What miraculous stories he's written!

TREPLYOV: *(Coldly)* I wouldn't know, I haven't read them.

NINA: It's hard to act in your play. There are no living characters in it.

TREPLYOV: Living characters! A playwright shouldn't present life in reality but only as it comes to us in dreams...

NINA: Nothing happens in your play, and there's nobody to talk to. I definitely think there should be a love story...

*They both exit behind the stage. Enter POLINA ANDREYEVNA and DORN.*

POLINA ANDREYEVNA: It is getting damp. Go back, put on your galoshes.

DORN: I am hot.

POLINA ANDREYEVNA: You don't take care of yourself. It's just stubbornness. You — a doctor. You should know perfectly well that damp air is bad for you, but you want me to suffer; you purposely sat on the terrace all last night...

DORN: *(He sings)* "Don't say, that my youth is ruined."

POLINA ANDREYEVNA: You were so carried away by your conversation with Irina Nikolayevna... you didn't even notice the cold. Admit it, you like her...

DORN: I'm 55 years old.

POLINA ANDREYEVNA: Don't be silly, that's not old for a man. You still look wonderful and women like you.

DORN: What do you want from me?

POLINA ANDREYEVNA: You're always ready to kiss the ground that actress walks on!

DORN: *(He sings)* "I am before you again…" If people treat artists differently than the rest of us, it's only natural. It's — hero worship.

POLINA ANDREYEVNA: Women have always fallen in love with you. They wrap themselves around your little finger. Is that what you call hero worship?

DORN: *(Shrugging his shoulders)* All right, I have always gotten on well with women. They loved me primarily because I was a very good doctor. Ten, fifteen years ago, if you remember, I was the only decent doctor who could deliver babies in the whole province. And besides, I've always been trustworthy.

POLINA ANDREYEVNA: *(She takes him by the hand)* My darling!

DORN: Quiet. They're coming.

*Enter ARKADINA on the arm of SORIN, TRIGORIN, SHAMRAYEV, MEDVEDENKO and MASHA.*

SHAMRAYEV: In 1873 at the Poltava fair she was brilliant. An absolute delight! Marvelous! And what's become of the comic Chadin these days, Pavel Semyonich Chadin? When he played Rasplyuyev he was astonishing, better than Sadovsky, I swear to you, most respected one. Where is he now?

ARKADINA: You're always asking about prehistoric characters. How should I know? *(She sits down)*

SHAMRAYEV: *(Sighing)* Pashka Chadin! There's nobody like him these days. The theater has certainly declined, Irina Nikolayevna! Before there were mighty oaks, but now we only see stumps.

DORN: There aren't many bright stars today, that's true, but the general level of talent is much better.

SHAMRAYEV: I cannot agree with you. However, it is a question of taste. *De gustibus aut bene, aut nihil.*

*TREPLYOV comes out from behind the stage.*

ARKADINA: *(To her son)* My darling son, when do we begin?

TREPLYOV: In a minute. Please be patient.

ARKADINA: *(Reciting from* Hamlet*)*
"My son! Thou turn'st mine eyes into my very soul,
And there I see such black and grained spots,
As will not leave their tinct!"

TREPLYOV: *(From* Hamlet*)*
"Nay, but to live in the rank sweat of an enseamed bed,
Stew'd in corruption, honeying and making love
Over the nasty sty."

*Behind the stage a small horn is heard.*

Ladies and gentlemen, we begin! Attention, please!

*Pause.*

I'm starting. *(He taps a stick and speaks loudly)* O you, honorable ancient shadows, which drift at evening's fall on this lake, lull us to sleep, and let us dream of that which will come to be in two hundred thousand years!

SORIN: In two hundred thousand years there will be nothing.

TREPLYOV: Then let them show us this nothing.

ARKADINA: Let them. We are asleep.

*The curtain rises; a view opens onto the lake; the moon on the horizon, its reflection on the water; NINA ZARECHNAYA sits on a large stone, all in white.*

NINA: People, lions, eagles and partridges, horned deer, geese, spiders, silent fishes dwelling in the water, starfish and those that cannot be seen with our eyes, — in a word, all lives, all lives, all lives, having accomplished their doleful circle: dead… Already thousands of centuries have passed since the earth has borne one living creature and in vain the poor moon shines her light. No longer do the cranes awaken the meadow, no longer do the maybugs sing in the linden groves. Cold, cold, cold. Empty, empty, empty. Horrible, horrible, most horrible.

*Pause.*

The bodies of living creatures have vanished into dust, and eternal matter has turned them into stone, into water, into clouds, and their souls have fused into one. The common world soul — it is I… I… In my soul is Alexander the Great, and Caesar, and Shakespeare, and Napoleon, and the lowliest of leeches. In my consciousness people have fused with instinctual beasts, and I remember everything, everything, everything, and every life that's in me I live again.

*The marsh fires appear.*

ARKADINA: *(Quietly)* I think this is supposed to be "High Art."

TREPLYOV: *(Imploring and with reproach)* Mama!

NINA: I am alone. Once in one hundred years I open my lips in order to speak, and my voice is heard in this cheerless emptiness, and no one listens… Even you, pale fires, do not hear me… Near morning the decayed marsh gives birth to you, and you roam until dawn, but without thoughts, without will, without the quivering of life. Fearing that in you, life will not arise, the father of eternal matter, the devil, every instant in you, as in stones and in water, carries out the exchange of atoms, and you are changing continuously. In the universe only the spirit remains constant and immutable.

*Pause.*

Like a captive, cast into a deep, hollow void, I do not know what waits for me. I see clearly, that in this stubborn, cruel struggle with the devil, the strongest force in this world, I am destined to conquer, and after that matter and soul will come together in beautiful harmony and the kingdom of world liberty will emerge. But that will only be, when little by little, over a long, long thousand-years, even the moon, and radiant Sirius, and the earth will revert to dust… But until that time, horror, horror…

*Pause; in the background lake appear two red dots.*

My powerful adversary, the devil comes closer. I see his terrible crimson eyes…

ARKADINA: It smells like sulphur. Is that necessary?

TREPLYOV: Yes.

ARKADINA: *(She laughs)* Oh I see, it's a theatrical effect.

TREPLYOV: Mama!

NINA: He is bored without man…

POLINA ANDREYEVNA: *(To DORN)* You took your hat off. Put it on, or you'll catch a cold.

ARKADINA: The doctor has tipped his hat to the devil, the father of eternal matter.

TREPLYOV: *(Jumping up, loudly)* The play is finished! Enough! Curtain!

ARKADINA: Why are you angry?

TREPLYOV: Enough! Curtain! Bring down the curtain! *(Stamping his foot)* Curtain!

*The curtain lowers.*

So sorry! I failed to realize that only a chosen few can write plays and act onstage. I violated the sacred law! To me... I... *(He tries to say something further, but waves his hand and exits left)*

ARKADINA: What's the matter with him?

SORIN: Irina, you can't treat a young man's pride like that, as it were.

ARKADINA: What did I say to him?

SORIN: You wounded him.

ARKADINA: He told us before it began that it was a joke, and I treated it like a joke.

SORIN: But my dear...

ARKADINA: Now it appears he wrote a great work of art! Oh, please excuse me! Now I see that he created this performance and perfumed it with sulphur not as a joke, but as a demonstration... He wanted to give us a bit of instruction on how to write and how to act. Sorry, but it's just boring. These constant attacks against my work and his caustic personal remarks would make anyone crazy. Willful, egotistical boy.

SORIN: He wanted to please you.

ARKADINA: Indeed? Why then couldn't he choose some ordinary play? No, he had to compel us to listen to his ravings. For the sake of some fun I was ready to listen, even to ravings, but his pretentious claims to new forms, a new era in art, have gone far beyond a joke. In my opinion, there are no new forms here, only the evidence of a nasty disposition.

TRIGORIN: Everyone writes as he wants and as he can.

ARKADINA: Then let him write as he wants and as he can, only tell him to leave me in peace.

DORN: Mighty Jove, once grown angry…

ARKADINA: I am not Jove, I am a woman. *(Lighting up a cigarette)* I am not angry, I'm disappointed, that a young man should spend his time so foolishly. I didn't want to hurt him.

MEDVEDENKO: There is no scientific evidence to separate spirit from matter, since the spirit is probably the sum total of material atoms. *(Lively, to TRIGORIN)* But someone should really write a play about a schoolteacher and how he lives. His life is so hard, so hard.

ARKADINA: Very true, but let's not talk about plays or about material atoms. The evening is so glorious! Listen, everyone — music. *(She listens)* Oh, it's so beautiful.

POLINA ANDREYEVNA: It's across the lake.

*Pause.*

ARKADINA: *(To TRIGORIN)* Sit by me. Ten, or fifteen years ago, here, on the lake, we listened to music and singing all night long, almost every night. There are six country houses along the shore. I remember laughter, lots of noise, fireworks, and all the love affairs, so many love affairs… The *jeune premier* and romantic idol of all these six houses was none other than — *(She nods to introduce DORN)*, Doctor Yevgenii Sergeyich Dorn. He's handsome now, but then he was irresistible. But my conscience is beginning to torment me. Why did I hurt my poor boy? I'm very upset. *(Loudly)* Kostya! Darling! Kostya!

*POLINA weeps quietly.*

SHAMRAYEV *(Reproachfully)* Polina, Polina…

POLINA ANDREYEVNA: It's nothing… Pardon me… I just felt a little sad.

MASHA: I'll go look for him.

ARKADINA: Yes, please, dear girl.

MASHA: *(She goes to the left)* Hello! Konstantin Gavrilovich!... Hello! *(She exits)*

NINA: *(Peering out from behind the stage)* Is it over? Are we going on?

ARKADINA: The author has departed! Come out, dear girl, and join us.

NINA: Yes. Hello! *(She kisses ARKADINA and POLINA ANDREYEVNA)*

SORIN: *Bravo! Bravo!*

ARKADINA: *Brava! Brava!* We all adored you. With such a face, with such a marvelous voice, it would be positively shameful for you to stay in the country. You have talent, believe me. You absolutely must go on the stage!

NINA: Oh, that is my dream! *(Sighing)* But it will never happen.

ARKADINA: Who knows? Here, allow me to introduce you to: Trigorin, Boris Alekseyevich.

NINA: Oh, I'm so thrilled... *(Embarrassed)* I've read all your —

ARKADINA: *(Seating her near)* Don't be shy, darling. He's a celebrity, but he has a simple soul! You see, he's shy too.

DORN: I think it would be good to open the curtain — it's eerie like this.

SHAMRAYEV: *(Loudly)* Yakov, open the curtain — Now, Yakov, open it!

*The curtain opens.*

NINA: *(To TRIGORIN)* It's a strange play, isn't it?

TRIGORIN: I didn't understand a word of it. But, I must admit, I watched it with pleasure. You were so sincere. And the scenery was beautiful.

*Pause.*

Are there many fish in this lake?

NINA: Yes.

TRIGORIN: I love to fish. I can think of nothing more enjoyable than to sit on the bank on a beautiful evening with a fishing pole in my hand.

NINA: But anyone who has experienced the joy of creation, surely nothing else can compare…

ARKADINA: *(Laughing)* Don't talk to him that way. When people say nice things to him, he curls up inside himself.

SHAMRAYEV: I remember, in Moscow at the opera once, the celebrated Silva sang a low "C." But as luck would have it, a bass from our church choir was sitting in the gallery, and all of a sudden, to our complete amazement, we hear from the gallery: "*Bravo, Silva!*" a full octave lower… Like this: *(With a low bass) Bravo*, Silva… Everyone sat frozen in their seats.

*Pause.*

DORN: The angel of silence has just flown over.

NINA: It's time for me to go. Good night.

ARKADINA: Where are you going? Why so early? We will not let you go.

NINA: Papa will be waiting for me.

ARKADINA: What kind of a person, really…*(They exchange kisses)* Well, what can we do? It's a shame, just a shame to let you go.

NINA: If only you knew, how difficult it is for me to leave!

ARKADINA: Someone should take you home, darling girl.

NINA: *(Frightened)* Oh, no, no!

SORIN: *(To her, imploring)* Stay!

NINA: I cannot, Pyotr Nikolayevich.

SORIN: Stay for one hour, as it were. Really, do…

NINA: *(Thinking for a moment, on the verge of tears)* Impossible! *(She shakes their hands and quickly exits)*

ARKADINA: Such an unlucky girl. They say, her late mother left her husband all of her huge fortune, every last *kopek*, and now he's leaving everything to his second wife. That little girl has nothing. It's disgraceful.

DORN: Yes, to be frank, her father is a complete swine.

SORIN: *(Rubbing his cold hands)* Shall we go in, ladies and gentlemen. It's getting damp. My legs are aching.

ARKADINA: Those sweet sorry legs are like stiff boards, they can hardly move. Well, let's go, you poor old man. *(She takes him under the arm)*

SHAMRAYEV: *(Offering his arm to his wife)* Madame?

SORIN: Oh, dear, the dog is howling again. *(To SHAMRAYEV)* Be so kind, Ilya Afanasyevich, please unchain her.

SHAMRAYEV: Can't do that, Pyotr Nikolayevich. I'm afraid that thieves will get into the barn. My millet is there. *(To MEDVEDENKO, walking next to him)* Yes, a whole octave lower: "*Bravo*, Silva!" And he wasn't a famous singer, just a church choir member.

MEDVEDENKO: And how much does a church choir singer make?

*Everyone exits, except DORN.*

DORN: *(Alone)* I don't know, maybe I don't understand anything or I've lost my mind, but I liked the play. There was something about it. When that girl talked about loneliness and then, when the red eyes of the devil appeared, my hands were shaking. Fresh, innocent… Oh, here he comes. I want to say something nice to him .

TREPLYOV: *(He enters)* No one's here?

DORN: I'm here.

TREPLYOV: Mashenka is looking for me everywhere. Intolerable creature.

DORN: Konstantin Gavrilovich, I liked your play very much. It's a bit strange, and I didn't hear the end, of course, but still it made a strong impression on me. You're a talented man, you need to continue.

*TREPLYOV squeezes his hand and fitfully hugs him.*

*(Makes a disparaging noise)* You're so high strung! Tears in your eyes… What was I trying to say… You took a subject from the realm of abstract ideas. That seems right to me because artistic creations certainly must express only great thoughts. To be beautiful, it must be serious. How pale you are!

TREPLYOV: What were you saying — don't stop.

DORN: Yes… You must write about something that is important and eternal. You know, I've had a pretty interesting life. I'm happy — but if

I felt just the slightest artistic impulse to create, I think I would shed my worldly existence and disappear into the ether.

TREPLYOV: Sorry, where is Nina?

DORN: And what's more. In any work of art there must be a clear, definite purpose. You must be sure about what you're writing, otherwise, you go down some picturesque road without a definite goal, you will lose your way and that will be your undoing.

TREPLYOV: *(Impatiently)* Where is Nina?

DORN: She went home.

TREPLYOV: *(In despair)* What the hell should I do? I want to see her… I must see her… I'm going…

    *MASHA enters.*

DORN: *(To TREPLYOV)* Calm down, my friend.

TREPLYOV: I've got to go. I've got to get out of here.

MASHA: Come home, Konstantin Gavrilovich. Your mama is waiting for you. She's worried.

TREPLYOV: Tell her that I left. And please everyone, leave me in peace! Leave me alone! Don't come looking for me!

DORN: But, but, but my dear… You can't do this… It's not good.

TREPLYOV: *(On the verge of tears)* Farewell, doctor. Thank you… *(He exits)*

DORN: *(Sighing)* Youth, youth!

MASHA: When people have nothing better to say, they say: youth, youth… *(She takes snuff)*

DORN: *(He takes the snuff-box from her and throws it into the bushes)* That is disgusting!

Pause.

I hear music from the house. Let's go in.

MASHA: Wait a minute.

DORN: What?

MASHA: I need to tell you something. I have to talk… *(Agitated)* I don't love my own father… but I feel close to you. I can't explain it but I feel you understand me… Help me. Help me, or I'll do something stupid, something crazy… I just can't help it. Help me…

DORN: What? Help you how?

MASHA: I'm suffering. No one, no one knows how much I'm suffering! *(She puts her head on his chest, quietly)* I love Konstantin.

DORN: How nervous everyone is! How fragile! And so much love… Oh, magic lake! *(Tenderly)* But what can I do, my child? Hmm?

*CURTAIN.*

# ACT II

*A croquet lawn. In the distance to the right is a house with a big terrace, to the left the lake is visible, with the glittering sun reflected. Flower beds. Midday. Hot. On one side, in the shadow of an old linden tree, ARKADINA, DORN and MASHA sit on a little bench. DORN has an open book on his lap.*

ARKADINA: *(To MASHA)* All right, let's stand up.

*They both stand.*

Come stand next to me. You are twenty-two years old, and I'm almost twice that. Yevgenii Sergeyevich, which of us looks younger?

DORN: You, of course.

ARKADINA: There, you see… And why? Because I work, I'm constantly doing something, I experience my life, but you sit still in one place, not really living… And I have a rule: never think about the future. I never think about old age, or death. What will come in life, will come.

MASHA: I feel like I was born hundreds of years ago. I drag my life around like an endless heavy train… And most of the time I have no desire to live at all. *(She sits)* Of course, this is all nonsense. I need to give myself a good shaking — cut out all this whining.

DORN: *(He sings quietly)* "You tell her, my flowers…"

ARKADINA: And besides, I am as neat as any Englishman. I hold myself straight and tall and I'm always dressed with my hair *comme il faut*. Would I ever go outside, even here to the garden, in working clothes without my hair perfectly coiffed? Never. That is why I look so good at my age. I never let myself go, like some people… *(She places her hands on her hips, walks around the area)* See, look at me, light as a feather. I could play a girl of fifteen.

DORN: Well… well… Nevertheless let me continue. *(He takes the book)* We stopped at the grain merchant and the rats…

ARKADINA: And the rats. Yes. Continue. *(She sits)* No, give it to me, I will read. My turn. *(She takes the book and looks for the place)* And the rats… Here it is… *(She reads)* "And, it should be understood that for women in society to indulge novelists and seduce them is as dangerous as when a grain merchant allows rats to get into his own barn. When a woman has selected a writer whom she desires to captivate, she besieges him with courtesies, compliments, with all of her charms, and he revels in these attentions." Well, that may be true with the French, but Russian women do nothing of the kind. We fall head over heels in love. Just look at me and Trigorin, I certainly didn't lay siege to him. When I met him all I needed to do was look at him and I'd turn to putty and cry. What kind of siege is that?

*Enter SORIN, leaning on a walking stick, and with NINA next to him; MEDVEDENKO rolls an empty chair behind them.*

SORIN: *(In a tone in which one comforts children)* Tell me. Are we happy? Are we having fun today? *(To his sister)* We are happy! Father and stepmother have gone to Tver, and we're now free for three whole days.

NINA: *(She sits next to ARKADINA and embraces her)* I am happy! I completely belong to you.

SORIN: *(He sits in his own chair)* Isn't she adorable!

ARKADINA: Nicely dressed, interesting… you're a clever girl. *(She kisses NINA)* But we mustn't praise her too much, or we'll cast the evil eye on her. *(She spits over her shoulder three times)* Where is Boris Alexseyevich?

NINA: He's down by the swimming hole, fishing.

ARKADINA: He never seems to get tired of it! *(She wants to continue reading)*

NINA: What are you reading?

ARKADINA: Maupassant's *"Sur l'Eau,"* sweetheart. *(She reads a few lines to herself)* Well, the rest is uninteresting and untrue. *(She closes the book)* My soul is troubled. Tell me, what's wrong with my son? Why is he so depressed, so dark? He spends whole days down at the lake, and I never see him.

MASHA: He's hurting inside. Please, do some more from his play!

NINA: *(Shrugging her shoulders)* Are you sure you want me to? It's so uninteresting!

MASHA: *(Holding back her rapture)* When he himself reads, his eyes burn and his face becomes pale. He has a beautiful, sad voice, like a poet.

*SORIN is heard snoring.*

DORN: Pleasant dreams!

ARKADINA: Petrusha!

SORIN: Eh?

ARKADINA: Are you asleep?

SORIN: Not in the least.

*Pause.*

ARKADINA: Why aren't you seeing a doctor? I'm not happy about this, Brother.

SORIN: I would be glad to see a doctor, but our doctor here doesn't want to see me.

DORN: At sixty, what's the use!

SORIN: Even at sixty one wants to live.

DORN: *(Irritably, makes a disparaging sound)* Well, take valerian drops.

ARKADINA: I think it would be good for him to go for a water cure.

DORN: Fine. He can go. Or he can not go.

ARKADINA: And what does *that* mean!

DORN: It doesn't mean anything. Everything is clear.

*Pause.*

MEDVEDENKO: Pyotr Nikolayevich should give up smoking.

SORIN: Rubbish!

DORN: No, it's not rubbish. Wine and tobacco sap you of your individuality. After a cigar or glass of vodka you aren't Pyotr Nikolayevich anymore, but Pyotr Nikolayevich plus someone else — some stranger.

SORIN: *(He laughs)* It is fine for you to talk this way. You've had plenty of fun in your day, but I? I worked in the Justice Department for twenty-eight years, and I have never lived, never played, never experienced anything and it stands to reason that I would still want to live. It's easy for you, so jaded and tired of life, to be a philosopher, but I want to live and that is why I drink sherry after lunch and I smoke cigars, as it were. And that is that.

DORN: Oh, please, be serious. To ask for treatment at sixty years of age, to regret all the fun you missed out on in your youth, that, if you'll pardon me, is ridiculous. It's time to start contemplating eternity…

MASHA: *(She rises)* It must be time for lunch. *(She walks unsteadily)* My foot fell asleep… *(She exits)*

DORN: She'll put away two glasses of vodka before lunch.

SORIN: Poor little thing, she's so unhappy.

DORN: *(Makes a disparaging noise)* Your Excellency.

SORIN: You talk like a man who's done everything.

ARKADINA: Ah! Can you think of anything more tedious than this sweet country boredom. It's hot, it's quiet, no one does anything, everyone philosophizes… Good for you, friends, it's lovely to listen to you, but… to sit alone in my hotel room and learn my lines — much better!

NINA: *(Enthusiastically)* Absolutely! I understand you.

SORIN: Of course, it's better in town. You sit in your own office, no one is let in unannounced, the telephone… cabs in the street, as it were…

DORN: *(He sings)* "You tell her, my flowers…"

*Enter SHAMRAYEV, behind him POLINA ANDREYEVNA.*

SHAMRAYEV: Yes, here's everybody. Good afternoon! *(He kisses ARKADINA's hand, then NINA's)* Very happy to see you in good health. *(To ARKADINA)* My wife tells me that you intend to go into town today with her. Is this true?

ARKADINA: Yes.

SHAMRAYEV: Hm… That is splendid, but how will you go, most respected one? They are carting rye today, all of the workers are busy. And, permit me to ask you, on which horses?

ARKADINA: Which? How do I know — which!

SORIN: We have carriage horses.

SHAMRAYEV: *(Agitated)* Carriage horses? And where will I get harnesses? Where will I get harnesses? This is marvelous! This is incomprehensible! Most honored ones! Pardon me, I am in awe of your talent, I am prepared to give you ten years of my life, but I cannot give you horses!

ARKADINA: And if I have to go? This is some business!

SHAMRAYEV: Most respected one! You don't seem to understand how to run a farm.

ARKADINA: *(Flaring up)* Same old story! In that case I am going to Moscow today. I order you to hire horses for me in the village, or I will walk to the station on foot!

SHAMRAYEV: *(Flaring up)* In that case I offer my resignation. Find yourself another manager! *(He exits)*

ARKADINA: Every summer it's like this, every summer I am offended! I will never set foot here again!

*She exits left, supposedly where the swimming hole is; after a minute she passes through to the house; TRIGORIN walks behind her with fishing rods and a bucket.*

SORIN: *(Flaring up)* What impertinence! The devil only knows! I am sick to death of him, as it were and so forth. Bring all of the horses here now!

NINA: *(To POLINA ANDREYEVNA)* To refuse Irina Nikolayevna, a famous actress! Every desire, every whim of hers is more important than your old farm. It's simply incredible!

POLINA ANDREYEVNA: *(In despair)* What can I do? Put yourself in my position, what can I do?

SORIN: *(To NINA)* Let's go to my sister… We will all plead with her, not to go. Don't you think? *(Looking in the direction SHAMRAYEV went)* Unbearable man! Despot!

NINA: *(Preventing him from standing)* Sit, sit… We'll take you…

*She and MEDVEDENKO roll the chair.*

Oh, how terrible it is!…

SORIN: Yes, yes, it is terrible… But he won't resign, I'll have a talk with him now.

*They exit; only DORN and POLINA ANDREYEVNA remain.*

DORN: People are so predictable. In truth, your husband ought to be thrown out on his ear, but you know how everything will end, that old baby Pyotr Nikoleyevich and his sister will wind up begging his forgiveness. You'll see!

POLINA ANDREYEVNA: He purposely sent the carriage horses into the field. He does what he wants. The third year we were here, he persuaded the old man to mortgage the estate. Why? Who needed that? He bought purebred pigs and turkeys and they died on him; he set up an expensive apiary and in the winter all the bees froze. He uses all the income from the estate on needless construction. He even takes the old man's pension and sends Irina Nikolayevna six hundred *rubles* a year from it, pretending it's part of the income from the farm. And she's happy with that arrangement, because she's such a miser. And every day there's all this fighting. If you knew how this upsets me! I'm sick; you see, I'm trembling… I can't stand his coarseness. *(Pleading)* Yevgenii, dear, beloved, help me… Let's run away together. We're running out of time, let's stop hiding, let's stop lying…

*Pause.*

DORN: I'm fifty-five years old, it's too late to change my life.

POLINA ANDREYEVNA: I know you have plenty of other women — you can't run away with all of us. I understand. Pardon me, I must be getting on your nerves.

*NINA appears near the house; she is picking flowers.*

DORN: No, it's fine.

POLINA ANDREYEVNA: I am tormented by jealousy. Of course, you're a doctor, it is impossible for you to avoid women. I understand… But can't you wait to look at them when I'm not around…

DORN: I'll try… *(To NINA, who is approaching)* What's happening?

NINA: Irina Nikolayevna is crying, and Pyotr Nikolayevich is having an asthma attack.

DORN: *(He stands)* I'll go give them both valerian drops.

NINA: *(She gives him the flowers)* My compliments!

DORN: *Merci bien. (He goes to the house)*

POLINA ANDREYEVNA: *(Going with him)* What pretty flowers! *(Near the house, in a muffled voice)* Give me those flowers! Give me those flowers! *(Having gotten the flowers, she tears them and throws them to the ground)*

*They both go into the house.*

NINA: *(Alone)* How funny to see a famous actress crying over something so silly! And isn't it funny that a famous writer, the darling of the public, written about in all the newspapers, his portrait for sale everywhere, his works translated into foreign languages, that he should spend every day fishing and then jumping for joy when he has caught two little perch. I thought famous people were supposed to be proud and distant. I thought they held their hordes of admirers in contempt — that the brilliance of their fame would make them even more glorious than royalty. But, no — they fish, play cards, laugh and get angry, like ordinary people.

TREPLYOV: *(Enters without a hat, with a rifle and a dead seagull)* Are you alone?

NINA: Alone.

*TREPLYOV places the seagull at her feet.*

What is this supposed to mean?

TREPLYOV: I was cruel enough to kill this seagull today. I lay it at your feet.

NINA: What's the matter with you? *(She picks up the seagull and looks at it)*

TREPLYOV: *(After a pause)* I will kill myself in the same way soon.

NINA: I don't know you anymore.

TREPLYOV: Yes, ever since I stopped knowing you. You've changed toward me, you're cold, my very presence upsets you.

NINA: Lately you've become irritable, you speak incomprehensibly — in symbols. And I suppose this seagull here is also a symbol, but, forgive me, I don't understand… *(She puts the seagull on the bench)* I'm too simple to understand you.

TREPLYOV: This began the night my play failed so completely. Women never forgive failure. I burned everything, every last shred. If you only knew how unhappy I am! Your coldness is horrible, unfathomable, it's as if I woke up and found the lake all dried up. You just said that you're too simple to understand me. Oh, what is there to understand? You didn't like the play, you despise my imagination, you see me as mediocre, insignificant, a nobody — like everyone else… *(Stamping his foot)* Believe me, I understand, I understand it all too well! I feel like I have a spike in my brain that is damning me and damning my pride which sucks my blood, like a snake… *(Seeing TRIGORIN, who walks, reading a little book)* Here comes the true genius; he walks like Hamlet, and see, he even has a little book in his hand. *(He teases)* "Words, words, words…" His sun hasn't even shone on you, but you are already smiling, your very gaze is melted into his beams. I will not stand in your way. *(He exits quickly)*

TRIGORIN: *(Making a note in the little book)* She takes snuff and drinks vodka… Always in black. The schoolteacher loves her…

NINA: Hello, Boris Alekseyevich!

TRIGORIN: Hello. Everything seems to have changed, we're leaving today. We'll probably never see each other again. And that's a pity. I don't often meet interesting young women. I can't possibly remember what they're like at eighteen, nineteen years old, and that's why young women are usually false in my stories. I would just love to have one hour in your shoes, just to get to know how you think and what makes you tick.

NINA: And I would love to be in your shoes.

TRIGORIN: Why?

NINA: So that I could know how it feels to be a famous, talented writer. What does fame feel like? What does it mean to you to be famous?

TRIGORIN: Mean? Probably nothing. I never thought about it that way. *(Thinking a little)* It's either one of two things: either you exaggerate my fame, or I don't have any real feelings about it.

NINA: But you must read about yourself in the newspapers?

TRIGORIN: When they praise me, it's nice, and when they attack me, I'm depressed for two days.

NINA: Incredible! How I envy you. If you only knew! People's destinies are so different. Some people can hardly drag themselves through their own boring, meaningless existences, everyone looking alike, everyone unhappy; but others, like you, for example— you are one in a million — your destiny in life turned out to be interesting, bright, completely meaningful... You are happy...

TRIGORIN: I? *(Shrugging his shoulders)* Hm... You talk about fame, about good fortune, about some kind of bright, interesting life, but for me all of your nice words, forgive me, are like sweet marmalade, which I never eat. You are very young and very kind.

NINA: Your life is so beautiful!

TRIGORIN: What's so beautiful about it? *(He looks at his watch)* I've got to go now and write. Excuse me, I don't have time... *(He laughs)* Uh oh, you just hit a nerve, as they say. I'm starting to feel a bit agitated and even a little angry. Well, all right, let's talk. Let's talk about my bright, beautiful life... And so, where do I begin? *(Thinks a little)* When a man thinks about one idea day and night, the moon, for example, he becomes obsessed by it. I have my own such moon. Day and night one obsessive thought overwhelms me: I must write, I must write, I must... I have barely finished a story, when I'm already drawn to write another, then a third, after the third a fourth... I write endlessly, without being able to stop. What's so bright and beautiful about that? It's such an impossible life! Here I am with you, I'm feeling excited and yet I can't stop thinking about the story I'm working on now. I look up at the sky, a cloud, hmmm, resembles a grand piano. I think: yes, I need to put that into a story somewhere, yes, a floating cloud looks like a grand piano. I smell a heliotrope. Immediately I make a mental note: sickly sweet smell, widow's color; mention it in a description of a summer evening. I angle for every word or phrase you say, then I reel it in and lock it in with all the other phrases and words in my secret literary stash. Maybe it'll come in handy! When I finish work, I run to the theatre or go fishing; I try to relax, forget myself for a moment, but oh no, my brain is already churning with the next idea and I rush back to my desk, not breathing until I've written it down. It's always like this — there's never any peace for me and I feel as if I'm destroying my whole life. In order to strew some honeyed petals before my readers, I rip out my own flowers and leave the roots to rot. You must admit I'm crazy! My best friends think I'm crazy. "What are you writing?" "What gifts will you bestow upon us next?" Always the same, always the same, and it seems to me that all their fawning attention, the praise, the flattery — that it's all a lie, that they are deceiving me as if I were a sick old man. I'm scared sometimes that they are going to sneak in and snatch me up and take me to the loony bin — like Poprischin, the madman in Gogol's story. And in those first years, my best years, when I first started writing, it was endless torture for me. An unknown minor writer, especially when he's unlucky, feels he's clumsy, awkward, inconsequential, his nerves are in knots, strained to the breaking point. He hangs around literary stars and artists, a nobody, hoping to get noticed, acknowledged by someone, yet afraid to look anyone directly in the eye, just like a compulsive gambler who has run out of money. Even now, I don't know my reader but I see him as unfriendly and disdainful. I'm afraid of my public, they terrify me, and when my play was first produced, I imagined all the brunettes in the audience were hostile and the blondes were coldly indifferent. Oh it was agony! Utter torture!

NINA: Excuse me, but I can't believe the creative process, the sheer inspiration, doesn't give you sublime, happy moments?

TRIGORIN: Yes. When I write, it's pleasant. And I like correcting the proofs, but... before it has barely left the printer's, I see that it's not right, that it shouldn't have been written at all, that it's one giant mistake and I become so upset and disappointed with myself, I feel like a worthless idiot. *(Laughing)* And the public reads it: "Yes, nice, talented... Nice, but he's no Tolstoy", or: "Beautiful work, but Turgenev's "Fathers and Sons" is so much better". Until I die it will always be "nice and talented, nice and talented" — that's it. And on my tombstone it will be engraved: "Here lies Trigorin. He was a nice writer, but he was no Turgenev."

NINA: Forgive me, I just don't accept that. You're simply spoiled by your success.

TRIGORIN: What success? I never liked myself. I don't think I'm a particularly good writer. Worst of all, when I'm obsessed with something, I don't even understand what it is I'm writing... I love this lake, the trees, the sky, I appreciate nature, it arouses passion in me, an irresistible desire to write. But the problem is, I'm not only a landscape painter, I see myself as a good citizen, I love Russia, I love the people and I feel, that if I'm a writer, then it's my responsibility to talk about them, about their struggles, about their future, to talk about science, the rights of man, etcetera etcetera. And so I write about everything, all the issues chase me, drive me on, get me angry until I can't run any longer. While life and science are always moving forward, I fall helplessly behind like a peasant running late for the train. And in the end, I feel I can only paint landscapes after all and in everything else I am false to the core.

NINA: You work too hard and you have neither the time nor the inclination to recognize your own importance. That's all right, you can be dissatisfied with yourself, but the rest of us think you're marvelous! If I were a writer like you, I would devote my whole life to the masses, and in return I would expect that it's their good fortune, indeed their happiness, to raise me above them and carry me off in a chariot.

TRIGORIN: Well, in a chariot... am I Agamemnon?

*Both smiling.*

NINA: If I were lucky enough to be an artist I would put up with petty dislikes, deprivations, disappointments. I would live in a garret and only eat stale bread, yes, suffer from my own inadequacies, my own awareness of my imperfections, but in return I would demand fame... genuine, resounding fame... *(She covers her face with her hands)* My head is spinning... Oof!

VOICE OF ARKADINA: *(From the house)* "Boris Alekseyevich!"

TRIGORIN: They're calling me... Probably to pack up. But I don't want to leave. *(He glances back at the lake)* Just look at that, isn't it amazing! Beautiful!

NINA: Do you see that house and garden across the lake?

TRIGORIN: Yes.

NINA: That was my mother's home. I was born there. I spent my whole life by this lake and I know every inch of it.

TRIGORIN: Yes, it's wonderful here! *(Seeing the seagull)* And what's this?

NINA: A seagull. Konstantin Gavrilovich killed it.

TRIGORIN: Beautiful bird. I really don't want to leave. See if you can convince Irina Nikolayevna to stay. *(He makes a note in his little book)*

NINA: What are you writing?

TRIGORIN: Just making a note... an idea... *(Putting away the little book)* A subject for a short story: a young girl has lived on the shores of a lake all her life, like you; she loves the lake, like a seagull, and is happy, and free, as a seagull. But by chance a man comes along, sees her, and for no particular reason destroys her, just like this seagull here.

*Pause. ARKADINA appears in the window.*

ARKADINA: Boris Alekseyevich, where are you?

TRIGORIN: I'm coming! *(He walks and glances at NINA; to the window, to ARKADINA)* What?

ARKADINA: We are staying.

*TRIGORIN exits to the house.*

NINA: *(She approaches the footlights; after a moment)* Dream...

CURTAIN.

# ACT III

*The dining room in SORIN's house. To the right and left are doors. A buffet. A cupboard with medicines. In the middle of the room, a table. A suitcase and cardboard boxes; noticeable preparation for departure. TRIGORIN eats breakfast, MASHA stands by the table.*

MASHA: I'm telling you all this because you're a writer. You can use it if you want. I'll be honest with you: if he had seriously hurt himself, I couldn't have lived another minute. But I'm trying to be brave. I've made up my mind once and for all: I'll tear this love from my heart, I'll tear it out by the roots.

TRIGORIN: How? How will you do that?

MASHA: I'll get married. To Medvedenko.

TRIGORIN: To the schoolteacher?

MASHA: Yes.

TRIGORIN: I don't understand, why do you need to do that?

MASHA: To love without hope, always waiting for something to happen… But when I get married, I won't have love on my mind, I'll have new problems to worry about. And anyway, it'll be a change. Shall we have another?

TRIGORIN: Haven't you had enough?

MASHA: Well, here! *(She pours them each a shot of vodka)* Don't look at me like that. Women drink more than you think. A few drink openly, like I do, but most do it in secret. Yes. And it's always vodka or cognac. *(She clinks glasses)* Na zdorovye. You're a nice man, it's a shame you're leaving.

*They drink.*

TRIGORIN: To be honest, I don't want to leave.

MASHA: Then tell her to stay.

TRIGORIN: No, she won't stay. Her son is acting like a crazy man. First he shoots himself, and now he challenges me to a duel. And for what? He grumbles, he grouses, he preaches new forms… But there's plenty of room for all of us, the new and the old — what's the fight about?

MASHA: Well, it's jealousy too. But it's none of my business.

> *Pause. YAKOV crosses left to right with a suitcase; NINA enters and comes to a stop by the window.*

My schoolteacher isn't very smart, but he's a good person, humble, and he really loves me. I feel sorry for him. And I feel sorry for his poor old mother. Well, permit me to wish you all the best. Remember me kindly. *(She strongly shakes his hand)* I'm very thankful to you for your interest. Do send me your books, and sign them please. Only don't write "Dear Madam", but simply: "To Marya, ancestry unknown, reason for living unknown." Farewell! *(She exits)*

NINA: *(Extending her hand to TRIGORIN with something gripped in her fist)* Even or odd?

TRIGORIN: Even.

NINA: *(Sighing)* No. There's only one pea. Should I be an actress or not? If only someone would advise me.

TRIGORIN: I can't advise you.

> *Pause.*

NINA: You'll leave and… we'll probably never see each other again. Please take this little memento. I had your initials engraved on it… and on this side the title of your book "Days and Nights".

TRIGORIN: How lovely! *(He kisses the medallion)* A delightful gift!

NINA: Remember me sometimes.

TRIGORIN: I will remember. I will remember you as you were on that clear day — do you remember? — A week ago, when you wore that light-colored dress... we were talking... the white seagull was lying on the bench between us.

NINA: *(Pensively)* Yes, the seagull...

*Pause.*

Shhh, they're coming... Before you leave, give me two minutes, I beg you... *(She exits to the left)*

*At the same time ARKADINA and SORIN enter from the right. SORIN is in a tailcoat with medals. Then YAKOV enters, busy with packing.*

ARKADINA: Oh please stay at home, my dear old man. Do you think you can go around paying visits to people with your rheumatism? *(To TRIGORIN)* Who was it that just left? Nina?

TRIGORIN: Yes.

ARKADINA: *Pardon*, we interrupted... *(She sits)* Yes, I packed everything. I'm worn out.

TRIGORIN: *(He reads on the medallion)* "Days and Nights", page 121, lines 11 and 12.

YAKOV: *(Clearing the table)* Should I pack the fishing rods?

TRIGORIN: Yes, I still need them. But give the books to someone.

YAKOV: Will do.

TRIGORIN: *(To himself)* Page 121, lines 11 and 12. What are those lines? *(To ARKADINA)* Do you have my books here in the house?

ARKADINA: My brother has them in his den, in the corner bookcase.

TRIGORIN: Page 121… *(He exits)*

ARKADINA: Really, Petrusha, you should stay at home…

SORIN: You're leaving. I'll be so bored without you here.

ARKADINA: And what's so interesting in town?

SORIN: Nothing much, but all the same… *(He laughs)* They're going to lay the cornerstone for the *zemstvo* building and that kind of thing. I would just like an hour or two to get away from here. I feel like an old fish from the lake. I've been lying around here too long like a smelly old fish. I ordered the horses for one o'clock. We'll both be going at the same time.

ARKADINA: *(After a pause)* I wish you'd stay here. Stay here and try not to get bored. Don't catch a cold. Take care of my son. Look after him. Keep him sensible.

    *Pause.*

Here I'm leaving, and I don't know why Konstantin shot himself. I have a feeling it was jealousy, and the sooner I take Trigorin from here, the better.

SORIN: How do I put this — there are other reasons. It is quite understandable, an intelligent young man lives in the country, in the backwoods really, without any money, without a position, without a future. He has nothing to do. He's ashamed and frightened of his own uselessness. I love him so much, and he is very attached to me, but in truth, he feels like he doesn't belong here, like a parasite, a hanger-on. It's understandable, his self esteem —

ARKADINA: Will I never be free of this! *(In thought)* What if he got a desk job somewhere...

SORIN: *(He whistles, then indecisively)* It seems to me, maybe, what if, if you were to... give him a little money. First of all, he needs to look like a human being. He's been wearing the same raggedy suit for three years. He doesn't even have an overcoat... *(He laughs)* And would it be so terrible if he had the chance to have fun once in a while... to go abroad or something... It wouldn't be all that expensive.

ARKADINA: Well... maybe I can manage a suit, but to go abroad... No, right now I can't even do the suit. *(Decisively)* I have no money!

*SORIN laughs.*

None!

SORIN: *(He whistles)* Yes, *Madame*. Forgive me, sweet, don't be angry. I believe you... You're a wonderful, generous woman.

ARKADINA: *(On the verge of tears)* I have no money!

SORIN: It's understandable — if I had any money, I would give it to him, but I have nothing, not a *kopek*. *(He laughs)* Shamrayev takes my whole pension and he spends it on farming, cattle-breeding, and pfft, it's all gone — gone to waste. The bees freeze, the cows die, the horses are never available...

ARKADINA: Yes, I have money, but you know I'm an actress; the costumes alone completely ruin me.

SORIN: You are so good, sweet... I respect you... Yes... But wait, something is... *(He staggers)* My head is spinning. *(He holds onto the table)* I feel faint, as it were.

ARKADINA: *(Frightened)* Petrusha! *(Trying to support him)* Petrusha, my dear... *(She shouts)* Help me! Help!...

*Enter TREPLYOV with a bandage on his head, and MEDVEDENKO.*

He's going to faint!

SORIN: It's nothing, nothing… *(He smiles and drinks water)* It has already passed… as it were…

TREPLYOV: *(To his mother)* Don't be scared, Mama, it's not dangerous. This happens a lot with uncle these days. *(To his uncle)* Uncle, dear, you need to lie down.

SORIN: Yes, lie down… But I'm still going to town. I will lie down and I will go… yes, it's understandable… *(He goes, supporting himself on the walking stick)*

MEDVEDENKO: *(He takes him by the hand)* There's a riddle: in the morning what goes on four legs, at noon on two, in the evening on three —

SORIN: *(He laughs)* Exactly. And at night flat on the back. Yes, thank you, I can walk myself…

MEDVEDENKO: Don't stand on ceremony with me!

*He and SORIN exit.*

ARKADINA: He frightened me to death!

TREPLYOV: It's not healthy for him to live in the country. He's depressed. Mama, if you were to feel a little generous and loan him fifteen hundred or two thousand *rubles*, he could live in town the whole year.

ARKADINA: I don't have any money. I'm an actress, not a banker.

*Pause.*

TREPLYOV: Mama, please change my bandage. You do it so well.

ARKADINA: *(She takes iodine from the medicine cabinet with some dressings)* The doctor's late.

TREPLYOV: He promised to be here at ten, but it's already noon.

ARKADINA: Here, sit. *(She takes the bandage from his head)* You look like you're wearing a turban. Yesterday a visitor in the kitchen asked what nationality you were. Oh, it's almost completely healed. Just a little scar remains. *(She kisses him on the head)* And when I'm gone you won't go bang-bang again?

TREPLYOV: No, Mama. That was a moment of utter despair, I wasn't able to control myself. It'll never happen again. *(He kisses her hand)* You have such golden hands. I remember, very long ago, when you were still working at the State theater — I was little then — there was a fight in the courtyard of our building. Someone was violently beating up a woman. Do you remember? They picked her up unconscious… you went right to her, brought her medicine, washed her children in the washtub. Don't you remember?

ARKADINA: No. *(She applies a new bandage)*

TREPLYOV: There were two ballerinas living in the same building… They used to come to our place and drink coffee…

ARKADINA: I remember them.

TREPLYOV: They were so religious.

  *Pause.*

These past few days, I have loved you as tenderly and completely as when I was a child. I have no one except you. Only why, why do you let that man come between us?

ARKADINA: You don't understand him, Konstantin. He's a noble person…

TREPLYOV: Oh, yes, noble, but when they told him I was going to challenge him to a duel, I notice his nobility didn't keep him from playing the coward. He is leaving. He's making a gutless retreat!

ARKADINA: Don't be silly! I'm the one taking him away from here. I understand that you are uncomfortable with our relationship, but you're intelligent and sophisticated, and I must demand that you respect my freedom.

TREPLYOV: I respect your freedom, but you must allow me the freedom to think of him any way I want. A noble person! Here we are almost fighting over him, and he is somewhere in the living room or in the garden laughing at both of us, "cultivating" Nina, trying to convince her once and for all, that he is a genius.

ARKADINA: I think you truly enjoy hurting me. I respect that man and I am asking you to speak well of him in my presence.

TREPLYOV: But I don't respect him. You'd like me to consider him a genius, but, forgive me, I cannot lie, his writing makes me sick.

ARKADINA: That's just envy. With pretentious, untalented people, all that's left is to speak ill of the genuinely gifted. That must be some consolation!

TREPLYOV: *(Ironically)* The genuinely gifted! *(Angrily)* I am more gifted than all of you put together! *(He tears the bandage from his head)* You old fashioned hacks only believe in your own work and when the truly innovative, young, talented artists come along, you try to suffocate them! I do not acknowledge any of you! I do not acknowledge you or him!

ARKADINA: You arrogant —

TREPLYOV: Go back to your darling theater and act in your pathetic, third-rate plays!

ARKADINA: I have never acted in third-rate plays. How dare you! You couldn't even write a pathetic vaudeville sketch. Kiev Provincial parasite!

TREPLYOV: Miser!

ARKADINA: Beggar!

*TREPLYOV sits and quietly cries.*

Nobody! You are a nobody! *(More and more agitated)* Don't cry. You mustn't cry… *(She cries)* Don't cry… *(She kisses him on the forehead, on the cheeks, on the head)* My sweet baby, forgive me… Forgive your sinful mother. Forgive your wretched mother.

TREPLYOV: *(He embraces her)* If you only knew! I've lost everything. She doesn't love me, I can't write anymore… everything I hoped for is gone…

ARKADINA: Don't despair. It'll all turn out. I'm taking him away from here, she'll fall in love with you again. *(She dries his tears)* There, there. We're good again, yes?

TREPLYOV: *(He kisses her hands)* Yes, Mama.

ARKADINA: *(Tenderly)* Make up with him, too. It's not necessary to fight a duel, now is it?

TREPLYOV: Fine… Only, Mama, don't let me see him again, please. It's more than I can bear… *(Enter TRIGORIN)* Uh oh, here he comes… I'm leaving… *(Quickly he puts the medicine in the cabinet)* Don't worry, the doctor will put the bandage on later…

TRIGORIN: *(He searches in the little book)* Page 121… lines 11 and 12… Here… *(He reads)* "If you ever need my life, come and take it".

*TREPLYOV picks up the bandage from the floor and exits.*

ARKADINA: *(Glances at her watch)* They'll be bringing the horses in a minute.

TRIGORIN: *(To himself)* If you ever need my life, come and take it.

ARKADINA: I hope you're all packed?

TRIGORIN: *(Impatiently)* Yes, yes… *(In thought)* Why does this appeal from such a pure soul touch me so deeply? If you ever need my life, come and take it. *(To ARKADINA)* Let's stay one more day!

   *ARKADINA shakes her head "no".*

Let's just stay!

ARKADINA: Darling, I know, I know why you want to stay. But get control of yourself. You're a little drunk, sober up.

TRIGORIN: You be sober too, be reasonable. Be a good friend to me… *(He presses her hand)* I know you're capable of sacrifice… Be my friend, let me go…

ARKADINA: *(In strong agitation)* Are you so far gone?

TRIGORIN: I'm entranced by her! Maybe this is just what I need.

ARKADINA: The love of a farm girl? Oh, how little you know yourself!

TRIGORIN: Sometimes people walk and talk in their sleep and that's how I feel — I'm talking to you, but I'm dreaming of her. And these sweet, marvelous dreams are taking hold of me… Let me go…

ARKADINA: *(Trembling)* No, no… I'm an ordinary woman, you're not allowed to talk to me like that… Don't torment me, Boris… I'm terrified…

TRIGORIN: You can be extraordinary if you want. Love is young, delightful, poetic, and once again it's filling me with hope and dreams — I just know that only she can bring me happiness, she can be my good luck charm. I've never experienced anything like it… When I was young, there was no time, I was so busy chasing after editors, wrestling with poverty. Now, finally, here she is, my love has come, she's calling me... How can I run away from her?

ARKADINA: *(With fury)* Have you lost your mind!

TRIGORIN: Maybe.

ARKADINA: Everyone has conspired to torment me today! *(She cries)*

TRIGORIN: *(He holds his head)* She doesn't understand! She doesn't want to understand!

ARKADINA: Am I so old and ugly that you can talk to me this way about another woman? *(She embraces and kisses him)* Oh, you have lost your mind! My beautiful, amazing... You are the last chapter of my life! *(She kneels)* My joy, my pride, my happiness... *(She embraces his knees)* If you abandon me, even for one hour, then I will not survive, I will lose my mind, my astounding, extraordinary lover, my king...

TRIGORIN: Someone'll come in. *(He helps her to stand)*

ARKADINA: Let them, I'm not ashamed of my love for you. *(She kisses his hands)* My treasure, my desperate darling, you want to behave like a raving maniac, but I won't let you... *(She laughs)* You are mine... you are mine... Yes, this forehead is mine, and these eyes are mine, and this beautiful silky hair is mine... You are all mine. You are so talented, so intelligent, the best of all our contemporary writers, you are the only hope of Russia... You are so sincere, simple, fresh, clever, funny... With one stroke you create the poetry of a landscape, your characters are so alive. Oh, to read you is to be in rapture! Do you think this is flattery? Am I flattering you? Well, look me in the eye... look... Do I look like a liar? Look at me, I'm the only one who appreciates you, the only one who'll tell you the truth, my sweet, magnificent magician... Can you go? Really? Will you leave me?

TRIGORIN: I have no will of my own... I have never had a will... I'm a dishrag, limp, always submissive — how can that possibly be attractive to women? All right, take me, take me away, but don't let me out of your sight for a moment...

ARKADINA: *(To herself)* Now he's mine. *(Freely and easily, like nothing took place)* Darling, if you really want, you can stay. I'll leave today and you can come later, in a week. What's the hurry?

TRIGORIN: No, let's go together.

ARKADINA: As you wish. Together, yes, together...

*Pause. TRIGORIN makes a note in his little book.*

What are you writing?

TRIGORIN: This morning I heard something good: "virgin forest"... I can use it one day... *(He stretches himself)* All right then, travel... the carriages, the stations, refreshment buffets, railroad food, conversations... words, words, words...

SHAMRAYEV: *(Enters)* I have the honor to announce, with great regret, that the horses are ready. It is time, most respected one, to go to the station; the train will arrive at five minutes past two. And will you, Irina Nikolayevna, be so kind as to find out where the actor Suzdaltsev is now? Still alive? Healthy? We had a drink together once... He was brilliant in "The Mail Robbery" in Yelizavetgrad. In the same play, I also remember the tragedian, Izmailov, who was just as excellent... Don't hurry, most respected one, we still have five minutes. In a melodrama I once saw, they played conspirators, and when they were caught, one of them was supposed to say: "We are caught in a trap", but Izmailov said — "We are traught in a clap"... *(He chuckles)* In a clap...

> *While he speaks, YAKOV busies himself around the suitcases, a HOUSEMAID carries ARKADINA's hat, coat, umbrella and gloves; everyone helps ARKADINA to dress. From the left door a COOK peeps out, and then enters tentatively. Enter POLINA ANDREYEVNA, then SORIN and MEDVEDENKO.*

POLINA ANDREYEVNA: *(With a small basket)* Here are some plums for you for the journey… Very sweet. I hope you'll treat yourself…

ARKADINA: You are very kind, Polina Andreyevna.

POLINA ANDREYEVNA: Farewell, my dear! If everything wasn't just so, please forgive us. *(She cries)*

ARKADINA: *(She embraces her)* Everything was fine, just fine. You mustn't cry.

POLINA ANDREYEVNA: Time's running out…

ARKADINA: What can we do!

SORIN: *(In an overcoat with a cape, in a hat, with a cane, enters from the left door; crossing the room)* It's time, Sister, we can't be late. I'm going to take my seat. *(He exits)*

MEDVEDENKO: And I'll walk to the station… to see you off. I'll be there in no time. *(He exits)*

ARKADINA: Bye bye, my dears… If we're alive and healthy, in the summer we'll see each other again…

   *The HOUSEMAID, YAKOV and COOK kiss her hand.*

Don't forget me. *(She gives the COOK a ruble)* Here is a ruble — for the three of you.

COOK: We humbly thank you, madam. Happy days to you!

MAID: *Do Svidanya.*

YAKOV: Good luck!

SHAMRAYEV: Farewell, Boris Alekseyevich! Be sure to write.

ARKADINA: Where is Konstantin? Tell him I'm leaving. I need to say goodbye. Well, remember me fondly. *(To YAKOV)* I gave the cook a ruble. It's for the three of you.

*Everyone exits to the right. The stage is empty. Offstage we hear the noise of people being seen off. The HOUSEMAID returns, in order to take the little basket with plums, and again exits.*

TRIGORIN: *(Returning)* I forgot my walking-stick. Oh, I think it's inside.

*He goes and by the left door meets NINA, who enters.*

You! We're leaving…

NINA: I just had a feeling I'd see you again. *(Excitedly)* Boris Alekseyevich, I have finally decided, the die is cast, I'm going on the stage. I'll be gone by tomorrow, I'll leave my father, leave everyone and start my new life… So I'm going to Moscow… like you. Maybe we can meet sometime?

TRIGORIN: *(Glancing back)* Stay at the Hotel Slavyanskii Bazaar… Let me hear from you immediately… Grokholskii House, Molchanovka Street… I've got to go…

*Pause.*

NINA: Just one more minute…

TRIGORIN: *(Quietly)* You are so beautiful… I'm so happy that I'll see you again.

*She puts her head on his chest.*

I'll see these lovely eyes, this inexpressibly beautiful, tender smile… this angelic face… My darling….

*A prolonged kiss.*

CURTAIN.

# ACT IV

*Between the third and fourth acts two years pass.*

*One of the sitting-rooms in SORIN's home, converted by KONSTANTIN TREPLYOV into a working office. To the right and left are doors, leading to interior rooms. Directly up center is the glass door to the terrace. Aside from the usual sitting-room furniture, in the right corner is a writing desk, near the left door a Turkish sofa, a cupboard with books, books on the windowsills, on the chairs. — Evening. A single lamp burns under a shade. Semi-darkness. The trees stirring and the wind is howling in the chimneys.*

*The WATCHMAN taps. MEDVEDENKO and MASHA enter.*

MASHA: *(Calls)* Konstantin Gavrilych! Konstantin Gavrilych! *(Looking around)* He's not in here. The old man is constantly asking, where's Kostya, where's Kostya... He cannot live without him...

MEDVEDENKO: He's afraid of being alone. *(Listening)* What terrible weather! It's been like this two days in a row.

MASHA: *(She turns up the lamp)* There are waves on the lake. Huge ones.

MEDVEDENKO: It's dark in the garden. We should tell them to tear down that stage. It's just standing there, bare and abandoned, and the curtain flaps in the wind. When I went past it last night I thought I heard someone crying.

MASHA: Hmmm...

*Pause.*

MEDVEDENKO: Masha, let's go home!

MASHA: *(She shakes her head)* No, I'll spend the night here.

MEDVEDENKO: *(Pleading)* Masha, let's go! Our baby must be hungry.

MASHA: Never mind. Matryona will feed him.

*Pause.*

MEDVEDENKO: It's really a shame. Three nights already without his mother.

MASHA: You're so boring lately. In the old days at least you would philosophize a little, but now it's always baby, home, baby, home — it's all you can talk about.

MEDVEDENKO: Let's go, Masha!

MASHA: Go yourself.

MEDVEDENKO: Your father won't give me horses.

MASHA: Yes he will. Ask him and he'll do it.

MEDVEDENKO: Maybe. I'll ask him. So, will you come tomorrow?

MASHA: *(She takes snuff)* Yes, yes, tomorrow. You're driving me crazy.

*Enter TREPLYOV and POLINA ANDREYEVNA; TREPLYOV carries pillows and a blanket, and POLINA ANDREYEVNA bed clothes; they put them on the Turkish sofa, then TREPLYOV walks to his desk and sits.*

What's this for, Mama?

POLINA ANDREYEVNA: Pyotr Nikolayevich asked to make his bed here near Kostya.

MASHA: Let me… *(She makes the bed)*

POLINA ANDREYEVNA: *(Sighing)* Old people are like little children.

*(She goes to the writing table, and, leaning her elbows on it, looks at the manuscript)*

Pause.

MEDVEDENKO: So I'm going. Farewell, Masha. *(He kisses his wife's hand)* Farewell, *Mamasha*. *(He tries to kiss his mother-in-law's hand)*

POLINA ANDREYEVNA: *(Annoyed)* Well! Go with God.

MEDVEDENKO: Farewell, Konstantin Gavrilovich.

*TREPLYOV silently offers his hand; MEDVEDENKO exits.*

POLINA ANDREYEVNA: *(Glancing at the manuscript)* No one ever guessed you'd turn out to be a real writer, Kostya. And look at you, thank God. You've even started to receive money from journals. *(She passes her hand over his hair)* And you've become so handsome... Sweet Kostya, be a little more affectionate with my Mashenka!...

MASHA: *(Making the bed)* Leave him alone, Mama.

POLINA ANDREYEVNA: *(To TREPLYOV)* She's a lovely girl.

Pause.

A woman doesn't need much, Kostya, just a tender look now and then. Believe me, I know.

*TREPLYOV stands from the desk and silently exits.*

MASHA: Now you've made him angry. Did you have to bother him?

POLINA ANDREYEVNA: I pity you, Mashenka.

MASHA: Just what I need!

POLINA ANDREYEVNA: My heart is sick for you. You know I see everything, I understand everything.

MASHA:  It's all ridiculous. Unrequited love—that's only in novels. Never mind. You can't sit around always hoping that something will happen... If you start to feel love in your heart, you've got to get rid of it. Listen, they promised to transfer Semyon to another school district. Once we move there — I will forget everything... I will tear this love from my heart by the roots.

*Two rooms away a melancholy waltz is heard.*

POLINA ANDREYEVNA: Kostya is playing. Hmm, he must be depressed.

MASHA:  *(She noiselessly does two-three turns of a waltz)* The main thing for me, Mama, is not to see him. If only Semyon's transfer comes through, then believe me, in one month I'll completely forget him. It doesn't mean a thing.

*The left door opens, DORN and MEDVEDENKO roll SORIN in a wheelchair.*

MEDVEDENKO:  There are six in the house now. And flour is five *kopeks* a pound.

DORN:  That's the way it goes, I'm afraid.

MEDVEDENKO:  It's easy for you to laugh. You're rolling in money.

DORN:  Money? From thirty years of practice, a difficult practice, mind you, when I didn't have a moment to myself night or day, I managed to save just two thousand, and I spent it all on a trip abroad. I have nothing.

MASHA:  *(To her husband)* You haven't left yet?

MEDVEDENKO:  *(Guiltily)* Oh, sure, when no one will give me any horses.

MASHA: *(With bitter vexation, under her breath)* I wish I had never laid eyes on you!

> SORIN's *chair comes to a stop in the left side of the room; POLINA ANDREYEVNA, MASHA and DORN sit nearby; MEDVEDENKO, doleful, withdraws to the side.*

DORN: My God, this room has changed! It used to be a drawing-room, now it's an office.

MASHA: Konstantin Gavrilych is more comfortable here. He can go out to the garden to think whenever he likes.

> *The* WATCHMAN *taps.*

SORIN: Where's my sister?

DORN: She went to the station to meet Trigorin. She'll be right back.

SORIN: If you needed to bring my sister down here, I must be very ill. *(He goes silent for a while)* Here's a good one for you, I am dangerously ill, and in the meantime, no one will give me any medication.

DORN: What do you want? Valerian drops? Sodium carbonate? Quinine?

SORIN: Ah yes, now comes the philosophy — leave me out of this! *(Nodding his head toward the sofa)* Is that fixed up for me?

POLINA ANDREYEVNA : For you, Pyotr Nikolayevich.

SORIN: Thank you kindly.

DORN: *(He sings)* "The moon floats along the night sky…"

SORIN: Listen, I want to give Kostya a subject for a story. It must be called: "The Man Who Wanted". "*L'homme qui a voulu*". In my youth I wanted to become a writer, a man of letters — I didn't; I wanted to speak beautifully — and instead I speak abominably *(He mocks himself)* "as it were and so on and so forth, this that and the other, etcetera…" I babble on and on until I run out of words; I wanted to marry — and I never did; I always wanted to live in town — and here I am ending my life in the country, as it were.

DORN: You wanted to become a State Councilor — and you became one.

SORIN: *(He laughs)* I never wanted that. That just happened to me.

DORN: To be filled with regrets at sixty-two, you have to admit — that's pretty useless.

SORIN: How ungenerous you are. One wants to live, can't you understand that!

DORN: That's just ridiculous. Everyone must die — it's the law of nature.

SORIN: You talk like a fat cat. You are just so satisfied with your life, that you don't understand anyone else's unhappiness. But believe me, when the time comes, even you will be afraid to die.

DORN: Fear of death — is an animal response… You've got to get a hold of it and suppress it. It's just those religious types who are afraid, facing eternity with their sins on their heads. In the first place, you don't believe in God. In the second place — what sins have you committed? You worked in the Justice Department for twenty-five years — that's the whole story.

> TREPLYOV *enters and sits on a little stool by* SORIN's *feet.* MASHA *does not take her eyes off of him the entire time.*

DORN: We are keeping Konstantin Gavrilovich from working.

TREPLYOV: No, that's fine.

*Pause.*

MEDVEDENKO: Permit me to ask, doctor, how much does a ream of paper cost abroad nowadays?

DORN: How should I know? I never bought any.

MEDVEDENKO: And which city did you like most in your travels?

DORN: Genoa.

TREPLYOV: Why Genoa?

DORN: In Genoa the crowds are marvelous. When you leave your hotel in the evening, the street seems to suddenly fill with people, and you move with the crowd without any specific destination, here and there, in and out, you become part of a living organism, merging with it psychically and you start to believe that indeed a single world soul is possible — just as Nina Mikhailovna spoke of in your play. By the way, where is Nina now? Where is she and how is she doing?

TREPLYOV: Probably, fine.

DORN: I hear she's supposed to be living some kind of peculiar life. What's going on?

TREPLYOV: That's a long story, Doctor.

DORN: Make it a short one.

   *Pause.*

TREPLYOV: She ran away from home and took up with Trigorin. Had you heard this?

DORN: Yes.

TREPLYOV: She had a child. The child died. Trigorin stopped loving her and returned to his "previous attachment" — no surprise to anyone.

In truth he never really left his "previous attachment" and he somehow devised a plan to go back and forth between both of them. The way I understand it, Nina's personal life was a disaster.

DORN: And on the stage?

TREPLYOV: Worse still. She debuted in a theatre outside Moscow, then left for a tour to the provinces. At the time I kept right up with her — wherever she went, I went too. She took on all of the big roles, but she acted coarsely, tastelessly, with lots of shrieking and ugly gestures. There were moments when you could see her talent — when she was crying or dying — but those were few and far between.

DORN: So when all is said and done, is there any talent?

TREPLYOV: It's hard to know. Probably. I went to see her, but she didn't want to see me, and her maid wouldn't let me into her hotel room. I understood what she was going through and I didn't insist.

*Pause.*

What else can I tell you? I got some letters from her when I returned home. The letters were intelligent, warm, interesting; she didn't complain, but I could feel that she was deeply unhappy — every line was forced. And her mind seemed a little confused. She signed her name "Seagull." Just like in Pushkin's *Rusalka* when the miller calls himself a raven, she always says she's a seagull. Now she's here.

DORN: What do you mean, here?

TREPLYOV: In town, at the local hotel. She's been here for five days already. I tried to see her, and Marya Ilyinishna went too, but she wouldn't let anyone in. Semyon Semyonovich is pretty sure he saw her after lunch yesterday walking in a field not far from here.

MEDVEDENKO: Yes, I saw her. She was walking toward the town. I bowed, asked if she'd come visit us. She said she would.

TREPLYOV: She won't come.

*Pause.*

Her father and stepmother don't even want to know her. They've hired watchmen all over their estate to keep her off. *(He walks with the doctor to the desk)* It's a lot easier, Doctor, to be a philosopher on paper than it is in real life!

SORIN: The girl was lovely.

DORN: Pardon?

SORIN: Lovely, I say, the girl was lovely. Even State Councilor Sorin was in love with her for a time.

DORN: You old Romeo!

*SHAMRAYEV's laugh is heard.*

POLINA ANDREYEVNA: I think they've arrived from the station…

TREPLYOV: Yes, I hear Mama.

*Enter ARKADINA, TRIGORIN, behind them SHAMRAYEV.*

SHAMRAYEV: *(Entering)* We're all growing old, we're all weather-beaten and worn down, but you, most respected one, are always young… A bright-colored blouse, liveliness… gracefulness…

ARKADINA: You're trying to jinx me again! *(She spits over her left shoulder three times)*

TRIGORIN: *(To SORIN)* Hello, Pyotr Nikolayevich! What's this about you being ill. That's not good! *(Seeing MASHA, joyfully)* Marya Ilyinichna!

MASHA: You recognized me? *(She presses his hand)*

TRIGORIN: Married?

MASHA: Long ago.

TRIGORIN: Happy? *(He exchanges bows with DORN and MEDVEDEN-KO, then tentatively approaches TREPLYOV)* Irina Nikolayevna said you're ready to let bygones be bygones.

*TREPLYOV extends a hand to him.*

ARKADINA: *(To her son)* Look, Boris Alekseyevich has brought the journal with your new story.

TREPLYOV: *(Taking the book, to TRIGORIN)* Many thanks. You are very kind.

*They sit.*

TRIGORIN: Your admirers send their regards… In Petersburg and Moscow there's a lot of talk about you, and everyone asks me about you. Lots of: what's he like, how old, light or dark. For some reason people don't realize you're so young and since you publish under a pen name, nobody knows who you are. You're an enigma, like The Man in the Iron Mask.

TREPLYOV: Are you staying long?

TRIGORIN: No, tomorrow I'll head back to Moscow. I've got to. I'm rushing to finish a story and after that I promised to contribute something to an anthology. In other words — it's the same old story.

*While they talk, ARKADINA and POLINA ANDREYEVNA open a card table in the middle of the room; SHAMRAYEV lights candles, places chairs. They take a lotto game from the cupboard.*

The weather seems to be against me. That wind is brutal. Tomorrow morning, if it calms down, I'll try to do some fishing in the lake. By the way, I really need to take a look at the garden and that place where —

remember? — you did your play. I've got a good idea for a story and I just need to refresh my memory.

MASHA: *(To her father)* Papa, give my husband a horse! He's got to go home.

SHAMRAYEV: *(He mimics)* Horse... go home... *(Severely)* You saw for yourself, the horses just came back from the station. They can't go out again.

MASHA: For heaven's sake, there are other horses... *(Seeing that her father is quiet, waves with her hand)* Oh, what's the point...

MEDVEDENKO: Masha, I'll walk. It's fine.

POLINA ANDREYEVNA: *(Sighing)* Walk, in this weather... *(She takes a seat at the card table)* Please, ladies and gentlemen.

MEDVEDENKO: It's only four miles... Farewell... *(He kisses his wife's hand)* Farewell, Mama.

*His mother-in-law reluctantly extends her hand to him to kiss.*

I don't want to be any trouble, it's just the baby... *(He bows to everyone)* Farewell... *(He exits; his gait is apologetic)*

SHAMRAYEV: He'll get there. He's not a general, you know.

POLINA ANDREYEVNA: *(She taps on the table)* Please, ladies and gentlemen. Let's not waste any time before they call us to dinner.

*SHAMRAYEV, MASHA and DORN take a seat at the table.*

ARKADINA: *(To TRIGORIN)* When the long autumn nights set in, we always play lotto here at this table. Take a look: this is the same lotto set our dear mother used to play with us when we were children. Do you want to join us 'til dinner? *(She sits with TRIGORIN at the table)* It's a boring old game, but it's fun when you get used to it. *(She deals everyone three cards)*

TREPLYOV: *(Leafing through the journal)* He's read his own story, but he hasn't even cut the pages of mine. *(He puts the journal on the desk, then makes for the left door; passing by his mother, he kisses her on the head)*

ARKADINA: Kostya?

TREPLYOV: Sorry, I just don't feel like it... I'll take a walk. *(He exits)*

ARKADINA: The ante is: one ten-*kopek* piece. Would you put it in for me, doctor.

DORN: At your service, *Madame*.

MASHA: Everyone in? I'm starting... Twenty-two!

ARKADINA: Got it.

MASHA: Three!

DORN: Indeed!

MASHA: Did you get three? Eight! Eighty-one! Ten!

SHAMRAYEV: Slow down.

ARKADINA: What a triumph I had in Kharkov, my dear old friend — my head is still spinning.

MASHA: Thirty-four!

*Offstage, a melancholy waltz is heard.*

ARKADINA: The students arranged a marvelous reception... Three baskets, two wreaths, and look at this... *(She takes from her dress a brooch and flings it on the table)*

SHAMRAYEV: Yes, that is something...

MASHA: Fifty!...

DORN: Just fifty?

ARKADINA: I looked gorgeous. You have to admit, I know how to dress.

POLINA ANDREYEVNA: Kostya's playing. He's depressed, poor boy.

SHAMRAYEV: The reviewers are saying awful things about him in the papers.

MASHA: Seventy-seven!

ARKADINA: Who cares what they say!

TRIGORIN: He's unlucky. He can't seem to find his own voice. One moment it's strange, vague and then it becomes gibberish — pure ravings. Not one living character.

MASHA: Eleven!

ARKADINA: *(Looking over at SORIN)* Petrusha, are you bored?

*Pause.*

He's asleep.

DORN: State Councilor Sorin is asleep.

MASHA: Seven! Ninety!

TRIGORIN: If I lived here, by the lake, would I be able to write? I think I'd be too obsessed with fishing all the time.

MASHA: Twenty-eight!

TRIGORIN: To catch a perch — Bliss!

DORN: I don't know, I believe in Konstantin Gavrilych. He's got something! Something! He thinks in vivid, colorful images, and they really touch me. Only it's a crime his stories seem so aimless. He creates an atmosphere, nothing more, and let's face it, you can't go too far with just atmosphere. Irina Nikolayevna, are you glad your son is a writer?

ARKADINA: Imagine, I still haven't read him. There never seems to be any time.

MASHA: Twenty-six!

*TREPLYOV quietly enters and goes to his own desk.*

SHAMRAYEV: *(To TRIGORIN)* We still have that thing you left with us, Boris Alekseyevich.

TRIGORIN: What thing?

SHAMRAYEV: That seagull Konstantin Gavrilovich shot. You asked me to have it stuffed.

TRIGORIN: I don't remember. *(Thinking)* I don't remember!

MASHA: Sixty-six! One!

TREPLYOV: *(He flings open the window, he listens)* It's so dark! I don't know why I feel so nervous.

ARKADINA: Kostya, close the window, it's drafty in here.

*TREPLYOV closes the window.*

MASHA: Eighty-eight!

TRIGORIN: I win, ladies and gentlemen.

ARKADINA: *(Happily)* Bravo! Bravo!

SHAMRAYEV: *Bravo!*

ARKADINA: This man is always lucky. *(She stands)* And now let's get something to eat. Our celebrity hasn't eaten all day. We'll come back to the game after dinner. *(To her son)* Kostya, leave your writing and come join us.

TREPLYOV: I don't want to, Mama, I'm not hungry.

ARKADINA: Whatever you want... *(Waking SORIN)* Petrusha, dinner! *(She takes SHAMRAYEV under the arm)* I must tell you more about my reception in Kharkov...

> *POLINA ANDREYEVNA puts out the candles on the table, then she and DORN wheel the chair. Everyone exits through the left door except TREPLYOV, who remains alone at the desk.*

TREPLYOV: *(He starts to write; he skims through what he has already written)* I've talked so much about new forms, but the truth is I'm just as much a hack as everyone else. *(He reads)* "The poster on the fence proclaimed... A pale face, framed by dark hair..." Proclaimed, framed by... Ekh, this is such garbage. *(He strikes it out)* I'll begin when the hero wakes up to the sound of the rain, and everything else must go. The description of the moonlit night is so clichéd. It's easy for Trigorin, he's got his style down perfectly... With him the neck of a bottle glitters on the dam and the mill wheel creates a dark shadow and *voila*, he's got his moonlit night — but I have to have a flickering light and quiet twinkling stars and the distant sound of a piano, dying out in the fragrant night air... Oh, God, it's agonizing.

> *Pause.*

Yes, I see the truth of it now, it's not a question of old or new forms that matter, but what comes from a man's soul.

> *Someone raps at the window nearest the desk.*

What's that? *(He looks at the window)* I don't see anybody… *(He opens the glass door and looks in the garden)* Someone ran down the steps. *(He calls)* Who's there?

> *He exits; we can hear him move quickly on the terrace; after a moment he returns with NINA.*

Nina! Nina!

> *NINA puts her head to his chest and sobs.*

*(Moved)* Nina! Nina! It's you… you… I just had a feeling all day long — it's been awful. *(He takes her hat and cloak from her)* Oh, my dear, my darling, she's come! Don't cry, we mustn't cry.

NINA: Someone is here.

TREPLYOV: No one.

NINA: Lock the doors, they'll come in.

TREPLYOV: No one will come in.

NINA: I know, Irina Nikolayevna is here. Lock the doors…

TREPLYOV: *(He locks the right door with a key, he approaches the left)* This one doesn't have a lock. I'll block it with a chair. *(He stands the chair by the door)* Don't be frightened, no one will come in.

NINA: *(Intently gazing at his face)* Let me look at you. *(Looking around)* It's warm, good… This was the drawing-room. Have I changed very much?

TREPLYOV: Yes… You're thinner, and your eyes are bigger. Nina, it is so strange to see you. Why wouldn't you let me visit you? Why did you wait 'til now to come here? I know, you've been staying here almost a week… Several times a day I went to see you. I stood under your window, like a poor beggar.

NINA: I was afraid that you hated me. Every night I dream that you see me and don't recognize me. If you only knew! I've been coming here every day since the moment I arrived… to the lake. I've been at your door so many times but I couldn't bring myself to come in. Let's sit.

*They sit.*

We'll sit and we'll talk, talk. It's nice here, warm, cozy… Listen — the wind? Turgenev has a passage: "Happy is he who has a roof over his head and a warm corner to rest on such nights." I — seagull… No, that's not right. What did I start to say? Yes… Turgenev… "And may the Lord help all homeless wanderers."… It's nothing. *(She sobs)*

TREPLYOV: Nina, please don't cry… Nina!

NINA: It's nothing, I need to do this… I haven't cried for two years. Yesterday late in the evening I went to the garden, to see if our theatre was still there. And it was! I started crying for the first time in two years, and suddenly I felt more clear. You see, I'm not crying anymore. *(She takes him by the hand)* So, you've become a writer… You're a writer, I — an actress… We're both right in the middle of it… I was so happy as a child — I used to wake up each morning and sing; I loved you, I dreamed about glory, and now? Tomorrow morning early I have to go to Yelets, third class… with the peasants, and in Yelets disgusting merchants who proclaim their love of art will paw me with compliments. Horrible!

TREPLYOV: Why Yelets?

NINA: I've got an engagement for the whole winter. It's time to go.

TREPLYOV: Nina, I cursed you, hated you, tore up your letters and photographs, but I've always known that my soul is bound to yours forever. I don't have the strength to stop loving you, Nina. Ever since I lost you, my life has been unbearable — I'm suffering… My youth seems to have vanished. I feel like I'm ninety years old. I call your name, I kiss the ground you walk on; I see your face everywhere, I see that tender smile, which used to shine on me in the best years of my life…

NINA: *(Confused)* Why do you talk to me like this? Why?

TREPLYOV: I'm so lonely, I don't feel close to anybody. I'm so cold, it's like I live in a cave, and everything I write is so cold and stale — dead. Stay here, Nina, I beg you, or at least let me go with you!

*NINA quickly puts on her hat and cloak.*

Nina, why? For God's sake, Nina… *(He watches, as she gets dressed)*

*Pause.*

NINA: My carriage is waiting at the gate. Don't see me off, I'll go by myself… *(On the verge of tears)* Give me some water…

TREPLYOV: *(He gives her something to drink)* Where are you going now?

NINA: To town.

*Pause.*

Is Irina Nikolayevna here?

TREPLYOV: Yes… On Thursday my uncle got worse, we telegraphed her to come.

NINA: Why did you say that you kiss the ground I walk on? I ought to be killed. *(She bends down on the table)* I'm so tired! I need to rest… to rest! *(She raises her head)* I — seagull… no, that's not right — actress. Oh, yes! *(Hearing the laughter of ARKADINA and TRIGORIN, she listens, then runs to the left door and looks through the key-hole)* And he is here… *(Returning to TREPLYOV)* Yes, yes… No, it's nothing… Yes… He didn't believe in the theatre, he always laughed at my dreams, and little by little I stopped believing in them too, I lost heart… And then came the miseries of love, jealousy and the constant fear for the baby's life… I became so petty, worthless really, my acting was so amateurish… I didn't know what to do with my hands, I didn't know how to stand on the stage, I wasn't in control of my voice. You have no idea how awful it is when you know you're acting badly. I — seagull... No, that's not right. Do you remember, you shot a seagull? Once upon a time a man comes along and for no reason at all kills it... A subject for a short story... That's not it... *(She rubs her forehead)* What was I saying?... Yes, I was talking about the theater. But now it's different — now I'm the real thing — an actress. I act with delight, with rapture. It's as if I'm intoxicated on the stage, and I feel so beautiful. And since I've been here, I've been walking back and forth, back and forth and I've begun to feel my strength coming back. I know now, I understand, Kostya, that in our business — it doesn't matter if it's acting or writing — the most important thing is not fame, or brilliance, or those things I always dreamed about, it's the ability to endure, to have patience. We have to be able to bear our own cross and believe. I believe and to me it's not so painful, and when I think about my own calling, then I'm not afraid anymore.

TREPLYOV: *(Mournfully)* You're on a journey — you know where you're going, but I'm still wandering around in a chaos of daydreams and images. I don't know where I am going or why. I don't know what my calling is.

NINA: *(Listening)* Ssh... I'm going. Farewell. When I become an important actress, be sure to come and see me. Do you promise? But now... *(She squeezes his hand)* It's late. I can barely stand on my feet... I'm so hungry. I need to eat...

TREPLYOV: Stay, I'll get you some supper...

NINA: No, no... Don't see me off, I'll go by myself... My carriage is nearby... So, she brought him with her? Yes, it makes no difference. When you see Trigorin, don't say anything... I love him. I love him more than ever, more than before... A subject for a short story... I love, I love passionately, I love desperately. It was so nice, Kostya! Remember? How warm, joyful, pure life felt — like gentle, graceful flowers... Remember? *(She recites)* "People, lions, eagles and partridges, horned deer, geese, spiders, silent fishes dwelling in the water, starfish and those that cannot be seen with our eyes, — in a word, all lives, all lives, all lives, having accomplished their doleful circle: dead... Already thousands of centuries have passed since the earth has borne one living creature and in vain the poor moon shines her light. No longer do the cranes awaken the meadow, no longer do the maybugs sing in the linden groves..." *(She fitfully embraces TREPLYOV and runs out through the glass door)*

TREPLYOV: *(After a pause)* I hope nobody sees her in the garden. That would upset Mama...

*For two minutes he rips up all of his manuscripts and throws them under the desk, then opens the right door and exits.*

DORN: *(Trying to open the left door)* That's odd. Door seems to be locked... *(He enters and places the chair in place)* Obstacle course.

POLINA ANDREYEVNA: *(Entering behind him)* You were looking at her the whole time. I am requesting, I am begging you by everything that is sacred to you, do not torment me. Do not look at her, do not talk with her.

DORN: All right, I'll try...

POLINA ANDREYEVNA: *(Presses his hand to her breast)* I know I'm too jealous. I'm so ashamed... You must be sick of me.

DORN: No, it's nothing. If you must keep talking, do...

*Enter ARKADINA, MASHA and YAKOV with bottles, then SHAMRAYEV and TRIGORIN.*

ARKADINA: Put the wine and the beer over here for Boris Alekseyevich. We'll play and drink. Let's take a seat, ladies and gentlemen.

POLINA ANDREYEVNA: *(To YAKOV)* Bring the tea now. *(She lights candles, sits at the card table)*

SHAMRAYEV: *(He leads TRIGORIN to the cupboard)* Here's the thing I was telling you about before... *(He takes the stuffed seagull from the cupboard)* Just what you ordered.

TRIGORIN: *(Looking at the seagull)* I don't remember! *(Pondering)* I don't remember!

*Offstage a shot is heard; everyone shudders.*

ARKADINA: *(Frightened)* What's that?

DORN: Nothing. It's probably something in my medicine bag, something must have burst. Don't worry. *(He exits through the right door, after a half minute he returns)* Yes, that was it. A bottle of ether exploded. *(He sings)* "I am before you again charmed..."

ARKADINA: *(Sitting at the table)* Phew, that scared me. It reminded me, how... *(She covers her face with her hands)* Everything went black...

DORN: *(Leafing through the journal, to TRIGORIN)* I saw this article a couple of months ago... a letter from America, and I wanted to ask you... *(he takes TRIGORIN by the arm and leads him downstage)* I'm very interested in this question... *(In a lower tone)* Take Irina Nikolayevna away from here quickly. Konstantin Gavrilovich has killed himself...

*CURTAIN.*

# Uncle Vanya

Scenes from Country Life
in Four Acts

(1899)

# CHARACTERS

**Aleksander Vladimirovich Serebryakov,** a retired professor.

**Yelena Andreyevna,** his wife, 27 years old.

**Sofya Aleksandrovna (Sonya),** his daughter from his first marriage.

**Maria Vasilyevna Voinitskaya,** a widow of Privy Councillor, the mother of the professor's first wife.

**Ivan Petrovich Voinitsky (Vanya),** her son.

**Mikhail Lvovich Astrov,** a doctor.

**Ilya Ilyich Telyegin (Waffles),** an impoverished landowner.

**Marina Timofeyevna,** an old nurse.

**Yefim,** a workman.

*The action occurs on SEREBRYAKOV's country estate.*

# ACT I

*A garden. Part of a house with a terrace is visible. On a path under old poplars is a table, laid for tea. Benches, chairs; on one of the benches lies a guitar. Not far from the table is a child's swing. — Between two and three o'clock in the afternoon. Overcast.*


*MARINA, a slow-moving old woman, sits by the samovar; she knits a stocking and ASTROV paces nearby.*

MARINA: *(She fills a glass)* Eat. Eat something.

ASTROV: *(Reluctantly takes the glass)* I'm not hungry.

MARINA: Maybe a little vodka?

ASTROV: No. I don't drink vodka every day. Anyway, it's so hot today.

*Pause.*

Sweetheart, how long have we known each other?

MARINA: *(Pondering)* How long? God help me, let's see…You arrived in these parts… when?… Sonyechka's mother, Vera Petrovna, was still alive. Two times you came here to help her… so it must be eleven years. *(Having thought)* Well, maybe more.

ASTROV: Have I changed much?

MARINA: Oh, sure. You were so young and handsome. Now you're old and not so good looking anymore. Besides — too much vodka… *(She makes a "tsk tsk tsk" sound)*

ASTROV: Yes… In ten years I've become a different man. And why? I work too hard, *Nyanya*. I'm on my feet all day long. I don't get a moment's rest until I'm in bed at night — and then I'm terrified they'll drag me out for another patient. In all these years here, I haven't had a single day off. How could I stay young? And anyway, life is boring, stupid, dirty… it drags you down. And everyone you meet is crazy — honest to God, everyone I know is crazy. Try living among them for a while and you become a crazy person too — no getting away from it. *(Twisting his long moustache)* Just look, look at this enormous moustache. Stupid moustache. I'm a crazy person, too, *Nyanya*. But the good news is I haven't become a stupid person. Thank God for that. I still have my brains — but I can't seem to feel anything anymore. I don't want anything, I don't need anything, I don't love anyone — only you — I still love you. *(He kisses her head)* When I was a kid, I had a *nyanya* just like you.

MARINA: Are you sure you don't want something to eat?

ASTROV: No. In the third week of Lent I was in Malitskoye because of the epidemic — typhus — wall to wall sick people. Filth, stench, smoke, animals lying next to sick people… calves, pigs… I was on my feet all day — not a drop of food or water touched my lips and when I finally got home, no rest there either. They brought me a railroad switchman; I put him on the table to operate and he died on me — under chloroform. And can you believe it — it was in that moment my feelings decided to wake up — and I started to believe that he died because of me. I sat down, closed my eyes — and I thought: will anyone remember us in a hundred or two hundred years? Will anyone speak well of us? No, *Nyanya*, no — we will be forgotten.

MARINA: People won't remember, but God will.

ASTROV: Thanks for that — well said.

*Enter VOINITSKY.*

VOINITSKY: Yes… *(He exits from the house; he had a nap after breakfast and has a rumpled appearance; he sits down on the bench, he adjusts his fancy tie)*

*Pause.*

Yes…

ASTROV: Good nap?

VOINITSKY: Yes... Very. *(He yawns)* Ever since the professor and his wife came to live with us, everything is upside down. I fall asleep at all the wrong times, we eat spicy foods, I drink too much wine — it's ridiculous. Sonya and I used to work all day long. Nowadays Sonya works and I eat, drink and sleep. Not good!

MARINA: *(Having shaken her head)* Yes, it's ridiculous! The professor wakes up at 12 noon, but the samovar boils from early morning, waiting for him. When they weren't around we ate lunch at one o'clock, like everybody does. But nowadays it's between six and seven. The professor reads and writes all night long, and about two o'clock in the morning, he rings. Now what's that about, my friends? Tea! Sure, wake everyone up and put the samovar on... Ridiculous!

ASTROV: How long are they staying?

VOINITSKY: *(He whistles)* A hundred years. The professor has decided to settle here permanently.

MARINA: And look — the samovar's been boiling for two hours and they are out for a stroll.

VOINITSKY: They're coming, they're coming... Calm down.

*Voices are heard; from the depths of the garden, returning from a stroll, enter SEREBRYKOV, YELENA ANDREYEVNA, SONYA, and TELYEGIN.*

SEREBRYAKOV: Excellent, excellent... remarkable views.

TELYEGIN: Yes, remarkable, Your Excellency.

SONYA: Tomorrow we'll take a walk in the woods, Papa. Does that sound nice?

VOINITSKY: Ladies and Gentlemen, tea!

SEREBRYAKOV: My friends, bring my tea to the study, if you please! I still have work to do.

SONYA: Oh, but you'll love the woods, Papa…

*YELENA ANDREYEVNA, SEREBRYAKOV and SONYA exit into the house; TELYEGIN goes to the table and sits near MARINA.*

VOINITSKY: It's boiling hot today, but our great scholar is in a topcoat, galoshes, with an umbrella and gloves.

ASTROV: Ergo, he takes good care of himself.

VOINITSKY: And did you get a look at her? Beautiful! I've never seen anyone more beautiful.

TELYEGIN: Whether I'm in the fields, Marina Timofeyevna, or wandering in the shady orchard, or just looking at this table, I experience indescribable joy! The weather is charming, the little birds are singing, we all live in peace and harmony — what more could we ask?
*(He accepts a glass)* I'm deeply grateful to you!

VOINITSKY: *(Dreamily)* Her eyes… Marvelous woman!

ASTROV: Talk to me, Ivan Petrovich.

VOINITSKY: *(Sluggishly)* What should I say?

ASTROV: Anything new?

VOINITSKY: Nothing. Everything is old. I'm the same as I was — only worse. I've gotten lazy. I grumble all day long like the old clown I've become. My ancient crow of a mother still prattles on about women's emancipation; she's got one foot in the grave, and the other at the edge of an "ennobled new life."

ASTROV: And the professor?

VOINITSKY: And the professor sits alone from morning 'til night in the study and writes:

> "Strained mind, strained brow,
> No rest will he allow.
> Must write all nights, must write all days,
> Sadly for him, there is no praise."

I pity the poor paper! He'd be better off writing his autobiography — now there's a topic! A retired professor, if you don't mind, a dried-up old geezer, a pedantic plodder… Gout, rheumatism, migraines, a liver swollen with jealousy and envy… This geezer lives on the estate of his first wife, lives here against his will, because he can't afford to live in the city. He whines endlessly about his own misfortunes, even though the truth is, he's been outrageously lucky. *(Irritably)* Just listen to this luck — son of a village sexton, a seminary student, who somehow got his academic degrees and chairmanship, became "His Excellency," the son-in-law of a councilman, etcetera, etcetera… But none of that is important. Just listen, there's more — Here's a man who spends twenty-five years reading and writing about art, and actually knows absolutely nothing about art. For twenty-five years he chews up and digests other scholars' ideas about realism, naturalism and other nonsense; for twenty-five years he reads and writes about stuff smart people knew all along and stupid people never cared about in the first place — so in reality, he has spent twenty-five years chasing his tail around a tree. Yet, have you noticed the conceit! The pretensions! He went into retirement, and there's not a living soul who has heard of him, he's a complete nobody — which means that for twenty-five years he hasn't made the tiniest dent in this world. But look at him: he strides around like a demigod!

ASTROV: I think you're jealous.

VOINITSKY: Yes, I'm jealous! And have you noticed his success with women! Don Juan never had such success! His first wife, my sister, a beautiful, gentle creature, as perfect as the blue sky above, generous, with more admirers than he had pupils, she loved him so, as only purest angels can love. My mother, his mother-in-law, to this day worships him, and yes, to this day he inspires in her wondrous awe. His second wife, a beauty, a clever girl — you just saw her — married him when he was old already, gave him her youth, beauty, freedom, her own brilliance. And for what? Why?

ASTROV: Is she faithful to the professor?

VOINITSKY: Unfortunately, yes.

ASTROV: Why unfortunately?

VOINITSKY: Because that kind of faithfulness is false from beginning to end. There's a lot of empty piousness in her faithfulness, but no logic. Sure, to betray an old husband, whom you can't endure, that's immoral; but to throw away your youth and brilliance, that's — yes, that's "honorable."

TELYEGIN: *(Crying out)* Vanya, I don't like it when you talk like that. Now, please… when someone is unfaithful to their husband or wife, then that person is capable of disloyalty to his country!

VOINITSKY: *(Irritated)* Oh, shut up, Waffles!

TELYEGIN: Please excuse me, Vanya. My wife ran away the day after our wedding with her lover, mostly because she couldn't stand to look at me. But I never strayed from my duty. To this day I love her and I remain faithful to her. I help her when I can — I sold my property to pay for her and her lover's children. I lost everything, all my happiness, but I still have my pride. And she? She's gotten old, her beauty has faded, her lover has died… What does she have?

> *Enter SONYA and YELENA ANDREYEVNA; a little later MARIA VASILYEVNA enters with a book; she sits and reads; they give her tea, and she drinks it without looking.*

SONYA: *(Hurriedly to the Nurse)* Nyanya dear, there are some peasants here. Go talk to them, and I'll pour the tea... *(She pours tea)*

> MARINA exits. YELENA ANDREYEVNA takes her teacup and drinks, sitting on the swing.

ASTROV: *(To YELENA ANDREYEVNA)* You know I came here to see your husband. You wrote that he's very ill — rheumatism or something — but he seems to be perfectly fine.

YELENA ANDREYEVNA: Last night he was depressed, he complained about pain in his legs, but today nothing...

ASTROV: And I galloped here, thirty-five miles at breakneck speed. Well, never mind, it's not the first time. Oh, alright, I'll stay with you until tomorrow and, maybe, I'll get a good night's sleep for once.

SONYA: Wonderful. You hardly ever stay overnight anymore. Have you had lunch?

ASTROV: No, Ma'am.

SONYA: Well you must have lunch! These days we eat lunch between six and seven o'clock.

*(She drinks)* Uh oh, the tea is cold!

TELYEGIN: The temperature in the samovar has lowered considerably.

YELENA ANDREYEVNA: Never mind, Ivan Ivanich, we'll drink it cold.

TELYEGIN: Please excuse me, Madam... Not Ivan Ivanich, but Ilya Ilyich, Madam... Ilya Ilyich Telyegin, or, as some call me, Waffles, on account of my pock-marked face. I am Sonyechka's godfather, and His Excellency, your husband, knows me very well. I live here, madam, on this estate, madam... You may have noticed, I dine with you every day.

SONYA: Ilya Ilych is our valued assistant, our right hand man. *(Tenderly)* Here, Godfather, I'll pour you some more.

MARIA VASILYEVNA: Akh!

SONYA: What's wrong, *Babushka*?

MARIA VASILYEVNA: I forgot to tell *Alexandre*... I must be losing my mind... today I received a letter from from Pavel Alekseyevich in Kharkov... He sent his new pamphlet...

ASTROV: Interesting?

MARIA VASILYEVNA: Yes, interesting, but strange somehow. He utterly refutes that which he himself defended seven years ago. It's terrible!

VOINITSKY: There is nothing terrible about it. Drink your tea, *Maman*.

MARIA VASILYEVNA: But I want to talk!

VOINITSKY: We've been talking and talking for fifty years and reading and reading pamphlets. Maybe it's time to be silent.

MARIA VASILYEVNA: My voice seems to annoy you lately, *Jean*. Forgive me, *Jean*, but in the last year you have changed so much that I absolutely don't recognize you anymore... You were a man with definite convictions, a clear point of view...

VOINITSKY: Oh, yes! I was so clear, no one could see me.

   *Pause.*

I was so clear that... oh, maybe I shouldn't make stupid jokes... I am forty seven years old. Until last year I was exactly like you, trying to immerse my mind in scholarly thinking — yes, I was so immersed I couldn't even see my nose in front of my face — and I thought I was being brilliant. But now — if only you knew! I don't sleep at night because I'm so furious that I wasted my time with all that. I lost my chance to live and now I'm too old!

SONYA: Uncle Vanya, please stop!

MARIA VASILYEVNA: *(To her son)* You are attacking all your former convictions... But they're not to blame, you yourself are! You forget, convictions are nothing in themselves, just words... One must take action, do something...

VOINITSKY: Do something? Not everyone is a *perpetuum mobile* writing machine like your *herr* professor.

MARIA VASILYEVNA: What are you talking about?

SONYA: *(Pleading) Babushka*! Uncle Vanya! I beg you!

VOINITSKY: I'll be quiet. I'll be quiet and I apologize.

*Pause.*

YELENA ANDREYEVNA: Isn't the weather lovely... not too hot...

*Pause.*

VOINITSKY: Yes, it's good weather for hanging yourself...

*TELYEGIN tunes his guitar. MARINA walks by the house and calls the chickens.*

MARINA: Chick, chick, chick...

SONYA: *Nyanya*, why did the peasants come?

MARINA: Always the same, always about that piece of land they want... Chick, chick, chick...

SONYA: Who're you calling?

MARINA: Pestrushka is out with her chicks… The crows might snatch them up… *(She exits)*

*TELYEGIN plays a polka; everyone listens quietly; YEFIM enters.*

YEFIM: Is the doctor here? *(To ASTROV)* Please, Mikhail Lvovich, some men are here to see you.

ASTROV: Where from?

YEFIM: From the factory.

ASTROV: *(Annoyed)* All right, thanks very much. It looks like I have to go. *(He looks for his hat)* It's so damn annoying.

SONYA: I'm so sorry. Come back later for lunch.

ASTROV: No, it'll be too late. Where the hell… Where's… *(To YEFIM)* Get me a glass of vodka, will you?

*YEFIM exits.*

Where the hell… Ah… *(He has found his hat)* In a play by Ostrovsky there's a man with a big moustache and no talent… that's me. Well, I have the honor, ladies and gentlemen… *(To YELENA ANDREYEVNA)* If you are in the neighborhood, please come visit me with Sofya Aleksandrovna. I have a small estate, fifty acres, but, if it interests you, it has a model orchard and nursery which you won't be able to find for a thousand miles around here. The State forest is right next to my place… the forest warden is old, always sick, so, in fact, I spend a lot of my time managing the forest business.

YELENA ANDREYEVNA: Yes, I've heard that you love forests. I'm sure you're very helpful, but doesn't it get in the way of your real work? You're a doctor, true?

ASTROV: Only God knows what our real work is.

YELENA ANDREYEVNA: Is it interesting?

ASTROV: Oh yes, very.

VOINITSKY: *(With irony)* Very!

YELENA ANDREYEVNA: *(To ASTROV)* You're still young... well, thirty-six or thirty-seven... I'll bet it can't be as interesting as you say. All those trees... it must be boring.

SONYA: No, it's extremely interesting. Mikhail Lvovich plants new trees every year, and they've given him a bronze medal and a certificate for his good work. He writes petitions to keep them from destroying the old forests. If you just listen to him, you'll agree completely. He says, forests bring grace to the earth, they teach man to understand what is beautiful and they inspire us to appreciate beauty in this world. Forests soften our harsh climate. In countries where there is a mild climate, people are less overwhelmed by the struggle with nature, and therefore men are gentler and more tender — more attractive, versatile, passionate — their speech is elegant, their movement is graceful. In those countries science and art flourish, their philosophy is not gloomy like ours, attitudes toward women are honorable and noble...

VOINITSKY: *(Laughing) Bravo, bravo!...* That's all very nice, but I'm not convinced. *(To ASTROV)* So permit me, my friend, to continue to heat my stove with firewood and build my shed with wood.

ASTROV: You can heat your stove with peat, and build your shed with stones. Well, I'll grant you, there is a need to chop down some trees, but why eliminate them entirely? Russian forests fall under the axe, billions of trees perish, they ravage the dwellings of wild animals and birds, rivers grow shallow and dry, the magical landscape irrevocably vanishes, and all because we are too lazy to stoop down and pick up the fuel from the ground. *(To YELENA ANDREYEVNA)* Isn't that right,

*Madame*? We must be reckless barbarians if we burn in our stoves that which we can never re-create. Man has been given reason and imagination, so that we may increase what is given to us. But up 'til now, we only destroy, not create. There are fewer and fewer forests, our rivers are drying up, our wildlife is becoming extinct, our climate is changing, and every single day the earth becomes poorer and uglier. *(To VOINITSKY)* Don't give me that look. Maybe you don't believe me and… and maybe you think I'm crazy, but… When I pass by the woods which I saved from the axe, or when I see a new tree growing that I planted with my own hands, I realize that maybe nature is just a little bit in my power after all, and if it could possibly make people happier, then I feel as if I have made a small contribution to this earth. When I plant a birch and I see how it grows green and sways with the wind, my soul fills with pride, and I… *(Seeing YEFIM, who has brought a glass of vodka on a tray)* However… *(He drinks)* it's time for me to go.

VOINITSKY: *(To YELENA)* He doesn't eat meat either.

ASTROV: Yes, I think it's a crime to kill living things. I must sound very strange to you… I have the honor to take your leave. *(He goes to the house)*

SONYA: *(She takes him by the arm and goes with him)* When will you be back to see us?

ASTROV: I don't know…

SONYA: In a month?…

> *ASTROV and SONYA exit into the house; MARIA VASILYEVNA and TELYEGIN remain by the table; YELENA ANDREYEVNA and VOINITSKY walk to the terrace.*

YELENA ANDREYEVNA: You, Ivan Petrovich, you were impossible! Why did you aggravate Maria Vasilyevna, and talk about *perpetuum mobile*! And today at breakfast you argued with Aleksander again. You are so petty!

VOINITSKY: I hate him!

YELENA ANDREYEVNA: There's nothing to hate. He's the same as everyone else. The same as you.

VOINITSKY: If you could just look at yourself — your face, the way you move... so lazy, so idle! It's hard for you to budge, to live, isn't it! Akh, what laziness...

YELENA ANDREYEVNA: Yes, lazy and bored! Everyone hates my husband, everyone looks at me with pity: poor darling, she has an old husband! Such sympathy — oh, how well I understand it! It's exactly as Astrov said: you recklessly destroy the forests, and soon nothing beautiful will remain on earth. In the same reckless way, you destroy man, and soon, thanks to you, there will be no truth or purity left, no capacity for self-sacrifice. Why can't you look at a woman with indifference — especially if she isn't yours? The doctor is right — a demon of destruction sits right inside you. You have no pity for the forests, the birds, women — no, not for anything...

VOINITSKY: Cut out the philosophy!

*Pause.*

YELENA ANDREYEVNA: That doctor has a tired, nervous face. It's an interesting face. Clearly, Sonya is fond of him, she's in love with him, and I understand her. He's been here to see us three times already, but I'm shy and I haven't yet talked with him as I'd like to. I haven't been too nice to him either. He probably thinks I'm awful. Ivan Petrovich, you know why we're such good friends? Because we're both such tedious, boring people! Tedious! Don't look at me like that, I don't like it.

VOINITSKY: How can I look at you differently? I love you. You are my happiness, my life, my youth! I know you'll never return these feelings, but at least permit me to look at you, to listen to your voice...

YELENA ANDREYEVNA: Be quiet, they can hear you!

*They walk to the house.*

VOINITSKY: *(Walking behind her)* Permit me to speak of my love, don't drive me away, that's all I need to be happy…

YELENA ANDREYEVNA: This is excruciating…

*They both exit into the house.*

*TELYEGIN plucks the strings and plays a polka; MARIA VASILYEVNA writes something in the margins of the pamphlet.*

CURTAIN.

# ACT II

*The dining room in SEREBRYAKOV's home. — Night. — In the garden the WATCHMAN can be heard tapping.*

*SEREBRYAKOV sits in an armchair before an open window and dozes and YELENA ANDREYEVNA sits beside him and also dozes.*

SEREBRYAKOV: *(Waking up)* Who's there? Sonya, is that you?

YELENA ANDREYEVNA: I'm here.

SEREBRYAKOV: You, Lenochka… The pain is unbearable!

YELENA ANDREYEVNA: Here, your blanket fell. *(She wraps up his legs)* I'll shut the window.

SEREBRYAKOV: No, I'm suffocating… I was just nodding off, and I dreamt that my left leg was attached to someone else. I woke up with such excruciating pain. No, this is not gout — probably rheumatism. What time is it?

YELENA ANDREYEVNA: Twenty minutes after twelve.

*Pause.*

SEREBRYAKOV: In the morning go look for Batyushkov in the library. I'm sure we have him.

YELENA ANDREYEVNA: What?

SEREBRYAKOV: Look for Batyushkov in the morning. I seem to recall, we have him. Why can't I breathe?

YELENA ANDREYEVNA: You're tired. This is the second night you haven't slept.

SEREBRYAKOV: They say Turgenev developed *angina pectoris* from gout. I'm afraid I'm getting it too. Damned, disgusting old age. The devil take it! Now that I'm old, I can't stand looking at myself. And I'm sure all of you must be repulsed by me too.

YELENA ANDREYEVNA: You make it sound as if it's our fault you got old.

SEREBRYAKOV: But I'm most disgusting to you.

*YELENA ANDREYEVNA walks away and sits at some distance.*

Of course, you're right. I'm not stupid, I understand. You're young, healthy, beautiful, you want to live, and I'm an old man, almost a corpse. True? I understand all too well. And of course, it's a terrible crime I have lived this long. But wait a little, soon you'll be free of me. I won't last much longer.

YELENA ANDREYEVNA: I'm exhausted... For God's sake be quiet.

SEREBRYAKOV: Yes, everyone is exhausted — all because of me. They're bored, they're wasting their time, they're wasting their youth. I'm the only one who's happy. I'm the only one having a good time. Well, yes, of course!

YELENA ANDREYEVNA: Be quiet! You've worn me out!

SEREBRYAKOV: Yes, I have worn everyone out! Of course.

YELENA ANDREYEVNA: *(On the verge of tears)* This is unbearable! Tell me what you want from me.

SEREBRYAKOV: Nothing.

YELENA ANDREYEVNA: Well, then be quiet. I beg you.

SEREBRYAKOV: It's so strange, Ivan Petrovich talks his head off, or that old idiot, Maria Vasilyevna, and it's just fine, everyone listens, but when I say one word, everyone suddenly feels desolate. Even my voice is offensive. Well, let's assume I am offensive, I'm an egoist, I'm a despot — don't I have the right to be an egoist, in my old age? Think about it. Haven't I earned it? I ask you, don't I have the right to a comfortable old age, surrounded by my admirers?

YELENA ANDREYEVNA: No one is taking away your rights.

*The window bangs from the wind.*

It's very windy, I'll close the window. *(She closes it)* It'll rain soon. No one's denying your rights.

*Pause; the WATCHMAN in the garden taps and sings a song.*

SEREBRYAKOV: All one's life to be dedicated to scholarship, to become accustomed to one's study, to the classroom, to respected colleagues — and suddenly, for no apparent reason, to find oneself buried in this tomb, every day to deal with stupid people, to listen to insignificant chatter... I want to live, I love success, I love fame, I love action — but here I'm in exile. Every minute I'm longing for the past, watching the success of others, fearing death... I cannot! I don't have the strength! And no one can forgive me for being old!

YELENA ANDREYEVNA: Wait a little, have patience: in five or six years I'll be old too.

*SONYA enters.*

SONYA: Papa, you sent for Dr. Astrov, but when he came, you refused to see him. That's so rude. You bothered this man...

SEREBRYAKOV: Why do I need your Astrov? He understands as much about medicine as I do astronomy.

SONYA: We cannot send for the entire medical faculty just for your gout.

SEREBRYAKOV: I won't talk to that idiot.

SONYA: As you wish. *(She sits)* It's all the same to me.

SEREBRYAKOV: What time is it?

YELENA ANDREYEVNA: Almost one.

SEREBRYAKOV: It's stifling... Sonya, give me the drops from the table!

SONYA: Yes, of course. *(She gives him the drops)*

SEREBRYAKOV: *(Irritatedly)* Akh, not these! I can't ask for anything!

SONYA: Please, stop acting like a baby. It may be fine for others, but spare me, please! I don't like it. I don't have time, I need to get up early tomorrow, I have the hay to mow.

*Enter VOINITSKY in a dressing-gown and with a candle.*

VOINITSKY: The storm's coming.

*Lightning.*

Here we go! *Hélène* and Sonya, go to sleep. I came to relieve you.

SEREBRYAKOV: *(Frightened)* No, no! Don't leave me with him! No. He'll talk my head off!

VOINITSKY: But they've got to get some rest! They didn't sleep at all last night.

SEREBRYAKOV: Let them go to sleep, but you go too. Thank you. I implore you. In the name of our former friendship, just go. We'll talk later.

VOINITSKY: *(With a grin)* Our former friendship... former...

SONYA: Be quiet, Uncle Vanya.

SEREBRYAKOV: *(To his wife)* My dear, don't leave me with him! He'll talk my head off.

VOINITSKY: Can you believe how ludicrous this is…

*MARINA enters with a candle.*

SONYA: You ought to be in bed, *Nyanya*. It's very late.

MARINA: The samovar is still boiling. You can't exactly expect me to go to bed.

SEREBRYAKOV: No one is sleeping, everybody is exhausted, I alone am in a state of bliss.

MARINA: *(She goes over to SEREBRYAKOV, tenderly)* What is it, my dear? Are you in pain? My legs ache too, they ache so. *(She adjusts the blanket)* You've been in pain such a long time. Vera Petrovna, Sonyechka's mother, may she rest in peace, never slept either, she nearly killed herself taking care of you… She loved you very much… oh yes…

*Pause.*

Old people are like children; they want someone to feel sorry for them, but no one feels sorry for the old. *(She kisses SEREBRYAKOV on the shoulder)* Let's go to bed, my dear… Let's go, my little boy… I'll make you some limeleaf tea, I'll warm your legs… I'll pray to God for you…

SEREBRYAKOV: *(Moved)* Let's go, Marina.

MARINA: My legs ache too, they ache so. *(She leads him together with SONYA)* Vera Petrovna nearly killed herself, always crying… You, Sonyechka, were still little then… Come, come, my dear…

*SEREBRYAKOV, SONYA, and MARINA exit.*

YELENA ANDREYEVNA: I'm completely exhausted with him. I can barely stand on my feet.

VOINITSKY: You're exhausted with him, and I with myself. This is the third night I haven't slept.

YELENA ANDREYEVNA: Something is wrong in this house. Your mother hates everything, except her own pamphlets and the professor; the professor is irritated, he doesn't trust me, he's afraid of you; Sonya is angry with her father, angry with me and hasn't talked to me for two weeks; you hate my husband and openly hold your own mother in contempt; I'm short-tempered and at least twenty times today I started to cry... There is something very wrong in this house.

VOINITSKY: Shall we cut the philosophy, please!

YELENA ANDREYEVNA: You, Ivan Petrovich, are educated, intelligent, and you must see that the world is not being destroyed by thieves and fires and wars, but rather by hatred, hostility, from all these petty squabbles... You shouldn't add to the noisy complaining around us, you should be helping to find peace in your own family.

VOINITSKY: Help me find peace in myself! My darling... *(He presses her hand to himself)*

YELENA ANDREYEVNA: Stop! *(She takes away her hand)* Go away!

VOINITSKY: Soon it'll stop raining, and everything in nature will be refreshed and alive. I alone will not be refreshed by the storm. Day and night, I'm strangled by the idea that my life is irrevocably lost — that I'm dead — that I wasted my life — that I spent my life on trifles. Here — take my life, take my love. What good are they to me, what have I done with them? My feelings are dying away in vain, like sun beams falling into a dark pit... I'm dying.

YELENA ANDREYEVNA: When you talk to me about your love, I just go numb and I don't know what to say. Forgive me, I have nothing to say to you. *(She tries to go)* Good night.

VOINITSKY: *(Blocking her way)* If you only knew how I suffer from the thought that next to me in this very house another life is dying — yours! What're you waiting for? What damned righteous morality stops you? Don't you see…

YELENA ANDREYEVNA: *(Intently staring at him)* Ivan Petrovich, you're drunk!

VOINITSKY: Possibly, possibly…

YELENA ANDREYEVNA: Where's the doctor?

VOINITSKY: He's here… he's spending the night. Possibly, possibly… Everything is possible…

YELENA ANDREYEVNA: Why are you drinking so much?

VOINITSKY: Because it makes me feel alive… Don't try to stop me, Hélène!

YELENA ANDREYEVNA: You never used to drink so much and you never talked so much… Go to sleep! I'm bored to death with you.

VOINITSKY: *(Pressing her hand)* My darling… beautiful, marvelous…

YELENA ANDREYEVNA: *(With vexation)* Leave me alone. This is just disgusting. *(She exits)*

VOINITSKY: *(Alone)* She's gone…

*Pause.*

I first met you ten years ago at my darling sister's remember? You were seventeen, and I was thirty-seven. Why didn't I fall in love with you and propose to you then? It would have been so easy! And today you would be my wife… Yes… Tonight both of us would be awakened by the storm; you would be afraid of the thunder, and I would take you in my arms and whisper: "Don't be afraid, little darling, I'm here." Oh, what marvelous thoughts, how wonderful, I'm laughing... but my God, I'm so mixed up... Why am I old? Why doesn't she understand me? The way she talks, her stupid morality, her silly prattling about making peace in the world... I hate it so much.

*Pause.*

Oh, how I've been deceived! I worshipped that professor, that pathetic, gout-ridden idiot! I worked for him like a slave! Sonya and I squeezed every drop out of this estate; we were like *kulaks*, haggling over vegetable oil, peas, starving ourselves with crumbs, just so we could save a few *kopeks* to send to him. I was so proud of him and his glorious scholarship, I lived for him, I breathed for him! Every word he wrote or uttered seemed like genius to me... God — and now? Now he's retired and it has become perfectly clear that the sum total of his life adds up to nothing. Not one word of his, not a single scholarly word, matters to anyone. A soap bubble! And I've been swindled... I see that now — stupidly swindled...

*Enter ASTROV in a frock-coat, without a waistcoat and without a tie; he is tipsy; behind him is TELYEGIN with a guitar.*

ASTROV: Play!

TELYEGIN: Everyone is sleeping, sir!

ASTROV: Play!

*TELYEGIN quietly strums.*

(*To VOINITSKY*) Are you alone here? No ladies? (*His arms akimbo, he quietly sings*) "Go to the peasant house, go to the fire, there is no place for the master to expire..." The storm woke me. Big storm! What time is it?

VOINITSKY: Who knows.

ASTROV: I thought I heard Yelena Andreyevna's voice.

VOINITSKY: She was just here.

ASTROV: What a gorgeous woman. *(Looking around at the bottles on the table)* Medicines, drugs… there's nothing missing! Kharkov, Moscow, Tulskaya… Every city is plagued with his gout. Is he really sick or faking it?

VOINITSKY: Sick.

*Pause.*

ASTROV: Why are you so sad today? Pity for the professor?

VOINITSKY: Quit it.

ASTROV: Or maybe, you're in love with the professor's wife?

VOINITSKY: She's my friend.

ASTROV: Already?

VOINITSKY: What does that mean "already?"

ASTROV: A woman can be friends with a man only in this order: first an acquaintance, then a lover, and then finally a friend.

VOINITSKY: Vulgar.

ASTROV: Oh? Yes… it's true — I'm becoming vulgar. I'm drunk. Usually I get drunk like this once a month. And when I'm drunk, I get completely vulgar — and fearless! Everything seems so easy to me! I take on the most difficult operations and do them brilliantly; I make daring plans for the future; when I'm drunk I no longer seem like a freak, and I actually believe I'm bringing some enormous benefit to humanity… enormous! And when I'm drunk, I see how valuable my own personal universe is — and the rest of you piddling creatures seem like insects... microbes. *(To TELYEGIN)* Waffles, play!

TELYEGIN: Dear one, I would love to play for you with all my soul, but understand — everyone is sleeping!

ASTROV: Play!

*TELYEGIN quietly strums.*

You need a drink. Ooh, I see there's some cognac left. In the morning, we'll go to my place. Rightch'are! I have a medical assistant who never says "right" but "rightch'are". Idiot — rightch'are. *(Seeing SONYA enter)* Pardon me, I forgot my tie. *(Quickly he exits; TELYEGIN follows)*

SONYA: And you, Uncle Vanya, you got drunk again with the doctor. A couple of juveniles — hanging around together... Well, he has always been like that, but what in heaven's name is wrong with you? At your age, you should know better.

VOINITSKY: Age has nothing to do with it. When you don't have a life, you live on soap bubbles. It's better than nothing.

SONYA: Our hay needs to be cut, it rains every day, everything is rotting, and all you can talk about is soap bubbles. You're completely neglecting the farm. I have to work alone, I'm strained to the breaking point... *(Frightened)* Uncle, you have tears in your eyes!

VOINITSKY: Tears? It's nothing... nonsense... The way you looked at me just now, just like your mother. My sweet... *(Greedily he kisses her hands and face)* My sister... my sweet, dear sister... Where is she now? If only she knew! Oh, if only she knew!

SONYA: Knew what? Uncle, what?

VOINITSKY: It's so hard... Nothing... Later... Nothing... I'm going... *(He exits)*

SONYA: *(Taps on the door)* Mikhail Lvovich! You're not sleeping, are you? Do you have a minute?

ASTROV: *(Behind the door)* One moment! *(A little later he enters: he is now in a waistcoat and tie)* What can I do for you?

SONYA: You can drink all you want if you can stand it, but, I beg you, don't let my uncle drink. It's not good for him.

ASTROV: Fine. We won't drink together again.

   *Pause.*

I'm going home now. Signed and sealed… The sun will be up by the time they harness the horses.

SONYA: It's still raining. Wait until morning.

ASTROV: The storm's almost over, we just caught a little bit of it. I'm going. And, please, don't send for me again to see your father. I tell him — it's gout, and he says rheumatism; I ask him to lie down, he sits up. And today he wouldn't even talk to me.

SONYA: He's spoiled. *(She looks at the sideboard)* Do you want to have a bite to eat?

ASTROV: Sure.

SONYA: I love to eat at night. There should be something in the sideboard. People say he was quite a ladies' man all his life, and his ladies have spoiled him. Here, have some cheese.

   *They both stand at the sideboard and eat.*

ASTROV: I ate nothing today, only drank. Your father is a difficult personality. *(He takes a bottle from the sideboard)* May I? *(He drinks a glass)* We're alone, so maybe I can speak more openly. You know, I don't think I'd last a month in this house, I'd be choked to death… Your father is completely buried in his own gout and in his books, Uncle Vanya in his depression, your grandmother... and finally, your stepmother...

SONYA: What about my stepmother?

ASTROV: To look at her, she's perfection: face, clothes, voice and soul. She is beautiful, there's no doubt, but... in reality, all she does is eat, sleep, stroll around, and bewitch us all with her beauty — nothing else. She has no responsibilities whatsoever, everyone waits on her... True? An idle life can't be a good one.

*Pause.*

But maybe I'm being too hard on her. I'm not happy with my life, like your Uncle Vanya, and both of us have become a couple of old grumblers.

SONYA: You're discontented with life?

ASTROV: Well of course I love life in general, but our Russian provincial life is so small-minded and mean — and I hate it with all my soul. As for my personal life, well, there's nothing good there either. You know, when you walk in the dark at night in the woods, and sometimes you're lucky enough to see a small light burning in the distance, then you're not bothered by your weariness, or the darkness, or the prickly branches that scratch your face... I work harder — you know this — than anyone in this district, I'm constantly hit with bad luck, and sometimes I suffer unbearably, but the truth is I see no light in the distance. I have no hope. I don't like people... I haven't loved anyone for a long time.

SONYA: No one?

ASTROV: No one. I feel some tenderness for your nurse — for old times' sake. The peasants are dull, backward, they live in filth, and it's just as hard to talk to the "intelligentsia." All of it exhausts me. I have plenty of nice acquaintances who can't think for themselves and see no further than their own noses — they're just stupid. And the ones who are more intelligent and more interesting are taken up with analyzing themselves with "self reflection"... They bellyache all the time, they hate everyone, they think everyone is beneath them and when they meet you, they label you immediately — "Oh, he's a psychopath, an eccentric, a freak." I love the forest — that's strange. I don't eat meat — that's really strange. It's impossible to have a true relationship with nature or with people any more — No, that doesn't exist! *(He goes to pour a drink)*

SONYA: *(She stops him)* No, please, I beg you, don't drink anymore.

ASTROV: Why?

SONYA: It's not right for you! You're elegant, noble, you have such a gentle voice... And you, more than anyone I know — you're wonderful. Why do you want to be like ordinary people who drink and play cards? Oh, don't do that, I beg you! You always say that people don't create, but only destroy all that is given to them from God. Why then, why are you destroying yourself? You shouldn't, you mustn't, I beg you, I implore you.

ASTROV: *(Extending his hand to her)* All right, I won't drink anymore.

SONYA: Give me your word.

ASTROV: Word of honor.

SONYA: *(Strongly pressing his hand)* Oh, thank you!

ASTROV: *Basta*! I'm sober! You see, I'm completely sober and will remain so until the end of my days. *(He looks at his watch)* So, let's continue. As I was saying: my time has already passed, it's too late for me... I've grown old, I'm overworked, I've become vulgar, I have no feelings left, and it looks like I'm no longer interested in making attachments. I don't love anyone and... I'm sure I'll never fall in love again. But what does still touch me, is beauty. I don't seem to be indifferent to it. I have a feeling that if Yelena Andreyevna wanted to, she could turn my head in a day... But you know that's not love, not real love... *(He covers his eyes with his hand and shudders)*

SONYA: What's wrong?

ASTROV: *(He sighs heavily)* During Lent a patient of mine died under chloroform.

SONYA: It's time to forget about that.

*Pause.*

Tell me, Mikhail Lvovich… If I had a friend, or a younger sister, and if you knew that she… well, let's just say, she loves you, what would you think?

ASTROV: *(Shrugging his shoulders)* I don't know. Probably, nothing. I would give her to understand that I cannot fall in love with her… and besides, I don't think about things like that. All right, if it's time to go, I've got to go. Say goodbye, my dear, or we'll keep talking till morning. *(He presses her hand)* I'll go through the back door, if that's alright, or I'm afraid your uncle will stop me. *(He exits)*

SONYA: *(Alone)* He didn't say anything to me… His soul and his heart are completely hidden from me, so why do I feel so happy? *(She laughs from joy)* I told him: you're elegant, noble, you have such a gentle voice… Should I have said that? His voice trembles, it caresses… I can still feel it in the air. When I tried telling him about a younger sister, he didn't understand… *(Wringing her hands)* Oh, how awful it is that I'm so plain! How awful! And I know, I know I'm plain, I know, I know… Last Sunday, when we were leaving church, I heard some people talking about me, and one woman said: "She is a kind, generous girl, but it's a pity she's so plain"… So plain…

*YELENA ANDREYEVNA enters.*

YELENA ANDREYEVNA: *(She opens the window)* The storm has passed. What lovely air!

*Pause.*

Where's the doctor?

SONYA: He left.

*Pause.*

YELENA ANDREYEVNA: *Sophie!*

SONYA: What?

YELENA ANDREYEVNA: How long are you going to ignore me? We haven't hurt one another. Why should we be enemies? Please, enough…

SONYA: Just what I wanted… *(She embraces her)* Enough being angry.

YELENA ANDREYEVNA: Excellent.

*They are both anxious.*

SONYA: Is papa in bed?

YELENA ANDREYEVNA: No, he is sitting in the drawing room… We haven't spoken to each other in weeks, God knows why… *(Seeing that the sideboard is open)* What's this?

SONYA: Mikhail Lvovich had something to eat.

YELENA ANDREYEVNA: There's wine… Let's drink *Bruderschaft*.

SONYA: Yes, let's.

YELENA ANDREYEVNA: From the same glass… *(She raises it)* So, much better. Well, friends?

SONYA: Friends.

*They drink and kiss.*

I wanted to make up a long time ago, but I was ashamed… *(She weeps)*

YELENA ANDREYEVNA: Why are you crying?

SONYA: It's nothing, no reason — that's just me.

YELENA ANDREYEVNA: Well, there, there... *(She weeps)* Silly you, now I've started to cry...

*Pause.*

You're angry with me, because you think I was scheming to marry your father... Please believe me, I swear — I married him out of love. I was captivated by him because of his fame, his brilliance as a scholar. It wasn't real love, I see that now, but it seemed like love then. Don't blame me, please. From the moment we married you have been punishing me with those suspicious eyes of yours.

SONYA: Please, peace, peace! Let's forget about it.

YELENA ANDREYEVNA: You shouldn't look at people that way — it doesn't suit you. You must believe in others — life is impossible without that.

*Pause.*

SONYA: Tell me honestly, as a friend... Are you happy?

YELENA ANDREYEVNA: No.

SONYA: I knew that. One more question. Tell me truthfully — would you have preferred a younger husband?

YELENA ANDREYEVNA: You're still such a baby! Of course I would! *(She laughs)* Well, ask me anything else, ask...

SONYA: Do you like the doctor?

YELENA ANDREYEVNA: Yes.

SONYA: *(She laughs)* I must look foolish... yes? He just left, but I can still hear his voice and his footsteps, and when I look at the dark window — I see his face. Please let me tell you... Oh, but I'm talking too loud, I'm embarrassed. Come, let's go to my room, we can talk there. Do I look foolish? Truth, now... Tell me something about him...

YELENA ANDREYEVNA: What?

SONYA: He's intelligent... He knows how to do everything, he can do anything... He takes care of people, and he also takes care of trees...

YELENA ANDREYEVNA: Oh, it's a lot more than trees and people, my darling — that man has talent! And do you know what talent means? Boldness, courage, a free mind, a vision... He plants a tree and already he's planning ahead — what this will be in a thousand years. He sees the benefit for humanity far into the future. Such people are rare, we must love them... He drinks, he's a bit coarse — but so what? A truly talented man in Russia can't stay pure. Think about it, what kind of life could this doctor lead! Impassable mud on the roads, frost, blizzards, huge distances, crude savage peasants, extreme poverty everywhere... And he struggles with all of this every day. It's hard to be pure and sober after forty. *(She kisses her)* From the bottom of my heart, I'm so happy for you... *(She rises)* But I'm such a boring person, so worthless, meaningless... In my music, and in my husband's home, in all my relationships — everywhere — in a word, I'm worthless... To tell you the truth, Sonya, when you really think about it, I'm very, very unhappy! *(She paces agitatedly)* No, there is no happiness for me in this world. None! Why are you laughing?

SONYA: *(She laughs, covering her face)* I'm so happy... so happy!

YELENA ANDREYEVNA: *(She goes to the piano)* I want to play... I would like to play something now.

SONYA: Play. *(She embraces her)* I can't sleep... Play!

YELENA ANDREYEVNA: Yes, soon. Your father's not asleep yet. When he's ill, music irritates him. Go ask. If he doesn't mind, then I'll play. Go.

SONYA: Yes, this minute. *(She exits)*

*In the garden YEFIM taps.*

YELENA ANDREYEVNA: I haven't played in a long time. I'll play and cry, cry like a baby. *(In the window)* Is that you tapping, Yefim?

YEFIM'S VOICE: Yep.

YELENA ANDREYEVNA: Don't tap, the master is ill.

YEFIM'S VOICE: Okay, I'm leaving now! *(He whistles)* Hey, you, Zhuchka, Zhuchka!

*Pause.*

SONYA: *(Returning)* He said no...

CURTAIN.

# ACT III

*The drawing room in SEREBRYAKOV's home. Three doors: on the right, on the left and in the center. — Day.*

*VOINITSKY, SONYA are sitting and YELENA ANDREYEVNA paces around the room, deep in thought.*

VOINITSKY: *Herr Professor* has expressed the desire that all of us congregate today here in the drawing room at precisely one o'clock in the afternoon. *(He looks at his watch)* It's a quarter to one. Surely he has an important announcement for the world.

YELENA ANDREYEVNA: Some kind of business probably.

VOINITSKY: He has no kind of business. He writes nonsense, he whines and he's jealous — that's his business.

SONYA: *(With a reproachful tone)* Uncle!

VOINITSKY: Okay, okay, it's all my fault. *(He points to YELENA ANDREYEVNA)* Look at her — she prowls around like a lazy tiger. Lovely! Just lovely!

YELENA ANDREYEVNA: All you do is buzz buzz buzz — aren't you getting tired of it? *(With melancholy)* I'm dying of boredom, I have absolutely nothing to do.

SONYA: *(Shrugs her shoulders)* There's lots to do — if you wanted to.

YELENA ANDREYEVNA: What?

SONYA: Help us with the house, teach, take care of people. Lots and lots to do. When you and papa weren't here Uncle Vanya and I were working around the clock.

YELENA ANDREYEVNA: I have no idea how to do those things. And anyway, they're so boring. It's only in romantic novels that people teach and take care of the peasants. How can you expect me to do those things?

SONYA: And I don't understand how you *can't* do them. Why don't you try, you might enjoy it. *(She embraces her)* Don't be bored, my dear. *(Laughing)* We're all catching your fever. Look: Uncle Vanya does nothing all day long but follow you around like a shadow, I've abandoned my own work and come running to you every minute, just to talk. I've gotten lazy. It's just awful! The doctor used to come here very rarely - maybe once a month. It was so hard to get him to come, but now he's here every day — he's abandoned his forests and his medicine. I think you've cast a spell on all of us.

VOINITSKY: Why are you so bored? *(Animatedly)* Well, my beauty, my splendid girl, be true to yourself. I'm sure mermaid's blood flows in your veins, so be a mermaid! Let yourself go for once in your life, let yourself fall madly in love — dive headlong into the water, leaving *Herr Professor* and the rest of us standing astonished on the shore!

YELENA ANDREYEVNA: *(With anger)* Do shut up! You are so cruel! *(She tries to leave)*

VOINITSKY: *(He does not allow her)* Well, well, my beautiful sprite, forgive me… I'm sorry. *(He kisses her hand)* Peace.

YELENA ANDREYEVNA: You have to agree that an angel couldn't endure your babble.

VOINITSKY: As a token of my desire for peace, I will bring you a bouquet of roses; I picked them for you this morning… Autumn roses — lovely, sad roses… *(He exits)*

SONYA: Autumn roses — so lovely, so sad…

*They both look out the window.*

YELENA ANDREYEVNA: It's September already. How will we ever get through the winter here!

*Pause.*

Where's the doctor?

SONYA: In Uncle Vanya's room. He's doing some writing. I'm glad that Uncle Vanya left, I need to talk with you.

YELENA ANDREYEVNA: About what?

SONYA: About what? *(She lays her head on YELENA'S chest)*

YELENA ANDREYEVNA: Well, shh, shh… *(She smoothes her hair)* Shh, my dear.

SONYA: I'm so plain.

YELENA ANDREYEVNA: You have beautiful hair.

SONYA: No! *(She looks around in order to see herself in the mirror)* No! When a woman is plain, they tell her: "you have beautiful eyes, you have beautiful hair"… I've been in love with him for six years, I love him more than my own mother; the minute I hear him arrive, I can already feel his hand in mine; and I wait at the door, I wait, and I have the feeling that any second now, he will walk in. I come to you to talk about him every spare moment. He's here every day, but he doesn't even look at me, he doesn't see… I'm in agony! I have no hope, none, no! *(In despair)* Oh, God, give me strength… I've been praying all night… I just need to talk to him, look at him, just be near him… I have no pride left, I can't control myself… Yesterday I even told Uncle Vanya that I love him — I have no shame at all… even the servants — everyone knows I love him, everyone…

YELENA ANDREYEVNA: Does he?

SONYA: No. He doesn't notice a thing.

YELENA ANDREYEVNA: *(In thought)* He's a strange man... You know what? Why don't I have a talk with him? I'll be careful — just a hint here or there...

*Pause.*

Really, how long can you live with this uncertainty... Shall I?

*SONYA nods her head "yes".*

Excellent. Either he loves you or he doesn't — it won't be difficult to find out. Don't be embarrassed, my darling, don't worry — I'll be very careful, he won't notice a thing. We just need to find out: yes or no?

*Pause.*

If no, then we can't have him come here again. Yes?

*SONYA nods her head "yes".*

It's easier when he's not around. Let's not put it off, I'll talk to him now. He wanted to show me some drawings... Go tell him that I'd like to see him.

SONYA: *(In strong agitation)* Will you tell me the honest truth?

YELENA ANDREYEVNA: Yes, of course. It seems to me that the truth, whatever it is, is better than living with uncertainty. Count on me, my darling.

SONYA: Yes, yes... I'll tell him that you want to see his drawings... *(She walks and comes to a stop near the door)* No, uncertainty is better... At least there's hope...

YELENA ANDREYEVNA: Did you say something?

SONYA: Nothing. *(She exits)*

YELENA ANDREYEVNA: *(Alone)* Oh, there's nothing worse than knowing someone else's secret and not being able to help. *(Pondering)*

He's not in love with her — that's obvious. But why shouldn't he marry her? She's not pretty, but for a country doctor, at his age, she'd be a wonderful wife. She's a clever girl, so kind, pure... No, something's wrong, all wrong...

*Pause.*

Poor darling... in this stifling atmosphere where the only people who come into her life are vulgar boors who live to eat, drink and sleep — and then, in comes this handsome, fascinating, intelligent man — and out of the darkness, a bright moon rises. How could she resist such a man... Uh oh, I think I'm a little in love with him myself. Yes, the truth is I'm bored without him — I smile when I think about him... Uncle Vanya says there's a mermaid in my veins. "For once in your life, let go"... Can I? Maybe I could... To fly like a bird far away from all of you, from your dead faces, from your boring conversations — oh, to forget you all exist on this earth... But I'm such a coward, I'm so timid... and it's always my conscience wearing me down... He's here every day, I know why he comes... and I feel guilty, I just want to fall on my knees before Sonya — to apologize, to cry...

ASTROV: *(He enters with a portfolio of maps)* Hello! *(He shakes her hand)* You wanted to see my drawings?

YELENA ANDREYEVNA: Yesterday you promised to show me your work... Are you free?

ASTROV: Yes, of course. *(He stretches the maps on the card table and fastens them with drawing pins)* Where were you born?

YELENA ANDREYEVNA: *(Helping him)* In Petersburg.

ASTROV: And where did you go to school?

YELENA ANDREYEVNA: At the conservatory.

ASTROV: Oh, then I don't think this will interest you.

YELENA ANDREYEVNA: Why? It's true, I don't know much about the countryside, but I've read a great deal.

ASTROV: I have my own desk in the house... in Ivan Petrovich's room. When I'm totally exhausted, completely dead to the world, I leave everything I'm doing and run here. I can lose myself for an hour or two... Ivan Petrovich and Sofya Aleksandrovna click away at their accounts, and I sit beside them at my own table — it's heaven — warm and peaceful. But I don't permit myself this pleasure often, maybe once a month... *(Showing her the maps)* Now look here. This is a map of our district as it was fifty years ago. The dark and light-green colors represent the forests; half of the entire area is dominated by forests. Where the red grid is lying over the green, that shows elk, goats... this shows you all the flora and fauna. In this lake lived swans, geese, ducks, and as the old ones used to say, a mess of birds, millions of them filling the sky as far as you could see. In addition to the villages you see here, look at these small farms, settlements, monasteries, water mills... many, many cattle and horses — you can see that in the light blue. For example, in this tiny village the light blue is particularly heavy — that's because there were whole herds of cattle, and on every farm at least three horses.

*Pause.*

Now look at this one. This is a map of the area twenty-five years ago. You'll notice the forests comprise only a third of the entire area. No more goats, but still elk. The green and light blue are much paler. And so on. Let us move to the third map: this is a drawing of our district today. Notice that the green is only spattered here and there, not throughout, only in spots; the elk have vanished, and the swans, and the woodgrouses... There's no trace of the settlements, small villages, monasteries, and mills. In general, it's a picture of gradual but total degeneration, and obviously in ten or fifteen years it will be complete. You would probably say, this is natural evolution, the old order giving way to the new. Yes, that's true too. However, if these desiccated forests were replaced by highways, railroads, and by factories or schools — then we would see healthier people, richer, more intelligent, but believe me, nothing of the kind is happening. This district is plagued by the same swamps, mosquitoes, the same non-existent roads, poverty, typhus, diphtheria, fires... Yes we have desiccation and degeneration not because of growth and progress but due to stagnation and complete carelessness — when a frozen, hungry, sick man tries to hang onto a shred of life, tries to protect his children, he'll do anything to satisfy hunger and grab some warmth — he'll even destroy everything around him, never thinking about tomorrow... So you see everything is being destroyed and for nothing — there's no chance to build a future... *(Coldly)* I see by your face this is not interesting to you.

YELENA ANDREYEVNA: I understand so little about this...

ASTROV: There's nothing to understand, it just doesn't interest you.

YELENA ANDREYEVNA: To tell you the truth, I've been thinking of something else. Forgive me. I need to interrogate you a little, and I'm embarrassed, I don't know how to begin.

ASTROV: Interrogate me?

YELENA ANDREYEVNA: Yes, just a little, but... innocently, I promise. Let's sit!

*They sit.*

This is in regard to someone we both know. We'll speak frankly, as friends — openly. We'll have this little talk and then we'll forget about it. Yes?

ASTROV: Yes.

YELENA ANDREYEVNA: It's about my stepdaughter Sonya. Do you like her?

ASTROV: Yes, I respect her.

YELENA ANDREYEVNA: Do you like her... as a woman?

ASTROV: *(Not at once)* No.

YELENA ANDREYEVNA: Just two or three more words — and then we're done. Have you noticed anything?

ASTROV: Nothing.

YELENA ANDREYEVNA: *(Takes him by the hand)* You don't love her, I see it in your eyes... She's suffering... Please understand this and... stop coming here.

ASTROV: *(He rises)* I'm too old for this... I have no time... *(Shrugging his shoulders)* When do I have time? *(He is embarrassed)*

YELENA ANDREYEVNA: Oh, what an unpleasant conversation! I'm so upset, I feel as if I was dragging along a thousand pounds. Well, thank God, it's finished. We'll forget it. It'll be as if we never spoke, and... and you will leave. You're an intelligent man, you understand...

   Pause.

I must be blushing all over.

ASTROV: If only you'd told me a month or two ago, then I, probably, would have thought about it, but now... *(He shrugs his shoulders)* And if she is suffering, then, of course... Only I don't understand one thing: why did *you* need to interrogate me? *(He looks her in the eyes and wags his finger at her)* You are something!

YELENA ANDREYEVNA: What does that mean?

ASTROV: *(Laughing)* All right, let's say Sonya's suffering, I'll admit that, but why did you have to talk to me about it — why you? *(He prevents her from speaking, animatedly)* Don't look so surprised, you know very well why I come here every day... You know all too well... Adorable little beast of prey, don't look so surprised, I'm an old hand at this...

YELENA ANDREYEVNA: *(In bewilderment)* Beast of prey? I don't understand what you're talking about.

ASTROV: Beautiful tigress… You need victims! Here I've been, doing absolutely nothing for a month, putting everything on hold — I ride here every day to find you and you just love it… Well, yes. I'm conquered, you knew that without an interrogation. *(Crossing his hands and bowing his head)* Tear me to pieces! Eat me up!

YELENA ANDREYEVNA: Have you lost your mind!

ASTROV: *(He laughs through his teeth)* You're shy…

YELENA ANDREYEVNA: Oh, I'm a lot better than you think! I promise you! *(She tries to leave)*

ASTROV: *(Blocking her way)* Today I'll leave, I won't stay, but… *(He takes her by the hand, and glances around)* Where shall we meet? Tell me quickly: where? They might come in here any moment… *(Passionately)* What a gorgeous, luscious… One kiss… Just to kiss your beautiful hair…

YELENA ANDREYEVNA: I swear to you…

ASTROV: *(He prevents her from speaking)* Why swear? Don't swear. Don't say anything… Oh, what a beauty you are! What hands! *(He kisses her hands)*

YELENA ANDREYEVNA: Oh, please… leave… *(She pulls her hands away)* You have completely forgotten yourself.

ASTROV: Just tell me where should we meet tomorrow? *(He takes her by the waist)* It's inevitable, darling, we must meet. *(He kisses her; at the same time VOINITSKY enters with a bouquet of roses and comes to a stop in the door)*

YELENA ANDREYEVNA: *(Not seeing VOINITSKY)* Oh, please, leave me alone… *(She puts ASTROV'S head on her chest)* No! *(She tries to leave)*

ASTROV: *(He grabs her by the waist)* Come to the forest tomorrow… around two o'clock… Yes? Yes? Will you come?

YELENA ANDREYEVNA: *(Seeing VOINITSKY)* Let me go! *(In strong confusion she withdraws to the window)* This is terrible.

VOINITSKY: *(He puts the bouquet on the chair; excited, he wipes his face with a handkerchief and behind the collar)* It's nothing… Yes… Nothing…

ASTROV: *(Sulking)* My friend Ivan Petrovich, the weather isn't too bad today. In the morning it was overcast, as if it might rain, but now it's sunny. Really, autumn has been quite beautiful… and the winter crops look good too… *(He rolls up the maps)* The only problem is the days are getting shorter… *(He exits)*

YELENA ANDREYEVNA: *(Quickly she crosses to VOINITSKY)* Please make sure that my husband and I leave here today! Do you hear me? This very day!

VOINITSKY: *(Wiping his face)* What? Well, yes… fine… *Hélène*, I saw everything, everything…

YELENA ANDREYEVNA: *(Nervously)* Did you hear me? I must leave here today!

*Enter SEREBRYAKOV, SONYA, TELYEGIN and MARINA.*

TELYEGIN: I myself, Your Excellency, am not very healthy. I've been feeling ill for two days. My head is simply…

SEREBRYAKOV: Where is everybody? I hate this house. It's like a labyrinth. Twenty-six enormous rooms, and everyone in a different room, so you can never find anyone. (*He rings*) Ask Maria Vasilyevna and Yelena Andreyevna to come here!

YELENA ANDREYEVNA: I'm here.

SEREBRYAKOV: I beg you, Ladies and Gentlemen, take a seat.

SONYA: (*Going to YELENA ANDREYEVNA, impatiently*) What did he say?

YELENA ANDREYEVNA: Later.

SONYA: You're trembling? Why? (*Scrutinizing in her face*) I understand… He said he won't be coming here anymore… yes?

*Pause.*

Say it: yes?

*YELENA ANDREYEVNA affirmatively nods her head.*

SEREBRYAKOV: (*To TELYEGIN*) One can find peace even with ill-health, but what I cannot abide is this life in the country. I feel as if I've dropped off the face of the earth and landed on some kind of foreign planet. Take a seat, Ladies and Gentlemen, please. Sonya!

*SONYA does not hear him, she stands, sadly hanging her head.*

Sonya!

*Pause.*

She doesn't hear me. (*To MARINA*) And you, Nurse, take a seat.

*The NURSE sits and mends a stocking.*

Please, friends, Romans and countrymen, lend me your ears. (*He laughs*)

VOINITSKY: (*Anxious*) I'm not needed here, am I? May I leave?

SEREBRYAKOV:  No, you're needed most of all.

VOINITSKY:  How may I help you?

SEREBRYAKOV:  Why are you angry?

*Pause.*

If I'm to blame for anything, then forgive me, please.

VOINITSKY:  Cut it out. Let's get to the point… What do you want?

*MARIA VASILYEVNA enters.*

SEREBRYAKOV:  Here is *Maman*. I will begin, Ladies and Gentlemen.

*Pause.*

I invited you, Ladies and Gentlemen, in order to announce that the Inspector General is coming. *(He laughs)* I couldn't resist, but let's get down to business. I have gathered you here, Ladies and Gentlemen, for serious business. I need to beg your help and advice, and since you are always so helpful and courteous, I am sure to receive it. As you know, I am a scholar who thinks about abstract matters, and I have always been a stranger to anything practical. I simply cannot manage without the assistance of such knowledgeable and experienced people. I call upon you, Ivan Petrovich, you, Ilya Ilyich, you, *Maman… manet omnes una nox*, that is all of us must walk under God; I am old, ill and therefore I feel it is time for me to get my affairs in order, especially those affairs which affect my family. My life is over, I'm not thinking about myself, but I have a young wife and an unmarried daughter.

*Pause.*

It is impossible for me to continue to live in the country. We are not built to live in the country. However, to live in the city without the resources we receive from this estate, is equally impossible. For example, if we sell the land, then we will lose the annual income. Thus, it is necessary to look for other measures which would guarantee us a permanent, yes, more or less a fixed income. I have thought of one such measure and have the honor to present it for your consideration. Leaving out the details, I will just give you the general outline. Our estate earns an average rate not greater than two percent. I propose to sell it. If we turn the money we earn from the sale into interest-bearing securities, then we will receive four to five percent, and I think, that will produce a surplus of a few thousand, which will permit us to buy a small *dacha* in Finland.

VOINITSKY: Hold on a minute. Did I hear you right? Repeat what you said.

SEREBRYAKOV: To turn the money we earn from the sale into interest-bearing securities and on the surplus, buy a *dacha* in Finland.

VOINITSKY: Not Finland… You said something else.

SEREBRYAKOV: I propose to sell the estate.

VOINITSKY: That's it. You're going to sell the estate — now that's a brilliant idea… And where do you plan to put me, my mother and Sonya?

SEREBRYAKOV: We have time to consider the details. Not everything at once, please.

VOINITSKY: Hold on, hold on. Obviously, until this moment I haven't had a sane thought in my head. Until this moment I was crazy enough to think that this estate belongs to Sonya. My late father bought this estate as a dowry for my sister. Until this moment I was so naïve, I didn't think we lived under Turkish law. I was under the misapprehension that this estate passed from my sister to Sonya.

SEREBRYAKOV: Yes, the estate belongs to Sonya. No one is arguing that. Without Sonya's agreement I will not think about selling it. Moreover what I propose is only for Sonya's good.

VOINITSKY: This is unbelievable! Either I've lost my mind, or… or…

MARIA VASILYEVNA: Jean, do not contradict Alexandre. He knows what is good for us better than we do.

VOINITSKY: No, give me water. *(He drinks water)* Fine, say what you want, whatever you want!

SEREBRYAKOV: I don't understand why you're so excited. I'm not saying that my plan is perfect. If everyone finds it unsuitable, then I won't insist.

*Pause.*

TELYEGIN: *(In embarrassment)* I, Your Excellency, have complete reverence for learning, and I even like to think I have kindred feelings with scholars. My brother Grigorii Ilyich's wife's brother, maybe you know him, Konstantin Trofimovich Lakedemonov, has a master's degree...

VOINITSKY: Hold on, hold on, Waffles, we're talking business here. Hold on, later... *(Suddenly grabbing hold of TELYEGIN; to SEREBRYAKOV)* Yes, here, ask him. This estate was bought from his uncle.

SEREBRYAKOV: Akh, what should I ask him? What?

VOINITSKY: This estate was bought for ninety-five thousand *rubles*. Our father paid only seventy and had a mortgage of twenty-five thousand. Now listen... This estate could never have been paid for, if I hadn't turned down my inheritance in favor of my sister, whom I ardently loved. And I worked for ten years, like an ox, to pay off the entire debt...

SEREBRYAKOV: I regret that I began this conversation.

VOINITSKY: The estate is finally clear of debt thanks to my personal efforts. And now, when I'm old, you want to throw me out of here on my —

SEREBRYAKOV: I don't understand what you're saying?

VOINITSKY: For twenty-five years I have managed this estate, I slaved away at it, and I sent you every penny, like the most conscientious steward, and in all that time not once did you thank me. All that time — when I was young and even now — I received from you a pitiful five hundred *rubles* a year — a pittance! — and you never, not once, thought to increase that money by one *ruble*!

SEREBRYAKOV: Ivan Petrovich, how could I know? I'm not a practical man and I don't understand such matters. You could have raised your salary any time you wanted.

VOINITSKY: Why didn't I steal? You all think I'm an idiot for not stealing? Oh sure, that would have been nice. And if I did steal I wouldn't be a beggar now!

MARIA VASILYEVNA: *(Severely)* Jean!

TELYEGIN: *(Agitated)* Vanya, my dear friend, don't do this, don't... I'm shaking... Why do you want to ruin a good friendship? *(He kisses him)* Don't, don't...

VOINITSKY: Twenty-five years I've been shut up here with my old mother — stuck... Every thought, every feeling was about you — only you. In the daytime we talked about you, about your work, we took pride in you, uttered your name with reverence; during the evenings we ruined our eyes reading your journals and books, which I now profoundly despise!

TELYEGIN: Please don't, Vanya, it's not necessary... I cannot...

SEREBRYAKOV: *(Angrily)* I don't understand, what do you want?

VOINITSKY: You were for us a supreme being, we memorized your articles by heart... But now my eyes are finally open! I see everything! You write about art, but you understand nothing about it! All your work, which I worshipped, is not worth one *kopek*! You sure fooled all of us.

SEREBRYAKOV: Ladies and Gentlemen! Stop him, please, please... I'm leaving!

YELENA ANDREYEVNA: Ivan Petrovich, please shut up! Do you hear me?

VOINITSKY: I will not be silent! *(Blocking SEREBRYAKOV's path)* Wait a minute, I'm not finished! You ruined my life! I never lived, never… The best years of my life were completely destroyed for your sake! You are my worst enemy!

TELYEGIN: I cannot… cannot… I'm leaving… *(He exits in strong agitation)*

SEREBRYAKOV: What do you want from me? And what right do you have to speak to me in such a tone? Nonentity! If this estate is yours, then take it, I don't need it!

YELENA ANDREYEVNA: I'm leaving this hell right now. *(She cries)* I can't stand it a moment longer!

VOINITSKY: My life is gone! I'm talented, intelligent, courageous… I could have been a Schopenhauer, a Dostoevsky… What am I talking about? I'm going crazy. Mother, I'm in despair! Mother!

MARIA VASILYEVNA: *(Severely)* Listen to Alexandre!

SONYA: *(She drops to her knees before the nurse and nestles up to her)* Nyanya! Nyanya!

VOINITSKY: Mother! What should I do? No, no, don't say it! I know what to do!

*(To SEREBRYAKOV)* You will never forget me! *(He exits through the center door)*

    *MARIA VASILYEVNA goes after him.*

SEREBRYAKOV: Ladies and Gentlemen, what just happened? Keep that madman away from me! I cannot live under the same roof with him! He sleeps in the next room from me… *(He gestures to the center door)* Let him move to the village, to the outhouse for all I care, or I will move away from here, but I cannot remain in the house with him one moment longer...

YELENA ANDREYEVNA: *(To her husband)* Let's leave today! We've got to get out of here this minute.

SEREBRYAKOV: That nonentity!

SONYA: *(Kneeling, she turns to her father; nervously, on the verge of tears)* Please, be kind, Papa! Uncle Vanya and I are so unhappy! *(Holding back despair)* Please, please be kind. Remember, a few years ago, Papa, Uncle Vanya and grandmother translated books for you, re-copied your papers... every night, every night! Uncle Vanya and I worked without rest, afraid of wasting a *kopek* on ourselves. We sent everything to you... We scrimped on the bread we ate. I'm not saying it right, but you must understand us, Papa. You must be merciful!

YELENA ANDREYEVNA: *(Anxiously to her husband)* Aleksander, for God's sake, calm him down... I beg you.

SEREBRYAKOV: Fine, good, I'll talk to him... I'm not accusing him of anything, I'm not angry, but, you have to agree, his behavior is, at the very least, strange. But if you wish, I'll go to him. *(He exits through the center door)*

YELENA ANDREYEVNA: Be gentle with him, calm him... *(She exits behind him)*

SONYA: *(Nestling up to the nurse)* Nyanya... Nyanya...

MARINA: It's nothing, my little girl. The geese honk, then they stop... They honk — then they stop...

SONYA: *Nyanya...*

MARINA: *(She strokes her head)* You're trembling, as if you were freezing! Well, well, little orphan girl, God is gracious. Some lime-leaf tea or maybe a little raspberry, it will pass... Don't grieve, sweet girl... *(Glancing at the center door, crossly)* Shoo you geese, the devil take you!

*Backstage a shot; YELENA ANDREYEVNA is heard crying out; SONYA shudders.*

God save us!

SEREBRYAKOV: *(Running in, staggering from fright)* Stop him! Stop him! He's lost his mind!

*YELENA ANDREYEVNA and VOINITSKY struggle in the doorway.*

YELENA ANDREYEVNA: *(Trying to take the revolver from him)* Give it to me! Give it to me, do you hear me!

VOINITSKY: Let go, Hélène! Let me go! *(Freeing himself, he runs and looks around for SEREBRYAKOV)* Where is he? Yes, here he is! *(He shoots at him)* Bang!

*Pause.*

I missed. How could I miss again? *(Irate)* Damn it, damn, damn, damn — *(He smashes the revolver on the floor and falls into a chair in exhaustion)*

*SEREBRYAKOV is stunned; YELENA ANDREYEVNA leans against the wall, she feels faint.*

YELENA ANDREYEVNA: Get me out of here! Get me out! Kill me, but... don't make me stay here... Get me out!

VOINITSKY: *(In despair)* Oh, what am I doing? What am I doing?

SONYA: *(Quietly)* Nyanya! Nyanya!

CURTAIN.

# ACT IV

*IVAN PETROVICH's bedroom. It is also the estate office. There is a large table with account books and many papers, a writing-desk, bookcases, scales. A slightly smaller table for ASTROV; on this table is his painting equipment; nearby is a portfolio. A cage with a starling. On the wall is a map of Africa, obviously not needed by anyone here. A huge sofa, covered with oil-cloth. To the left — a door, leading to other rooms; to the right — a door to the entrance-hall; beside the right door lies a mat for the peasants to wipe their feet. An autumn evening. Silence.*

*TELYEGIN and MARINA sit across from one another and wind wool.*

TELYEGIN: Please hurry, Marina Timofeyevna, they're going to call us any minute to say goodbye. The horses are ordered already.

MARINA: *(She tries to wind faster)* There's not much left.

TELYEGIN: They're going to Kharkov. They'll live there.

MARINA: Better that way.

TELYEGIN: They were really scared… Yelena Andreyevna was screaming, "I can't live here one more hour… we must leave…" She says, "We'll live in Kharkov, let's leave immediately and we'll send for our things later…" Can you imagine, they're leaving without their suitcases. It's God's will, Marina Timofeyevna, it's God's will. God doesn't want them to live here. God's will… ah, God…

MARINA: Better that way. My God, they raised such a racket… ekh, shame on them, shame…

TELYEGIN: Aivazovsky could have painted that scene…

MARINA: I wish I had never seen it!

*Pause.*

Thank the lord we'll begin to live like we used to. Eight o'clock in the morning tea, one o'clock lunch, and in the evening — we'll sit down for supper — everything as it should be for people... Christians. *(With a sigh)* It's been so long since I've eaten *lapshi*, sinner that I am.

TELYEGIN: Yes, it's been a long time since we've eaten noodles.

*Pause.*

...Ages... This morning, Marina Timofeyevna, I was going to the village, and one of the shop-keepers called out to me: "Hey, you, sponger!" It hurt me so much!

MARINA: Don't pay any attention, old friend. We're all sponging off God. All of us, you, Sonya, Ivan Petrovich — we all work hard, all of us... Where's Sonya?

TELYEGIN: In the garden. She's still with the doctor, they're looking for Ivan Petrovich. They're afraid he'll do harm to himself.

MARINA: And where's his pistol?

TELYEGIN: *(With a whisper)* I hid it in the cellar!

MARINA: *(With a smile)* You old sinner!

*Enter VOINITSKY and ASTROV from outside.*

VOINITSKY: Leave me alone. *(To MARINA and TELYEGIN)* Get out, leave me alone for one minute! I can't bear everybody looking at me.

TELYEGIN: This minute, Vanya. *(He exits on tiptoe)*

MARINA: Goose — honk, honk, honk! *(She gathers the wool and exits)*

VOINITSKY: Leave me alone!

ASTROV: I'd love to, I wanted to go hours ago. However, I repeat, I will not leave until you give me back what you took from me.

VOINITSKY: I didn't take anything from you.

ASTROV: C'mon — don't make me wait. I should have gone a long time ago.

VOINITSKY: I didn't take anything from you.

*They both sit.*

ASTROV: Really? All right, I'll wait a minute longer, but then, if you don't mind, I'm going to do my best to force you. We'll tie you up and we'll search you. I really mean it.

VOINITSKY: Do as you wish.

*Pause.*

Such an idiot! To shoot him twice and to miss both times! I'll never forgive myself.

ASTROV: The moment you felt like shooting someone, you should have fired at your own head.

VOINITSKY: *(Shrugging his shoulders)* It's strange. I attempt murder, but no one arrests me, no one takes me to jail. I guess that means they think I'm crazy. *(With an evil laugh)* Well — I am crazy, but no, they're not crazy — those who pretend to be a professor, an erudite genius, who hide their lack of talent, their mediocrity, their utter heartlessness — they're not crazy. No, nor are those who marry old men and cheat on them. I saw, I saw, how you kissed her!

ASTROV: Yes sir, I kissed her, and this is for you. *(He thumbs his nose)*

VOINITSKY: *(Looking at the door)* No, the truth is you're all crazy!

ASTROV: Now that's a stupid thing to say.

VOINITSKY: That's all right — remember I'm crazy — I can say anything I want…

ASTROV: You're not going to get away with this — you're not crazy, you're just a freak. A clown. I used to think freaks were sick, but now I see it's the normal condition of mankind to be freaks. You're absolutely normal.

VOINITSKY: *(He covers his face with his hands)* I'm so ashamed! If you only knew how ashamed I am! There's no pain worse than this shame. *(With anguish)* It's unbearable! *(He bends to the table)* What should I do? Tell me, what should I do?

ASTROV: Nothing.

VOINITSKY: Give me something! Oh, my God… I'm forty-seven years old; if I live to be sixty — oh God, that's thirteen years. Too long — how will I survive thirteen years? How will I fill them? Oh, I know you understand… *(Convulsively squeezes ASTROV's hand)*… you must understand, if I have to live any longer, I'll need to start my life all over again. I have to wake up in the clear, quiet morning and feel that I've started all over again, that my whole past is erased, like smoke. *(He weeps)* To begin again… Please tell me how… how do I start…

ASTROV: *(Vexedly)* Oh, to hell with you! New life? Our lives, yours and mine, are hopeless.

VOINITSKY: Really?

ASTROV: I'm sure of it.

VOINITSKY: Give me something… *(Pointing at his heart)* It's burning here.

ASTROV: *(He cries angrily)* Stop! *(Softening)* People who'll live a hundred years, two hundred years from now will despise us for wasting our lives so stupidly and so needlessly — maybe they'll find the secret to happiness, but we... You and I have only one hope — yes, indeed. We hope, that when we're sleeping in our graves, ghosts will visit us, and if we're lucky, they'll be nice ghosts. *(Sighing)* Yes, Brother. For a hundred miles, the only two decent, honest, educated men are you and me. But ten years of this crude, narrow-minded, despicable life has dragged us down; this life with its rotten stink has poisoned our blood, and we've become as vulgar as everyone else. *(Quickly)* But, please, don't distract me with philosophy. Give me back what you took from me.

VOINITSKY: I didn't take anything from you.

ASTROV: You took a vial of morphine from my medicine bag.

*Pause.*

Listen, if you want to kill yourself, then go into the woods and shoot yourself. But give me back the morphine, or they'll think I gave it to you... It's bad enough I'll have to do your autopsy... Do you think I'll enjoy that?

*Enter SONYA.*

VOINITSKY: Leave me alone.

ASTROV: *(To SONYA)* Sofya Aleksandrovna, your uncle walked off with a vial of morphine from my medical bag and he won't give it back to me. Please tell him that this... is ridiculous. I have no time for this. I've got to go.

SONYA: Uncle Vanya, did you take the morphine?

*Pause.*

ASTROV: He took it. I'm sure of it.

SONYA: Give it back. Why are you trying to scare us? *(Gently)* Give it back, Uncle Vanya! I may be as unhappy as you, but I don't give in to despair. We must all accept life as it is given to us — until we die... And you must accept it too...

*Pause.*

Give it back! *(She kisses his hands)* Dear, sweet Uncle, dearest, give it back! *(She weeps)* You're so good, you mustn't hurt us, you must give it back. You must accept this life, Uncle! Please, accept it!

VOINITSKY: *(He takes the vial from the desk and gives it to ASTROV)* Here, take it! *(To SONYA)* But we've got to get back to work, right away, right now — we must do something, otherwise I can't... I can't...

SONYA: Yes, yes, to work. First we have to say goodbye, then we'll get to work... *(Nervously she looks through the papers on the table)* Everything has fallen apart... everything.

ASTROV: *(He puts the vial in the medical bag and fastens the strap)* Finally I can go.

YELENA ANDREYEVNA: *(She enters)* Ivan Petrovich, are you here? We're leaving. Go to Aleksander, he wants to say something to you.

SONYA: Come, Uncle Vanya. *(She takes VOINITSKY by the hand)* We'll go. Papa and you must make peace. You must.

*SONYA and VOINITSKY exit.*

YELENA ANDREYEVNA: I'm leaving. *(She offers her hand to ASTROV)* Farewell.

ASTROV: Already?

YELENA ANDREYEVNA: The carriage is here.

ASTROV: Farewell.

YELENA ANDREYEVNA: You promised me, that you'd leave here today too.

ASTROV: I remember. I'm leaving now.

*Pause.*

Are you frightened? *(He takes her by the hand)* Is it so terrible?

YELENA ANDREYEVNA: Yes.

ASTROV: Then stay! Yes? Tomorrow in the forest…

YELENA ANDREYEVNA: No… It's already decided… And that's why I can look at you so courageously, because we're leaving… I ask one thing of you: please think well of me. I want you to respect me.

ASTROV: Please! *(A gesture of impatience)* Stay, I beg you. Admit it, you have nothing better to do on this earth, your life is meaningless, you don't do anything, so sooner or later you'll have to give in to your feelings — it's inevitable. So why do it in Kharkov or Kursk. Wouldn't it be better here, in this beautiful countryside… it's poetic, at least… Here in this lovely autumn with the forest and the tumbledown, romantic estates — the way Turgenev wrote about them…

YELENA ANDREYEVNA: You're so silly… I'm a little angry at you, but all the same… I'll remember you fondly. You're an interesting, special man. We'll never see each other again, so why — why hide it? I fell a little in love with you, too. Well, let's shake hands and part as friends. Please think well of me.

ASTROV: *(Shakes her hand)* Yes, go… *(In thought)* I know you are a good, sincere person, but there's something strange about you. You came here with your husband this summer, and all of us who work here suddenly threw everything aside to dance attendance on you and your husband's gout. Both of you have infected us all with your idleness. I was completely captivated. I've done nothing for a whole month, and during that time people fell ill, the peasants let their cattle trample on my plantings in the forests… Everywhere you and your husband set foot, destruction follows… I'm joking, of course, but all the same… it's strange… and I'm absolutely sure if you had stayed any longer, the devastation would have been complete. I would certainly perish, and you… well, it wouldn't be so good for you either. Yes, you're leaving. *Finita la commedia!*

YELENA ANDREYEVNA: *(She takes a pencil from his table and quickly puts it away)* I'll take this pencil to remember you.

ASTROV: It's funny, isn't it… We start to get to know one another and suddenly, with one stroke… we'll never see each other again. I guess it's always like that in this world… Well, since we're alone and before Uncle Vanya comes in with his bouquet of roses, permit me… to kiss you… to say farewell… Yes? *(He kisses her on the cheek)* Well — here… Fine.

YELENA ANDREYEVNA: I wish you all the best. *(Glancing back)* Oh, the hell with it, for once in my life! *(She embraces him tightly, and both immediately move away from one another)* I've got to go.

ASTROV: Yes, go, hurry. If the carriage is here, you'd better leave.

YELENA ANDREYEVNA: Yes, I hear them coming.

*They both listen.*

ASTROV: *Finita!*

*Enter SEREBRYAKOV, VOINITSKY, MARIA VASILYEVNA with a book, TELYEGIN and SONYA.*

SEREBRYAKOV: *(To VOINITSKY)* I can promise you I bear no grudge. After all I've lived through these past few hours, and all I've thought about, I am sure I could write a great treatise for humanity on how one must live one's life. I willingly accept your apology and I ask you to forgive me. Farewell! *(He exchanges three kisses with VOINITSKY)*

VOINITSKY: You will receive exactly the same amount as you've received in the past. Everything will be as it was.

    *YELENA ANDREYEVNA embraces SONYA.*

SEREBRYAKOV: *(He kisses MARIA VASILYEVNA's hand)* Maman...

MARIA VASILYEVNA: *(Kissing him) Alexandre*, have your photograph taken again and send it to me. You know how dear you are to me.

TELYEGIN: Farewell, Your Excellency! Don't forget us!

SEREBRYAKOV: *(Kissing his daughter)* Farewell... farewell everyone! *(Offering his hand to ASTROV)* I thank you for your pleasant company... *(To everyone)* I respect your thinking, your enthusiasm, passion, even your little outbursts, but permit an old man to give you one piece of advice as I say farewell: you must get to work, Ladies and Gentlemen, to work! *(General bow)* Best wishes to all! *(He exits; MARIA VASILYEVNA and SONYA walking behind him)*

VOINITSKY: *(He kisses YELENA ANDREYEVNA's hand firmly)* Farewell... Forgive me... We'll never see each other again.

YELENA ANDREYEVNA: *(Touched)* Farewell, dear friend. *(She kisses him on the head and exits)*

ASTROV: *(To TELYEGIN)* Waffles, tell them to bring my horses.

TELYEGIN: Sure thing, my friend. *(He exits)*

    *Only ASTROV and VOINITSKY remain.*

ASTROV: *(He takes paints from the table and puts them away in a suitcase)* So you're not going to see them off?

VOINITSKY: Let them go... I can't. It's too painful for me. I've got to get busy right away... Yes, to work, to work! *(He rummages in the papers on the table)*

*Pause; bells are heard.*

ASTROV: They're gone. The Professor is probably very happy. He'll never come back here again for love or money.

MARINA: *(She enters)* They're gone. *(She sits and knits a stocking)*

SONYA: *(She enters)* They're gone. *(She wipes her eyes)* God grant them a safe journey. *(To her uncle)* Well, Uncle Vanya, let's get started.

VOINITSKY: Yes, work, work...

SONYA: It's been a long time, a long, long time, since we sat together at this table. *(She lights the lamp on the table)* Oh dear, there's no ink... *(She takes the ink-well, goes to the cupboard and fills the ink)* But I'm sad they left.

MARIA VASILEVNA: *(She slowly enters)* They're gone! *(She sits and plunges right into her reading)*

SONYA: *(She sits at the table and leafs through the account book)* Let's work on the bills first, Uncle Vanya — what a mess our accounts are in! Today they sent more bills. Here. You do that one — I'll do this...

VOINITSKY: *(He writes)* "Dear Sir..."

*They both write in silence.*

MARINA: *(She yawns)* It's beddy-bye for me.

ASTROV: Such silence. The pens scratch, the crickets sing. It's so warm and comfortable... I don't want to leave.

*Little bells are heard.*

Ah, my horses... Looks like I'll have to say goodbye to you, my friends, to say goodbye to my table and — just go! *(He puts his map in his portfolio)*

MARINA: What's the hurry? Sit.

ASTROV: Can't.

VOINITSKY: *(He writes)* "Still remaining two seventy-five in arrears…"

   YEFIM *enters.*

YEFIM: Mikhail Lvovich, the horses are ready.

ASTROV: So I hear. *(He hands him his medical bag, suitcase and portfolio)* Here, take that. See that you don't squash the portfolio.

YEFIM: Yes sir. *(He exits)*

ASTROV: Well *Madame*… *(He goes to say goodbye)*

SONYA: When will we see you again?

ASTROV: Not before summer, I should think. Definitely not this winter… Of course, if something happens, let me know — I'll come. *(He shakes her hand)* Thank you for the bread, for the salt, for the kindness… in a word, for everything. *(He goes to the NURSE and kisses her on the head)* Farewell, old one.

MARINA: You're leaving without tea?

ASTROV: I don't want any, Nurse.

MARINA: Maybe, a little vodka?

ASTROV: *(Hesitantly)* Maybe…

   *MARINA exits.*

*(After a pause)* My trace-horse is limp. I noticed it yesterday, when Petrushka brought him to drink.

VOINITSKY: You'll need to reshoe him.

ASTROV: I'll have to stop at the blacksmith at Rozhdestvennoye. No way to get around it. *(He goes to the map of Africa and looks at it)* Ah, it must be hotter than hell right now in Africa — must be terrible!

VOINITSKY: Yes, probably.

MARINA: *(Returning with a tray, on which are a glass of vodka and a slice of bread)* Eat something too.

*ASTROV drinks the vodka.*

Na zdorovye, dear one. *(She bows low)* But take a little bread.

ASTROV: No, I'm fine... Good luck. *(To MARINA)* Don't see me off, Nurse. It's not necessary.

*He exits; SONYA goes after him with a candle, to see him off; MARINA sits in her own chair.*

VOINITSKY: *(He writes)* "On the second of February vegetable oil twenty pounds... On the sixteenth of February vegetable oil twenty pounds... Buckwheat..."

*Pause. Little bells are heard.*

MARINA: He's gone.

*Pause.*

SONYA: *(Returning, she places the candle on the table)* He's gone...

VOINITSKY: *(Counting on his abacus and making notes)* Total... fifteen... twenty-five...

*SONYA sits and writes.*

MARINA: *(She yawns)* God be merciful...

*TELYEGIN enters on tiptoe, he sits by the door and quietly tunes the guitar.*

VOINITSKY: *(To SONYA, running his hand through her hair)* My child, it's so painful! If only you knew how painful it is!

SONYA: What can we do, we must go on living!

*Pause.*

We'll live, Uncle Vanya. We'll live through many long days, many long nights; we'll patiently endure all the ordeals that God sends us. We'll work for others, never knowing rest. And in our old age, when our time comes, we'll humbly die and there beyond the grave we'll speak of how we suffered, how we wept, how we knew bitterness, and God will take pity on us — you and I — Uncle, sweet Uncle, ahead of us is a radiant, wonderful, graceful life, and we'll rejoice. Then we'll look back on our present unhappiness with sadness and tenderness, and with a smile — and we will rest. I have faith, Uncle, I truly believe, truly…

*SONYA is on her knees and she puts her head on his hands; with a weary voice.*

We will rest!

*TELYEGIN quietly plays on the guitar.*

We will rest! We will hear the angels, we will see all of the heavenly diamonds in the sky, we will see how all the evils of the earth, all of our suffering will be covered with mercy — mercy over the entire world. And our life will be as quiet, gentle, sweet, as a caress. I believe, I believe… *(She wipes his tears with a handkerchief)* Poor, poor Uncle Vanya, you're weeping… *(On the verge of tears)* In your life you never knew joy, but wait a little, Uncle Vanya, wait a little… We will rest… *(She embraces him)* We will rest!

*The WATCHMAN taps.*

*TELYEGIN quietly strums. MARIA VASILYEVNA writes in the margins of her pamphlet; MARINA knits a stocking.*

We will rest!

*CURTAIN.*

# *Three Sisters*

## A Drama in Four Acts

### (1901)

## CHARACTERS

**Andrei Sergeyevich Prozorov.**

**Natalya (Natasha) Ivanovna,** his fiancée, later wife.

His sisters: **Olga Sergeyevna.**

    **Maria (Masha) Sergeyevna.**

    **Irina Sergeyevna.**

**Fyodor Ilyich Kulygin,** high school teacher, husband of Masha.

**Aleksander Ignatyevich Vershinin,** lieutenant-colonel, battery commander.

**Nikolai Lvovich Tuzenbakh,** Baron, lieutenant.

**Vasilii Vasilyevich Solyony,** staff-captain.

**Ivan Romanovich Chebutykin,** military doctor.

**Aleksei Petrovich Fedotik,** second lieutenant.

**Vladimir Karlovich Roday,** second lieutenant.

**Ferapont Spiridonych,** a messenger from the *zemstvo* council.

**Anfisa,** a nurse, an old woman of 80 years, frequently referred to as "*Nyanya*".

*The action takes place in the principal town of a province.*

# ACT I

*The home of the PROZOROVs. The drawing-room with columns, behind which a large dining area can be seen. Midday; outside it is sunny, cheerful. In the dining area a table is laid for lunch.*

*OLGA, in the dark blue uniform of a girls' high school teacher, continually corrects student exercise books, stands and paces; MASHA, in a black dress, with a hat sitting on her lap, reads a little book. IRINA, in a white dress, stands pensive.*

OLGA: Father died a year ago. *(Discovers)* Today! May fifth, on your birthday, Irina. I remember it was very cold, snowing. I didn't think I'd live through it; you lay there like a dead person. But it's a year already, and we can talk about it again. You can wear a white dress now, and you have a smile on your face. *(A clock strikes twelve)* Yes, I remember the clock too.

*Pause.*

I remember at the cemetery there was music and a gun salute. He was an important general, with his own brigade. But there were so few people at the funeral. It was raining, raining and snowing.

IRINA: Forget about that!

*Behind the columns, in the hall near the table appear BARON TUZENBAKH, CHEBUTYKIN and SOLYONY.*

OLGA: It's warm today — enough to keep the window open. But the birches are still bare. Father was assigned his new brigade and we moved from Moscow eleven years ago. —Yes, I remember so perfectly in Moscow, by the beginning of May all the trees are in bloom, it's warm, and everything is flooded with sun. Yes, it's been eleven years, but I remember everything — as if we just left yesterday. My God! This morning when I woke up, it was so sunny — spring was finally here, and I was filled with joy. And I just wanted to go home again.

CHEBUTYKIN: To hell with both of you!

TUZENBAKH: So sorry, it's ridiculous of course.

*MASHA, meditating upon her little book, quietly whistles a song.*

OLGA: Don't whistle, Masha. Please!

*Pause.*

My head aches so much when I've been teaching all day and I feel like I've gotten so old. Honestly, after four years at the high school, I feel as if I'm losing my strength day by day… and the only thing that keeps me going is our dream —

IRINA: To go to Moscow. To sell this house, to put an end to everything here and — go back to Moscow…

OLGA: Yes! As soon as we can —

*CHEBUTYKIN and TUZENBAKH laugh.*

IRINA: Andrei will probably become a professor, and then he'll move away from here. The only problem is poor Masha.

OLGA: Masha will come to Moscow for the whole summer, every year.

*MASHA quietly whistles a song.*

IRINA: Let's hope so… *(Looking out the window)* The weather is really beautiful today. My soul feels very light — I don't know why. I got out of bed and remembered today is my birthday and I suddenly felt so much joy. I remembered when Mama was still alive and I was just a little girl… Oh, such marvelous memories, wonderful!

OLGA: You are particularly beautiful today — just beaming. Even Masha is beautiful. Andrei would be handsome, only he's really gained weight lately and it doesn't suit him. And I've gotten old — and so thin… I'm sure that's why I'm always so irritated with my students. But today I'm free, I'm home, and my headache is gone, I actually feel younger than yesterday. I mean, I'm only twenty-eight… Everything is good, everything is from God — but I still think, if I were married and stayed at home, my life would be better.

*Pause.*

I wish I had a husband.

TUZENBAKH: *(To SOLYONY)* Ridiculous! I'm tired of listening to you. *(Entering the drawing room)* Oh, I forgot to tell you — Today you'll have a visit from our new battery commander, Vershinin. *(He sits at the piano)*

OLGA: Well that'll be nice.

IRINA: Is he old?

TUZENBAKH: No, so-so. At most forty, forty-five. *(He quietly plays)* He seems to be a decent guy — intelligent — probably. But he talks a lot.

IRINA: Interesting?

TUZENBAKH: Yes, not too bad — only he has a wife, a mother-in-law and two little girls and this is his second marriage. When he walks into anyone's house he always says he has a wife and two little girls. And I'll bet you anything he says it here. His wife is a little crazy, dresses like a schoolgirl and talks philosophy all day long. I hear she's always attempting suicide — probably to punish him. I wouldn't be able to live with such a person but apparently he suffers through it — and then complains to everybody.

SOLYONY: *(Entering from the hall to the drawing room with CHEBUTYKIN)* With one arm I can lift only about forty pounds, but with two, a hundred and fifty, even two hundred pounds. From this I conclude, two men aren't twice as strong as one, but three times — maybe more…

CHEBUTYKIN: *(He reads the paper, pacing)* When your hair falls out… 15 ounces of naphthaline in half a bottle of alcohol… shake up and drink daily… *(He writes note in a little book)* Yes, we'll just make a note of that! *(To SOLYONY)* As I was saying, stick a stopper into a little bottle and put a glass tube through it… Then take the tiniest bit of ordinary alum…

IRINA: Ivan Romanych, sweet Ivan Romanych!

CHEBUTYKIN: What, my little girl, my darling?

IRINA: Tell me, why am I so happy today? It's as if I have wings and I'm flying away with big white birds in the sky. Why is that? Why?

CHEBUTYKIN: *(Kissing her on both hands, tenderly)* You're my little white bird…

IRINA: When I woke up today, I just started smiling, and everything seemed to be covered with a bright, shining light and I suddenly understood how I must live. Sweet Ivan Romanych, I understand everything! A person must work, work by the sweat of his brow, whoever he is, whatever he does! This is the only way to know true happiness in life. It must be so wonderful to be a worker, someone who rises at daybreak and builds roads, herds sheep, or teaches children, or works on a railroad… My God, something's wrong with being human, better to be an ox, better to be a simple workhorse, than a young woman, who wakes up at noon, drinks coffee in bed, takes two hours to get dressed… oh, that is so terrible! I'm as desperate to begin work as a thirsty man craves water. And if I don't get up early and go to work, then don't ever talk to me again, Ivan Romanych.

CHEBUTYKIN: *(Tenderly)* I won't. I won't ever talk to you ever again, I promise.

OLGA: Father trained us to get up at seven o'clock. Now Irina gets up at seven and lies back down, daydreaming until at least nine. Oh, what a face! *(She laughs)*

IRINA: You always see me as a little girl, you never let me be serious. I am twenty years old!

TUZENBAKH: I long for work too. Oh my God, how well I understand you! I never worked a day in my life. I was born in cold, empty Petersburg, into a family who never knew real labor, who never had a care in the world. I remember, when I came home from military school, I would let a footman pull off my boots. I was so awful to the servants, and my mother would just smile at me with pride and joy — but everyone else saw what a spoiled brat I was. My parents thought they were protecting me from hard work. Some protection! The times have changed, there are huge clouds over our heads, a big storm is moving in— it's already close and soon it will blow away laziness, indifference, prejudice against the workers and corruption. I will work, and in some twenty-five to thirty years every man will work. Every one of us!

CHEBUTYKIN: I won't be working!

TUZENBAKH: You don't count.

SOLYONY: In twenty-five years you won't be around, thank God. In two or three years you'll die of *kondrashok* [apoplexy], or, believe me, I'll get so angry, I'll put a bullet through your brain, my angel. (*He takes a flask of perfume from his pocket and sprinkles himself on the chest and hands*)

CHEBUTYKIN: (*He laughs*) And honestly, I've never done anything. Since I left the university I haven't lifted a finger, haven't read one book. I only read newspapers... (*He takes from his pocket another newspaper*) Here... I just learned from this newspaper that there's an important writer named Dobrolyubov — never read a word he wrote... God help me...

*Knocking can be heard on the floor from the lower floor.*

Uh oh... They're calling for me downstairs, someone has come for me. I'm coming, I'm coming... wait a minute, one minute... (*He hastily exits, combing his beard*)

IRINA: Uh oh indeed, there's a surprise coming.

TUZENBAKH: Yes. He left with such a sneaky smile. I'll bet he's bringing you a present.

IRINA: Oh, too much fuss!

OLGA: Yes, yes, he's terrible. He's always doing something silly.

MASHA: "At the sea, a green oak stands, with a golden chain wound round." *(She stands and quietly sings)*

OLGA: You're unhappy today, Masha.

*MASHA, singing, puts on her hat.*

Where're you going?

MASHA: Home.

IRINA: Terrible...

TUZENBAKH: You can't leave a birthday party!

MASHA: It's fine... I'll come back tonight. Farewell, my dear... *(She kisses IRINA)* Once again I wish you health and happiness. In the old days, when father was alive, every time we had a party thirty or forty officers would come. It was so noisy, but today just a few people and it's quiet — like a monastery... I'm leaving... Today I am in *merlekhlyundiya* [melancholy] — unhappiness has been visited upon me! You're not listening to me! *(On the verge of tears)* We'll talk later, but for now farewell, my dear, I'm leaving...

IRINA: *(Displeased)* What's wrong with you?

OLGA: *(With tears)* I understand you, Masha.

SOLYONY: If a man talks a lot, you might get philosophy or even sophistry; if one or two women talk, you get blah, blah, blah.

MASHA: What do you mean by that, you weird man!

SOLYONY: Nothing. Before he knew what hit him, the bear bit him.

*Pause. OLGA is crying.*

MASHA: *(To OLGA, angrily)* Stop howling!

*Enter ANFISA and FERAPONT with a cake.*

ANFISA: In here, my friend. Come in, your shoes are clean. *(To IRINA)* From the *zemstvo* council, from Protopopov, Mikhail Ivanych... a birthday cake.

IRINA: Thank you. I thank you.

FERAPONT: Huh?

IRINA: *(Louder)* I thank you!

OLGA: *Nyanechka*, give him a piece of cake. Ferapont, go, they will give you some cake.

FERAPONT: Huh?

ANFISA: Let's go, my friend. Come, Ferapont Spiridonych. Let's go... *(She exits with FERAPONT)*

MASHA: I don't like Protopopov, that Mikhail Potapych, or Ivanych. Don't invite him here.

IRINA: I didn't invite him.

MASHA: Great.

*Enter CHEBUTYKIN, behind him a orderly with a silver samovar; rumble of amazement and displeasure.*

OLGA: *(She covers her face with her hands)* A *samovar*! You are so terrible! *(She walks to the table in the hall)*

Together{      IRINA: My dear Ivan Romanych, what're you doing?

TUZENBAKH: *(He laughs)* I told you.

MASHA: Ivan Romanych, you simply have no shame!

CHEBUTYKIN: My sweet, my darling, you're my only... you're the most dear to me, you're the only one who matters... I'll soon be sixty, I'm an old man, lonely, a worthless old man... I have nothing good in me, except my love for you, and if it weren't for you, I wouldn't even be alive... *(To IRINA)* Sweet child, I've known you since you were a baby... I carried you in my arms... I loved your mama...

IRINA: But why such expensive gifts!

CHEBUTYKIN: *(On the verge of tears, angrily)* Expensive gifts... Well aren't you something! *(To the ORDERLY)* Take it away!... *(He teases)* Expensive gifts...

*The ORDERLY takes the samovar to the hall.*

ANFISA: *(Walking across the drawing room)* Dearest, a stranger — a colonel! He's taken off his coat already, dear ones, he's coming in here. Irinushka, please be polite... *(Exiting)* It's high time we had lunch... good heavens...

TUZENBAKH: It must be Vershinin.

*VERSHININ enters.*

Colonel Vershinin!

VERSHININ: *(To MASHA and IRINA)* Allow me to introduce myself, Vershinin. I am so happy — to finally see you again. My goodness, how you've grown! *Ai! ai!*

IRINA: Please, have a seat. It's our pleasure.

VERSHININ: *(Happily)* I feel so happy, so happy! But aren't there three sisters? I remember — three little girls. I don't remember your faces, but I do remember your father, Colonel Prozorov, had three little girls. I remember meeting all three... How time flies! Oh yes, how time flies!

TUZENBAKH: Aleksander Ignatyevich is from Moscow.

IRINA: From Moscow? You're from Moscow?

VERSHININ: Yes, I'm from Moscow. Your late father was the battery commander there, and I was an officer in his brigade. *(To MASHA)* Yes, I seem to remember your face a little.

MASHA: And I yours — no!

IRINA: Olya! Olya! *(She shouts into the hall)* Olya, come here!

OLGA *enters from the dining area to the drawing room.*

Colonel Vershinin is from Moscow.

VERSHININ: You must be Olga Sergeyevna, the oldest... And you are Maria... And you are Irina — the youngest...

OLGA: You're from Moscow?

VERSHININ: Yes. I studied in Moscow and then began my military service there. I served there a long time, but I finally received my own command here — I just moved here, as you see. I don't remember you individually. I just remember three sisters. I remember your father so well, I can close my eyes and see him now. I came to visit you in Moscow...

OLGA: I thought I remembered everything... but...

VERSHININ: My name is Aleksander Ignatyevich...

IRINA: Aleksander Ignatyevich, you're from Moscow... What a surprise!

OLGA: Yes, we'll be moving back to Moscow soon.

IRINA: We plan to be there by autumn. Our home town — we were born there... On Old Basmanny street...

*They both laugh from joy.*

MASHA: I can't believe you're from Moscow! *(Vividly)* Now I remember! Yes, you remember, Olya — they used to call you — "Captain Romeo." You were a lieutenant then and you were always in love with someone, and everyone teased you about it for some reason...

VERSHININ: *(He laughs)* That's right, that's right... "Captain Romeo," yes...

MASHA: I remember you had a mustache then... Oh how old you've gotten! *(On the verge of tears)* So old!

VERSHININ: Yes, when they called me "Captain Romeo," I was still very young, I was in love. That's not true anymore.

OLGA: But you don't have a single grey hair. You've aged, but you're not really old.

VERSHININ: Yes... I'm forty-three. Have you been away from Moscow a long time?

IRINA: Eleven years. What's wrong with you, Masha, why are you crying, silly!... *(On the verge of tears)* And now I'm starting to cry...

MASHA: Nothing's wrong with me. Where did you live? On what street?

VERSHININ: On Old Basmanny.

OLGA: Oh, we lived there too…

VERSHININ: At one point I lived on Nemetsky Street. From Nemetsky Street I could literally walk to the barracks. On the way you had to cross a gloomy grey bridge, with the water murmuring below it. A solitary man can feel very sad and lonely on that bridge.

*Pause.*

But here, such a wide, beautiful river! A glorious river!

OLGA: Yes, but it's cold. It's cold here and there are mosquitoes…

VERSHININ: No, no! It's so healthy here, a good Russian climate. Forests, rivers… and plenty of birches. Graceful, modest birches, I love them more than any other tree. It's good to live here. Only it's a little strange — the railroad station is eighteen miles away… why is that?

SOLYONY: I know why.

*Everyone looks at him.*

Because if the station were close, then it wouldn't be far, but if it is far, then it can't be close.

*Awkward silence.*

TUZENBAKH: Very funny, Vasilii Vasilyevich.

OLGA: Now I remember you. I remember…

VERSHININ: I knew your lovely mother.

CHEBUTYKIN: She was so wonderful. God rest her soul.

IRINA: Mama is buried in Moscow.

OLGA: In Novo-Devichy…

MASHA: I can't believe I'm already beginning to forget her face. And we'll be forgotten too. Yes, we'll be forgotten.

VERSHININ: Yes, we'll be forgotten. That's our fate, there's nothing you can do about it. Everything that seems important to us, so meaningful — before long — that will be forgotten too.

*Pause.*

And it's interesting, it's not possible to really know what will be important and meaningful to people and what will seem trivial and foolish. At first didn't they laugh at Copernicus and even Columbus — their discoveries were considered unimportant and ridiculous — and at the same time really shallow, nonsensical beliefs were considered the truth? It's possible that what we believe today will someday seem strange, stupid, awkward, and maybe even sinful…

TUZENBAKH: Who knows? It's also possible that what we believe will be considered sublime, truthful, and people will remember us with respect — maybe even reverence. Today there's no torture, no capital punishment, no war. But of course the truth is there is so much suffering!

SOLYONY: *(With a thin voice)* Tsyp, tsyp, tsyp… Don't feed the Baron any birdseed — just let him philosophize.

TUZENBAKH: Vasilii Vasilych, I beg you please leave me alone… *(He sits in a different chair)* You are getting on my nerves.

SOLYONY: *(With a thin voice)* Tsyp, tsyp, tsyp…

TUZENBAKH: *(To VERSHININ)* There's so much suffering today, yes, but that's because society has gotten so far…

VERSHININ: Yes, yes, of course.

CHEBUTYKIN: You just said, Baron, they will call our life sublime; but in fact all humanity is base… *(He rises)* Look, how base I am! But I appreciate the support — thank you for saying that my life is sublime and intelligent.

*Offstage a violin plays.*

MASHA: That's our brother Andrei playing.

IRINA: He's the scholar in the family. He'll probably be a professor. Papa was a military man, but his son chose a scholarly career.

MASHA: Just as Papa wanted.

OLGA: We were teasing him mercilessly today. He seems to be a bit in love.

IRINA: With a local girl. She'll probably come here today.

MASHA: Akh, the way she dresses! It's not that she's unattractive, but she has no sense of style — it's really a shame. She'll wear a strange, colorful, yellowish skirt with a vulgar fringe and a red blouse. And her cheeks are scrubbed raw — horrible! Andrei cannot be in love with her — I will not permit it! Surely he has some taste — I'm sure he's just teasing us. Just yesterday I heard she's going to marry Protopopov, chairman of the local *zemstvo* council. Excellent… *(To the side door)* Andrei, come here! Darling, come in here.

*Enter ANDREI.*

OLGA: This is my brother, Andrei Sergeyich.

VERSHININ: Vershinin.

ANDREI: Prozorov. *(He wipes sweat from his face)* You're the new battery commander?

OLGA: Aleksander Ignatyich is from Moscow.

ANDREI: Really? Well, congratulations, now my sisters will never leave you in peace.

VERSHININ: I've already succeeded in boring your sisters.

IRINA: Look, what a lovely frame Andrei gave me today! *(She shows the frame)* He made it himself.

VERSHININ: *(Looking at the frame and not knowing what to say)* Yes… that's something…

IRINA: And that frame on the piano, he made that too.

*ANDREI waves his hand and walks away.*

OLGA: He's the scholar among us and he plays the violin, and he creates all kinds of wonderful things with his hands — in other words, he can do anything. Andrei, don't leave! You're always walking away. Come here!

*MASHA and IRINA take him by the arms and with laughter lead him back.*

MASHA: Come, come!

ANDREI: Leave me alone, please.

MASHA: You're so funny! Aleksander Ignatyevich used to be called "Captain Romeo," and he wasn't a bit angry.

VERSHININ: Not a bit!

MASHA: And I will have to call you: "Professor Romeo!"

IRINA: Or "*Maestro* Romeo," the violinist!

OLGA: He's in love! Andryusha is in love!

IRINA: *(Applauding) Bravo, bravo! Bis!* Andryusha is in love!

CHEBUTYKIN: *(Approaches ANDREI from behind and puts his arms around his waist)* We've been put on this earth for love alone! *(He chuckles; he has a newspaper the entire time)*

ANDREI: Enough, enough… *(He wipes his face)* I didn't sleep all night and I'm really not myself today. I was reading until four, then I closed my eyes, but nothing happened. I couldn't turn off my mind and suddenly it was dawn and the sun was pouring into my room. This summer, if I'm still here, I'd like to translate a book from English.

VERSHININ: Ah, you read English?

ANDREI: Yes. Father, God rest his soul, stuffed us with education. It's funny — even a little crazy — but the fact is, after he died I started to put on weight. I have put on so much weight that I feel my body is bloated with all that education. Thanks to our father my sisters and I know French, German and English, and Irina even knows Italian — for all the good it does!

MASHA: What's the point of knowing three languages around here? In truth, in this town, it's a burden, like an extra finger.

VERSHININ: Ah, I see! *(He laughs)* You know too much! If you ask me, no place on earth can exist without intelligent, educated people. For example, let's take this town — let's say that among the hundred thousand inhabitants — probably all backward and crude — there are only three like you. Obviously, you can't conquer the stupidity around you all by yourselves, and it's true that little by little you may lose some of your brilliance and become lost in the crowd — you may even feel as if you're drowning — but you won't disappear entirely, you'll still have influence among these people. Then there will be six of you, maybe twenty, and so on, until finally, you will be the majority. In two hundred, three hundred years life on earth will be unimaginably beautiful, astounding. Of course, everyone wants such a life now and you must have faith that it will come. You must wait for it, dream about it, prepare for it. Undoubtedly you know more than your parents and your grandfather. *(He laughs)* And you complain that you know too much!

MASHA: *(She takes off her hat)* I'm staying for lunch.

IRINA: *(With a sigh)* Really, we should have written all that down…

*ANDREI has slipped out quietly.*

TUZENBAKH: In many years you say life on earth will be beautiful, astounding. That's true. But, in order to prepare for that life — though it may be in the far distant future — we need to do something now, we need to work…

VERSHININ: *(He stands)* Yes. You have so many flowers here! *(Looking around)* And your home is marvelous. I envy you! All my life I've been living in tiny apartments with two chairs, one sofa, and with stoves that are always smoking. Obviously what I've needed all my life are these lovely flowers!… *(He rubs his hands)* Ekh! Well, that's it!

TUZENBAKH: Yes, it's necessary to work. No doubt, you're probably thinking: the German is being romantic. But on my honor, I am Russian — I don't even speak German. My father was Russian Orthodox…

*Pause.*

VERSHININ: *(He walks about)* I often think if only we could start all over again and much more consciously this time. The life we've already lived can be a rough draft for what we would do the next time. Then there's always the chance we wouldn't repeat our mistakes — we could at least find a better place to live — a place filled with flowers, filled with light… I have a wife and two daughters. My poor wife is ill, yes, yes… Yes, if only we could start all over again — I surely wouldn't get married…

*Enter KULYGIN in a uniform.*

KULYGIN: *(He approaches IRINA)* Dear sister, permit me to congratulate you on your birthday. I sincerely wish you, from my soul, good health and everything a young lady of your age wishes for herself. Permit me to present you with this gift. *(He gives her a book)* The history of our high school over the past fifty years, written by yours truly. A trifling little book, written when I had nothing better to do, but I hope you will read it nonetheless. Good afternoon, ladies and gentlemen! *(To VERSHININ)* Kulygin, a teacher at the local high school. Civil servant, 7th class! *(To IRINA)* In this book you will find a list of all those who graduated from our high school in the past fifty years. *Feci quod potui, faciant meliora potentes.* ["I did what I could; let he who can, do better."] *(He kisses MASHA)*

IRINA: You already gave me this book for Easter.

KULYGIN: *(He laughs)* Impossible! In that case, give it back, or better yet give it to the colonel. Please accept it, colonel. Read it sometime when you have nothing better to do.

VERSHININ: I thank you. *(He prepares to leave)* I'm so very happy to see you again…

OLGA: You're leaving? No, no!

IRINA: You'll stay and have lunch with us. Please.

OLGA: I beg you!

VERSHININ: *(He bows)* It seems I have walked in on a birthday party. Forgive me, I didn't know, I haven't yet congratulated you… *(He exits with OLGA to the dining room)*

KULYGIN: Today, ladies and gentlemen, is Sunday, a day of rest, we will rest, we will enjoy ourselves each in keeping with our own age and position. These carpets must be taken up and stored for summer, don't take them out until winter… Insect-powder or naphthalene… The Romans were healthy, because they labored, and then they rested, *mens sana in corpore sano* ["A healthy soul in a healthy body"]. Their life had order to it. Our headmaster says, the most important thing in life is order… Without order, there is no life — and it's the same for all of us. *(He takes MASHA by the waist, laughs)* Masha loves me. My wife loves me. And the window curtains must go — along with the carpets… Today I'm happy, I'm in excellent spirits. Masha, at four o'clock today we are due at the headmaster's house. He's arranging a special walk for the staff and their families.

MASHA: I'm not going.

KULYGIN: *(Distressed)* Dear Masha, why?

MASHA: We'll talk about it later… *(Angrily)* Fine, I'll go, only leave me alone, please… *(She moves away)*

KULYGIN: And then we'll spend the evening with the headmaster. In spite of his own poor health, that man always endeavors to be friendly. An outstanding, brilliant man. A splendid man. Yesterday after a conference he said to me: "I'm tired, Fyodor Ilych! Tired!" *(He looks at the wall clock, then at his own)* Your clock is seven minutes fast. Yes, he said, tired!

   *Offstage a violin plays.*

OLGA: Ladies and gentlemen, welcome! Luncheon is served. *Pirogi*!

KULYGIN: Akh, kind Olga, my kind friend! Yesterday I worked from morning until eleven at night, I'm tired and yet today I feel so happy. *(He exits to the table)* My kind…

CHEBUTYKIN: *(He puts the newspaper in his pocket, combs his beard) Pirogi*? Magnificent!

MASHA: *(Severely to CHEBUTYKIN)* Listen to me — nothing to drink today. Do you hear me? Drinking is killing you.

CHEBUTYKIN: Nonsense! That's all over. It's been two years since I was drunk. *(Impatiently)* And in any case, *Babushka* [grandma], what difference does it make!

MASHA: And in any case, don't drink. You hear me, don't drink! *(Angrily, but so that her husband cannot hear)* Damn it, another boring evening with the headmaster!

TUZENBAKH: Don't go… just don't go.

CHEBUTYKIN: Don't go, my darling.

MASHA: Oh sure, don't go… this goddamn life! *(She walks to the hall)*

CHEBUTYKIN: *(He goes to her)* Oh, well…

SOLYONY: Tysp, tysp, tysp…

TUZENBAKH: Enough, Vasilii Vasilych. Stop it!

SOLYONY: Tysp, tysp, tysp…

KULYGIN: *(Happily)* To your health, Colonel. I'm an educator, but in this house I'm just one of the family, Masha's husband… She is good, very good…

VERSHININ: I'll have that dark vodka… *(He drinks) Vashe zdorevye!* *(To OLGA)* I feel so at home here…

*In the drawing room only IRINA and TUZENBAKH remain.*

IRINA: Masha is so depressed today. She was only eighteen when she got married — he seemed to her the most intelligent man in the world. Not anymore — he's the kindest, but not the most intelligent.

OLGA: *(Impatiently)* Andrei, come on!

ANDREI: *(Offstage)* Coming. *(He enters and goes to the table)*

TUZENBAKH: What are you thinking about?

IRINA: Hmmm. I hate that Solyony of yours — I'm afraid of him. He says such stupid things...

TUZENBAKH: He's a strange man. I feel sorry for him, and I'm also annoyed with him, but I think it's more like pity. He's so shy... When we're together, just the two of us, he can be very intelligent and gentle, but in company he's rude, a bully. Don't go, they can wait. Let me be close to you. What are you thinking about?

> Pause.

You're twenty years old, I'm still not thirty. There are so many years ahead of us — a future of long days, all filled with my love for you...

IRINA: Please, Nikolai Lvovich, don't talk to me about love.

TUZENBAKH: *(Not hearing)* I'm craving life, struggle, labor, and this craving in my soul perfectly blends with my love for you, Irina. You're so beautiful, and it makes me feel that life is beautiful! What are you thinking about?

IRINA: You say life is beautiful. Yes, but what if it only seems to be! For us three sisters, believe me, life hasn't been beautiful — it's choking us, like weeds in a garden... I'm crying. How stupid! *(She quickly wipes her face, she smiles)* We must work, work. We're unhappy and we're depressed because we don't work. We were born into families who never had to work for a living...

> *NATALYA IVANOVNA enters; she is in a pink dress, with a green belt.*

NATASHA: Oh dear, they've sat down already... I'm late... *(She glances in passing in the mirror, fixes herself)* My hair looks good... *(Seeing IRINA)* Sweet Irina Sergeyevna, congratulations! *(She gives IRINA a long, firm kiss)* You have so many guests, I'm embarrassed… Hello, Baron!

OLGA: *(Entering the drawing room)* Well, Natalya Ivanovna. Hello, my dear!

*They kiss.*

NATASHA: Happy birthday. You have so much company, I'm so embarrassed…

OLGA: No, no — everyone is welcome here. *(Under her breath, aghast)* You're wearing a green belt! Dear girl, that's not right!

NATASHA: Did I do something wrong?

OLGA: No, it simply doesn't go… it looks… funny…

NATASHA: *(With a weepy voice)* Really? But it's not really green — it's darker than green. *(She follows OLGA to the dining room)*

*In the dining room they settle in to eat lunch; no one is left in the drawing room.*

KULYGIN: Irina Sergeyevna, I wish for you a suitable suitor. It's high time you got married.

CHEBUTYKIN: Natalya Ivanovna, I wish for you a suitable suitor.

KULYGIN: Natalya Ivanovna already has a suitable suitor.

MASHA: *(She raps on the plate with her fork)* Let's have another glass of vodka! What the hell! We won't live forever!

KULYGIN: That's an F-minus for conduct!

VERSHININ: This vodka is delicious. What's it made from?

SOLYONY: Cockroaches.

IRINA: *(With a weepy voice)* Ekh, that's disgusting!

OLGA: We're going to have roast turkey and sweet apple pie for dinner. Thank goodness, I'm home all day today and tonight — home... Everyone, please come back.

VERSHININ: May I return too?

IRINA: Please.

NATASHA: They don't stand on ceremony here.

CHEBUTYKIN: We've been put on this earth for love alone... *(He laughs)*

ANDREI: *(Angrily)* Please! Stop teasing us! It's getting old...

*FEDOTIK and RODAY enter with a big basket of flowers.*

FEDOTIK: They're eating already.

RODAY: *(Loudly and with an accent)* Lunch? Great...

FEDOTIK: Wait a minute! *(He takes a photograph)* Hold still...Just a little minute... *(He takes another photograph)* Alright, everybody breathe.

*They take the basket and go into the dining area, where everyone greets them.*

RODAY: *(Loudly)* Congratulations, I wish you everything wonderful! Isn't it a gorgeous day! I spent the whole morning today hiking with my young hooligans. I teach gymnastics at the high school...

FEDOTIK: *(Taking a photograph)* Yes, you can move now, Irina Sergeyevna. Today you are the star attraction. *(He takes a top from his pocket)* Here's a top for you… it makes an astonishing sound…

IRINA: How lovely!

MASHA: "At the sea, a green oak stands, with a golden chain wound round…" *(Pathetic)* What the hell am I saying? I can't get that poem out of my head today…

KULYGIN: Thirteen at table!

RODAY: *(Loudly)* And what is that supposed to mean?

*Laughter.*

KULYGIN: If there are thirteen at table, then, it means there are lovers here. Surely you're not one of them, Ivan Romanovich…

*Laughter.*

CHEBUTYKIN: Me! I'm an old sinner — but why is Natalya Ivanovna so red — why? Why?

*Loud laughter; NATASHA runs from the dinner table to the drawing room, ANDREI follows.*

ANDREI: Stop it! That's enough! *(To NATASHA)* Don't pay any attention…

NATASHA: I'm so embarrassed… I don't know what's wrong with me — why are they all making fun of me? I know it wasn't right to leave the table, but I can't… I can't… *(She covers her face with her hands)*

ANDREI: My dear, I beg you, I implore you, don't be upset. They're just joking, they're all good-hearted. My dear, my sweet girl, they're all good, sincere people and they love me and they love you. Come over to the window, they can't see us there… *(He looks around)*

NATASHA: I'm just not used to this much company!...

ANDREI: Oh, you are so young, so beautiful! My dear, my sweet, don't be upset!... Believe me, believe... I'm so full of love right now, so full of joy... Don't worry, they can't see us! When did I fall in love with you? How? Where? Oh, I don't understand anything. My dear, sweet, pure darling, be my wife! I love you, I love you... like no one ever...

*Kiss.*

*Two OFFICERS enter and, seeing the kissing pair, come to a stop in amazement.*

CURTAIN.

# ACT II

*Same as first act. January, twenty-one months later.*

*Eight o'clock in the evening. Offstage, on the street, barely audible, someone plays an accordion. There is no fire in the stove.*

> *Enter NATALYA IVANOVNA in a house-coat, with a candle; she stops at the door to ANDREI's room.*

NATASHA: Andryusha, what're you doing? Are you reading? Never mind, it's nothing, I just… *(She walks, turns away toward another door and, looking in it, shuts it)* Just wanted to check if there was a light…

ANDREI: *(He enters with a book in hand)* What's wrong, Natasha?

NATASHA: I'm just checking if there was a light… It's carnival week, and the servants are acting up, I have to keep a careful eye on everything. Yesterday at midnight I walked into the dining room, and there was a candle burning. No one will admit who did it… *(She places the candle)* What time is it?

ANDREI: *(Glancing at the clock)* Quarter past eight.

NATASHA: And Olga and Irina are still out — not home yet. The poor dears — always working. Olga at the high school and Irina at the telegraph office… *(She sighs)* This morning I told your sister, I said, "take better care of yourself, Irina, my dear". But she doesn't listen. Quarter past eight, you say? I'm worried our Bobik is sick. Why is he so cold? Yesterday he had a fever, and today he's cold all over… I'm so worried!

ANDREI: It's nothing, Natasha. The boy is healthy.

NATASHA: But I think I'd better put him on a special diet. I'm worried. And tonight at ten, the carnival people will arrive. It would be better if they didn't come, Andryusha.

ANDREI: Alright… I don't know. They were invited, you know.

NATASHA: Our little boy woke up this morning and looked at me, and suddenly smiled — he knew me! So I said, "*Bobik*, hello! Hello, little sweetheart!" And he laughed. Children understand, they know everything. So, so then, Andryusha, let's cancel the carnival people.

ANDREI: *(Indecisively)* Isn't it up to my sisters? It's their house too.

NATASHA: Yes, it's theirs too — I'll tell them. They are so kind… *(She walks)* For dinner, I ordered you some yoghurt. The doctor says you need to eat only yoghurt, otherwise you won't lose any weight. *(She stops)* Bobik is cold. I'm worried, he's too cold in his room. Maybe we should move him to another room until the weather warms up. Irina's room, for example, is perfect for a child: it's dry and sunny all day. We need to tell her — for the time being she and Olga can share a room… It won't make any difference to her, she's away all day, she only sleeps here…

 *Pause.*

Andryushanchik, why are you so quiet?

ANDREI: Nothing, I was thinking… nothing…

NATASHA: Wait… what was I going to say?… Oh, yes. Ferapont from the council is here. He's asking for you.

ANDREI: *(He yawns)* Send him in.

 *NATASHA exits; ANDREI sits by the candle she left, reads a book. FERAPONT enters; he wears an old tattered overcoat, with the collar raised, ears covered.*

Hello, old friend. What's up?

FERAPONT: The chairman sent a book and some papers. Here... *(He gives the book and parcel)*

ANDREI: Thanks. Good. Why did you come so late? It's after eight, you know.

FERAPONT: What?

ANDREI: *(Louder)* I said, you've come late, it's already after eight.

FERAPONT: Uh huh. I came here when it was still light outside but they wouldn't let me in. They said, the master is busy. Well, okay. Busy is busy, I'm not in a hurry — I have nowhere else to go. *(Thinking that ANDREI is asking him about something)* Huh?

ANDREI: Nothing. *(Examining the book)* Tomorrow is Friday, we have the day off — well anyway, I'll go in... I'll keep myself busy. It's boring at home...

*Pause.*

Sweet *Dyedushka* [granddaddy], life is so crazy — it keeps changing, it's all a lie! Today, with nothing but time on my hands, I starting reading this book again — some old university lecture notes of mine, and suddenly I started laughing out loud... My God, I'm the secretary of the *zemstvo* council, the council where Protopopov is chairman, I'm secretary, and the best I can hope for — is to be a member of the *zemstvo* council! Me, a member of the local *zemstvo* council, me, who dreams every night I'm a professor at Moscow University, a famous scholar, a national hero.

FERAPONT: Sorry, I don't... I can't hear you...

ANDREI: If you could hear me, I wouldn't be talking to you. I need somebody to talk to— my wife doesn't understand, I'm afraid of my sisters for some reason — afraid — maybe they'll laugh at me, make me feel ashamed... I don't drink, I don't like taverns, but oh, what pleasure it would be to be in Moscow, to be sitting at Testov's or at the Grand Moscow, what joy....

FERAPONT: At the council, I heard a story about some merchants eating *blini*, and one guy ate forty *blini*, and I guess he died. Forty or fifty. I don't remember.

ANDREI: In Moscow, you can sit in a big restaurant — you don't know anybody and nobody knows you — yet you don't feel like an outsider. Here you know everybody and everybody knows you, but you feel like a stranger, a stranger… uncomfortable and alone.

FERAPONT: Huh?

　*Pause.*

And the same guy was saying — maybe he was lying — it seems they're gonna stretch a rope across all of Moscow.

ANDREI: Why?

FERAPONT: I don't know. The guy said…

ANDREI: Nonsense. *(He reads the book)* Were you ever in Moscow?

FERAPONT: *(After a pause)* Never. It wasn't God's will, I guess.

　*Pause.*

Can I go?

ANDREI: Yes. Take care.

　*FERAPONT exits.*

Take care. *(Reading)* Come tomorrow morning, take these papers…

　*Pause.*

He's gone.

　*Bell.*

Yes, business... *(He stretches and unhurriedly exits to his room)*

*From offstage the NURSE sings, rocking the baby to sleep. MASHA and VERSHININ enter. While they talk, a maid lights the lamps and candles.*

MASHA: I don't know.

*Pause.*

I don't know. Of course, maybe it's just habit... After father's death, for example, for a long time we couldn't get used to the fact that we didn't have orderlies around. But no, it seems to me — yes, I think I'm being fair — maybe in other places it's not true — but in our town the most respectable, the most noble, the most courteous people — are in the military.

VERSHININ: I'm dying of thirst. I would love some tea.

MASHA: *(Looking at the clock)* They'll bring it in a minute. I got married when I was eighteen, and I looked up to my husband because he was a teacher, and I had just graduated high school. He seemed so terribly distinguished, so intelligent and important. But now... sadly...

VERSHININ: Ah... yes.

MASHA: I never talk about my husband, I'm used to having him around. But when it comes to civilians in general, I'd say they are crude, disrespectful, ill-bred. I am deeply offended by their rudeness, I suffer when someone is coarse and impolite. I can't stand it when I'm in the company of my husband's colleagues — I actually feel pain.

VERSHININ: I see... But I think military men are just as crude and boring as civilians — at least around here. Exactly the same! Listening to "intellectuals" — whether civilian or military — all I hear is how worn out they are by their wives, by their houses, by their estates, by their horses... Russians are probably capable of higher thinking — so tell me, why are they always complaining? Why?

MASHA: Why?

VERSHININ: Because they're worn out by their children, by their wives? And because their wives and children are worn out by them?

MASHA: You seem so sad today.

VERSHININ: Maybe. I didn't have any lunch, I haven't eaten since morning. My daughter was a little sick, and when my daughters are sick, I get worried — I start feeling guilty that they have such a mother. Oh, you should have seen her today! What a fool I am! We started to fight at seven a.m., and at nine I slammed the door and left.

*Pause.*

I never talk about this. Why is it that I only complain to you? *(He kisses her hand)* Don't be angry with me. Except for you, I have no one, no one...

*Pause.*

MASHA: The stove is noisy. Just before father's death there was a hum in that stove. Just like this.

VERSHININ: Are you superstitious?

MASHA: Yes.

VERSHININ: That's strange. *(He kisses her hand)* You're a splendid, marvelous woman. Splendid, marvelous! It's dark in here, but I can still see the brilliance of your eyes.

MASHA: *(She takes a different chair)* There's more light over here...

VERSHININ: I love, love, love... Love your eyes, your every movement — I see you in my dreams. Splendid, marvelous woman!

MASHA: *(Quietly laughing)* When you speak to me like this, I don't know why, but I laugh — but the truth is it terrifies me. Don't say it again, I beg you... *(In a half-voice)* Oh, please speak... it doesn't matter... *(She covers her face with her hands)* It doesn't matter... Someone's coming, talk about something else...

*IRINA and TUZENBAKH walk across the hall.*

TUZENBAKH: I have three family names. My name is Baron Tuzenbakh-Krone-Altschauer, but I'm Russian, Russian Orthodox, like you. There's practically no German left in me, except perhaps the patience and stubbornness I bother you with every evening when I walk you home.

IRINA: I'm so tired!

TUZENBAKH: And I will continue to bother you and come to the telegraph office and walk you home every evening — I will for ten-twenty years, until you throw me out... *(Seeing MASHA and VERSHININ, joyfully)* Oh, it's you? Hello.

IRINA: Hooray, I'm home at last. *(To MASHA)* Just before I left work, a woman comes in and wants to telegraph her brother in Saratov — her son died today, and she can't remember the address. So she sent it without an address, just to Saratov. She was crying. And I was so rude to her — for no reason at all. "I don't have time," I told her. I was horrible. Aren't the carnival people coming tonight?

MASHA: Yes.

IRINA: *(She sits in the armchair)* Ooh, I'm so tired.

TUZENBAKH: *(With a smile)* When you come home from work, you seem so tiny, so vulnerable...

*Pause.*

IRINA: I'm tired. No, I don't like the telegraph office, I don't like it at all.

MASHA: You've lost too much weight... *(She whistles)* And you look younger — like a little boy.

TUZENBAKH: That's because of her haircut.

IRINA: I must find another job — this one's not for me. Everything I yearned for, dreamed about — forget about it in the post office! What is work without poetry, without intellect...

*Tap on the floor.*

The doctor is tapping. *(To TUZENBAKH)* Dear friend, knock for me. I can't... I'm too tired...

*TUZENBAKH taps on the floor.*

He's coming now. We've got to do something. Yesterday the doctor and Andrei were at the club and they lost again. I heard Andrei lost two hundred *rubles*.

MASHA: *(Indifferently)* What are we supposed to do about it!

IRINA: Two weeks ago he lost, he lost in December. The sooner he loses everything, maybe, the sooner we can get out of this town. Good God, I dream about Moscow every night. I'm going completely insane. *(She laughs)* We'll move away from here in June... February, March, April, May... *(She sighs deeply)*... almost half a year!

MASHA: We'd better not let Natasha hear anything about him losing.

IRINA: It doesn't matter to her.

*CHEBUTYKIN, having just gotten up from bed — he took a nap after dinner — enters the hall and combs his beard, then takes a seat there at the table and takes a newspaper from his pocket.*

MASHA: Here he comes... Did he pay his rent?

IRINA: *(She laughs)* No. Not a *kopek* in eight months. Apparently he has forgotten.

MASHA: *(She laughs)* How imperious he is!

*Everyone laughs; pause.*

IRINA: Why are you so quiet, Aleksander Ignatyich?

VERSHININ: I don't know. I want tea. My kingdom for a cup of tea! I haven't eaten since this morning…

CHEBUTYKIN: Irina Sergeyevna!

IRINA: What do you want?

CHEBUTYKIN: Please come here. *Venez ici.*

*IRINA goes and takes a seat at the table.*

I can't live without you.

*IRINA plays Solitaire.*

VERSHININ: What's happening? If they're not bringing the tea, then let's talk.

TUZENBAKH: Let's. About what?

VERSHININ: About what? Let's imagine… the life to come after us, in two hundred-three hundred years.

TUZENBAKH: What? After us… they'll be flying in air balloons, wearing different clothes, and maybe they'll discover a sixth sense and learn how to use it — but life itself will remain the same, life will always be difficult, full of mystery with glimpses of happiness. And in a thousand years man will still say: "akh, life is so hard!" — and just like today, we'll be afraid to die.

VERSHININ: *(Having thought of something)* How can I explain this? It seems to me, everything on this earth must evolve slowly — in fact it's already evolving before our eyes. In two hundred-three hundred years, maybe a thousand years — the exact time isn't important — we'll know a new, happy life. Well, of course we won't know it in our lifetime, but for now we must live, we must work, we must suffer, and someday it will happen. That's what we're striving for, why we exist — to create future happiness.

*MASHA laughs quietly.*

TUZENBAKH: What's the matter with you?

MASHA: I don't know. I haven't stopped laughing all day.

VERSHININ: I'm just as educated as you are — though it's true, I didn't go to the military academy. I read a great deal — any book I can get my hands on — though they're probably not what I should be reading — but the longer I live, the more I want to learn. My hair is getting gray, I'm practically an old man, but I feel I don't know anything — akh! What I do know — and this is the really important thing — we will never know happiness in our lifetime — happiness is not for us… But we must keep on working, working — happiness is for future generations.

*Pause.*

It's not for us…

*FEDOTIK and RODAY appear in the hall; they sit and sing quietly, playing the guitar.*

TUZENBAKH: So according to you we're not even allowed to dream of happiness! What if I'm happy already!

VERSHININ: No.

TUZENBAKH: *(Clasping his hands and laughing)* Evidently, we don't agree. Well, how can I convince you?

*MASHA laughs quietly.*

*(Pointing at her)* Go ahead, laugh! *(To VERSHININ)* Life won't change in two or three hundred years, in fact it will be the same in a million years. The laws of nature have their own course, which will follow regardless of what you and I think or do. Migratory birds, cranes for example, fly and fly, and whatever thoughts they have, lofty or trivial, they will keep on flying and never know why or where they're going. Whatever we philosophers say, they will keep on flying. So talk all you want, they will still be flying…

MASHA: But what does it all mean?

TUZENBAKH: Mean… It's snowing. What does that mean?

MASHA: It seems to me, we have to believe in something or else life is empty… empty… To live and not know why cranes fly, why children are born, why there are stars in the sky… not to know — why then it's all meaningless…

*Pause.*

VERSHININ: Still, it's a shame youth goes by so fast…

MASHA: You know what Gogol says, it's a long, sad life, my friends.

TUZENBAKH: I must say, it's hard to argue with you, Ladies and Gentlemen. You are so…

CHEBUTYKIN: *(Reading the paper)* Balzac got married in Berdichev.

*IRINA sings quietly.*

I must make a note of that in my little book. *(He makes a note)* Balzac got married in Berdichev. *(He reads the paper)*

IRINA: *(Plays Solitaire)* What was Balzac doing in Russia?

*Pause.*

TUZENBAKH: The die is cast, my friends. Maria Sergeyevna, I am tendering my resignation.

MASHA: I heard. And I can't see anything good to come of it. I hate civilians.

TUZENBAKH: It doesn't matter... *(He rises)* I'm not a handsome man, so what kind of soldier does that make? Well, yes, it doesn't matter... however... I'm going to work. If I could work just one day in my life, come home in the evening and collapse into bed and fall asleep immediately. *(Walking to the hall)* I'm sure workers sleep very soundly!

FEDOTIK: *(To IRINA)* I bought you some colored pencils at Pyzhikov's on Moscow Street. And this little knife...

IRINA: You still treat me like a little girl — Don't you see, I'm all grown up! *(She takes the pencils and knife, joyfully)* Oh, how lovely!

FEDOTIK: I bought myself a knife... look at this... a blade, another blade, and a third, this one is for picking my ears, these are scissors, this is to clean my toe nails...

RODAY: *(Loudly)* Doctor, how old are you?

CHEBUTYKIN: Me? Thirty-two.

*Laughter.*

FEDOTIK: Let me teach you another kind of Solitaire... *(He shuffles and lays out the cards)*

*They bring the samovar; ANFISA sits next to the samovar; after a little time passes NATASHA enters and fusses at the table; SOLYONY enters and, greeting them, takes at seat at the table.*

VERSHININ: It's so windy outside!

MASHA: Yes. I hate winter. I can't even remember what summer was like.

IRINA: Look, I'm going to win! That means we'll be in Moscow soon.

FEDOTIK: No — sorry... You see, the eight has fallen on the two of spades. *(He laughs)* That means you'll never get to Moscow.

CHEBUTYKIN: *(Reading the paper)* Hmmm, Tsitsikar. Smallpox is raging there.

ANFISA: *(Approaching MASHA)* Masha, have some tea, *Matushka*. *(To VERSHININ)* Please, Your Excellency... forgive me, my dear, I forgot your name...

MASHA: Bring it here, *Nyanya*. I won't go in there.

IRINA: *Nyanya!*

ANFISA: I'm coming, I'm coming...

NATASHA: *(To SOLYONY)* Little babies understand everything. I say to Bobik, "Hi, sweetness!" And the way he focuses right on me! I know you think it's because I'm his mother, but believe me, he's an extraordinary baby.

SOLYONY: If that child were mine, I would sauté him in a frying pan and eat him for supper. *(He goes with a glass to the parlor and sits in the corner)*

NATASHA: *(Covering her face with her hands)* Disgusting man!

MASHA: Happy is he who doesn't even notice the winter. I'm sure if I were in Moscow, I would be completely indifferent to the weather...

VERSHININ: The other day I was reading the diary of a French minister who is in prison. He had been convicted in Panama. He writes about the birds he sees from his prison window with such rapture — and he's sure he never noticed them before, when he was a minister. Now, of course, the minute he's released, he'll never notice them again. In the same way, when you live in Moscow, you'll never really see it. There is no such thing as happiness, there is only the desire for it.

TUZENBAKH: *(He takes a small box from the table)* Where's the candy?

IRINA: Solyony ate it.

TUZENBAKH: All of it?

ANFISA: *(Pouring tea)* There's a letter for you, dear sir.

VERSHININ: For me? *(He takes the letter)* It's from my daughters. *(He reads)* Yes, of course… Forgive me, Maria Sergeyevna, I must sneak out of here. I won't have any tea. *(He rises agitatedly)* These endless dramas…

MASHA: What is it? Is it a secret?

VERSHININ: *(Quietly)* My wife poisoned herself again. I must go. I'll leave quietly. God, it's so terrible. *(He kisses MASHA's hand)* My dear, sweet, lovely woman… I'll just leave quietly… *(He exits)*

ANFISA: Where's he going? I just poured him tea… What's going on…

MASHA: *(Becoming angry)* Stop it! Leave me alone! You never shut up… *(She goes with her teacup to the table)* I'm sick of you, old woman!

ANFISA: What's the matter? Dear heart!

ANDREI'S VOICE: Anfisa!

ANFISA: *(She teases)* Anfisa! And he just sits there… *(She exits)*

MASHA: *(At the table in the hall, angrily)* I want to sit here! *(She messes up the cards on the table)* You're taking up the whole table with your cards! Just drink your tea!

IRINA: Mashka, you're being very nasty.

MASHA: If I'm very nasty, don't talk to me. Don't touch me!

CHEBUTYKIN: *(Laughing)* Don't touch her, don't touch…

MASHA: You're sixty years old, but you act like a little boy — always making some goddam trouble.

NATASHA: *(Sighing)* Dear Masha, don't speak that way in public. You are so beautiful and the truth is, you would be very popular in fashionable society, if it weren't for that mouth of yours. *Je vous prie, pardonnez moi, Marie, mais vous avez des manières un peu grossières.* ["I beg you pardon me, Marie, but you sometimes have course manners."]

TUZENBAKH: *(Holding back laughter)* Give me… give me… There — I see some… cognac…

NATASHA: *Il parait, que mon* Bobik *déjà ne dort pas*, he woke up. My sweet little boy is feeling unwell today. I must go to him, *pardonnez moi…* (She exits)

IRINA: Where did Aleksander Ignatyevich go?

MASHA: Home. Problems with his wife again.

TUZENBAKH: *(He goes to SOLYONY, with a decanter of cognac)* You're always sitting alone, always thinking — but about what? Well, let's make up. Let's drink some cognac.

   *They drink.*

I've had such an urge to play the piano all day — I want to play all sorts of silly things… Well, be that as it may…

SOLYONY: Why make up? I wasn't fighting with you.

TUZENBAKH: You always make me feel as though something's gone wrong between us. You must agree you have a very strange personality.

SOLYONY: Yes, I'm strange, but who isn't strange! *(Declaiming)* "Don't be angry, Aleko!"

TUZENBAKH: Who's Aleko…

*Pause.*

SOLYONY: When I'm alone with someone, then I'm all right. I'm like everybody else — but in company I get depressed, shy and… I say all kinds of crazy things. Well, in any case, I'm more honest and noble than many, many other people. And I can prove it.

TUZENBAKH: I get so angry with you, you're always picking on me when we're with other people, but I still like you somehow. Well, be that as it may… Let's get drunk. Let's drink!

SOLYONY: Yes, let's drink.

*They drink.*

I have nothing against you, Baron. But I'm a lot like Lermontov, don't you think? *(Quietly)* I even look a little like Lermontov… so they say… *(He takes a flask from his pocket with perfume and pours it on his hands)*

TUZENBAKH: I'm resigning from the army. *Basta*! I've been thinking about it for five years and now I have finally decided to do it. I will go to work.

SOLYONY: *(Declaiming)* "Don't be angry, Aleko"… Oh, cut it out with your ridiculous fantasies…

*While they talk, ANDREI enters with a book quietly and sits by a candle.*

TUZENBAKH: I will work.

CHEBUTYKIN: *(Walking to the parlor with IRINA)* And the food was genuinely from the Caucasus: soup with onions, and for the entrée — *chekhartma* meat.

SOLYONY: *Cheremsha* is not meat at all, but a vegetable like onions.

CHEBUTYKIN: No, my angel. *Chekhartma* is not an onion, but an entrée from mutton.

SOLYONY: No, I'm telling you, *cheremsha* — is onion.

CHEBUTYKIN: And I'm telling you, *chekartma* — is mutton.

SOLYONY: And I insist, *cheremsha* — is onion.

CHEBUTYKIN: Why am I arguing with you! You've never been to the Caucasus and you haven't eaten *chekhartma*.

SOLYONY: I didn't eat it, because I can't stand it. *Cheremsha* smells like garlic.

ANDREI: *(Imploring)* Enough, gentlemen! I beg you!

TUZENBAKH: When are the carnival people coming?

IRINA: They promised by nine. That's right now.

TUZENBAKH: *(He embraces ANDREI and sings)* "*Akh, vy seni, moi seni, seni novye moi...*" ["Ah you hall of welcome, my new welcoming hall..."]

ANDREI: *(He dances and sings)* "*Seni novye, klenovye...*" ["Welcoming hall, wonderful hall..."]

CHEBUTYKIN: *(He dances)* "*Reshetchaty — e!*" ["Lacy trellised..."]

   Laughter.

TUZENBAKH: *(He kisses ANDREI)* Goddamn it, let's have a drink. Andryusha, let's drink to you. And I'm going to go with you, Andryusha — to Moscow — to the university.

SOLYONY: To which university? Moscow has two universities.

ANDREI: There's only one university in Moscow.

SOLYONY: I'm telling you — two.

ANDREI: Alright, let there be three. That's better yet.

SOLYONY: In Moscow there are two universities!

*Grumbling and catcalls.*

In Moscow there are two universities: the old one and the new one. And if you don't like to listen to me, if what I say irritates you so much, then I won't talk. I can even go to another room… *(He walks to one of the doors)*

TUZENBAKH: *Bravo, bravo! (He laughs)* Ladies and Gentlemen, let's begin, I'm going to play the piano now. That Solyony is so strange… *(He sits at the piano and plays a waltz)*

MASHA: *(She dances the waltz alone)* The Baron is drunk, the Baron is drunk, the Baron is drunk!

*NATASHA enters.*

NATASHA: *(To CHEBUTYKIN)* Ivan Romanych! *(She says something to CHEBUTYKIN, then quietly exits)*

*CHEBUTYKIN touches TUZENBAKH on the shoulder and whispers something to him.*

IRINA: What is it?

CHEBUTYKIN: It's time we left. Be well.

TUZENBAKH: Good night. It's time to go.

IRINA: I'm sorry but… what about the carnival people?…

ANDREI: *(Embarrassed)* They won't be coming. You see, my sweet sister, Natasha says Bobik isn't feeling well, and so… to tell you the truth, I don't know, it makes no difference to me.

IRINA: *(Shrugging her shoulders)* Well, if Bobik isn't feeling well —

MASHA: We're finished! They're running us out of here, we've got to leave. *(To IRINA)* If Bobik isn't sick, then believe me, she is… Here! *(She taps her finger on her forehead)* Small town bitch!

> ANDREI exits through the right door to his own room, CHEBUTYKIN follows him; they bid farewell in the hall.

FEDOTIK: What a shame! I intended to spend the whole evening here, but if the little boy is sick, then, of course… But where can I go with a guitar…

RODAY: *(Loudly)* I took a long nap today on purpose, so I could dance all night. It's only nine o'clock, you know!

MASHA: Let's go outside, we can talk there. We'll decide what to do next.

> "Farewell! Have fun!" is heard. TUZENBAKH's happy laughter is heard. Everyone exits. ANFISA and the MAID clear the table, put out the lights. The NURSE can be heard singing. ANDREI in an overcoat and hat and CHEBUTYKIN quietly enter.

CHEBUTYKIN: I never had time to get married — whoosh, life just flew by — and the truth is I was always madly in love with your *matushka*, who was of course already married…

ANDREI: There's no reason to get married — it's boring.

CHEBUTYKIN: Yes, probably — but then there's loneliness… Whatever you want to say, loneliness is a terrible thing, my dear friend… However… what's the difference… it's all the same!

ANDREI: Let's hurry.

CHEBUTYKIN: What's the rush? We have time.

ANDREI: I'm afraid my wife will see me.

CHEBUTYKIN: Ah!

ANDREI: I won't play tonight. I'll just sit and watch. I'm feeling a little unwell… Ivan Romanych, what should I do for shortness of breath?

CHEBUTYKIN: How should I know! I don't remember, my dear friend. I don't know.

ANDREI: Let's go through the kitchen.

*They exit.*

*The doorbell, then another ring; voices are heard, laughter.*

IRINA: *(She enters)* Who's there?

ANFISA: *(In a whisper)* The carnival folks.

*Doorbell.*

IRINA: Tell them no one's home, *Nyanechka*. Tell them to forgive us.

*ANFISA exits. IRINA walks about the room thinking; she is agitated. SOLYONY enters.*

SOLYONY: *(Perplexed)* No one here... Where is everyone?

IRINA: They went home.

SOLYONY: Strange. You're alone?

IRINA: Yes, alone.

*Pause.*

Good night.

SOLYONY: Tonight I've been very tactless. But you aren't like the others, you're sublime and pure, you see the truth... You alone — only you alone — can understand me. I love you, deeply, love you endlessly...

IRINA: Good night! Please leave.

SOLYONY: I can't live without you. *(Going to her)* Oh, my bliss! *(On the verge of tears)* Oh, happiness! Splendid, magical, amazing eyes, I have never seen such eyes in a woman...

IRINA: *(Coldly)* Stop it, Vasilii Vasilych!

SOLYONY: This is the first time I can speak of my love for you — I know I must be out of my mind — on another planet. *(He rubs his forehead)* Well, it doesn't matter. You can't force someone to love you, of course... But I cannot have any rivals... can not... I swear to you by all that is holy, I will kill any rivals... Oh, you beautiful woman!

*NATASHA passes through with a candle.*

NATASHA: *(She looks in one door, in another and passes by the door leading to her husband's room)* Andrei's in there. I'll let him read. *Pardonnez moi*, Vasilii Vasilych, I didn't know you were here, I'm in my dressing gown.

SOLYONY: It makes no difference to me. Farewell! *(He exits)*

NATASHA: Oh, you're so tired, my poor, darling little girl! *(She kisses IRINA)* You ought to go to bed earlier.

IRINA: Is Bobik in bed?

NATASHA: Yes, in bed. But he's not sleeping well. By the way, darling, I wanted to tell you — since you're never home… Bobik's bedroom is cold and damp. But your room is so perfect for a child. Sweetie, please, move to Olya's room for a while!

IRINA: *(Not understanding)* Where?

*A troika with little bells is heard pulling up to the house.*

NATASHA: You and Olya will be in one room, so that Bobik will have your room. He's such a sweet boy. Today I said to him: "Bobik, you are mine! Mine!" And he looked at me with his dear little eyes.

*Bell.*

It must be Olga. She's so late!

*The MAID goes to NATASHA and whispers something in her ear.*

Protopopov? What a crazy man! Protopopov's here, he wants to take me for a ride in his *troika*. *(She laughs)* Men are so silly…

*Bell.*

Uh oh, someone else is here. Maybe I'll go for a little ride with him — maybe just fifteen minutes… *(To the MAID)* Tell him I'm coming.

*Bell.*

More people?… Oh, that must be Olga. *(She exits)*

*The MAID runs out; IRINA sits thinking; KULYGIN and OLGA enter, behind them, VERSHININ.*

KULYGIN: Well, for goodness sake. I thought you were having a party.

VERSHININ: That's funny. I left about a half hour ago — just a half hour ago — and they were waiting for the carnival people…

IRINA: Everyone left.

KULYGIN: Masha too? Where did she go? And why is Protopopov waiting downstairs in a *troika*? Who's he waiting for?

IRINA: Don't ask me… I'm tired.

KULYGIN: Well, Miss *Kapriznitsa* [moody]…

OLGA: The meeting just ended. I'm worn out. Our headmistress is sick, and I'm stuck taking her place. My head, oh my head hurts, my head… *(She sits)* Andrei lost two hundred rubles at cards yesterday… The whole town is talking about it…

KULYGIN: Yes, and I'm tired too from that meeting. *(He sits)*

VERSHININ: My wife took it into her head to give me a fright — she tried to poison herself. Everything turned out alright, and I'm fine now. I can relax… But it looks like we need to get out of here — yes? Well, permit me to wish you all the best. Fyodor Ilych, let's go somewhere! I can't go home, I can't… Let's go!

KULYGIN: No, I'm tired. I'm not going. *(He rises)* I'm tired. Did my wife go home?

IRINA: Probably.

KULYGIN: *(He kisses IRINA's hand)* Good night. Tomorrow and the day after I'll be able to rest all day. All the best! *(He goes)* I really wanted some tea. I counted on spending the evening in pleasant company and — *o, fallacem hominum spem!*… ["Oh, illusory human hope!"] Accusative case for exclamations…

VERSHININ: So that means I'll have to go alone. *(He exits behind KULYGIN, whistling)*

OLGA: My head hurts, oh my head... Andrei lost... everyone's talking... I'm going to lie down. *(She goes)* Tomorrow I'm free... Oh, my God, what a lovely thought! Tomorrow I'm free, the day after that I'm free... My head hurts, my head... *(She exits)*

IRINA: *(Alone)* Gone. They've all left.

*On the street an accordion, the NURSE sings a song.*

NATASHA: *(In a fur coat and hat she walks across the hall; her MAID trails behind her)* I'll be home in a half-hour. I'm only going for a little ride. *(She exits)*

IRINA: *(Alone, she is miserable)* Moscow! Moscow! Moscow!

CURTAIN.

# ACT III

*Two and one-half years later.*

*OLGA and IRINA's room. To the left and to the right are beds, screened off from one another. It's after two a.m. Offstage fire alarm bells sound. They've been ringing for a while. No one has gone to bed in the house. MASHA lies on the couch, clothed, as usual, in black.*

> *OLGA and ANFISA enter.*

ANFISA: Now, they're under the stairs... I said to them — "you're welcome to come upstairs, don't worry about it, it's all right to come upstairs" — they're crying, "Where's our *papasha*? God forbid he was burned up." Can you believe it! And in the courtyard there's someone walking around naked...

OLGA: *(She takes clothes from the closet)* Here take this grey one... And this one... The blouse too... And take this skirt, *Nyanechka*. My God, what's going on? I heard Kirsanovsky Street is completely in flames — Do you think it's true? Take this... And this... *(She throws clothes into ANFISA's arms)* The poor Vershinins had such a scare... Their house nearly burned. Let them stay the night with us... They mustn't go home... Everything of Fedotik's burned, all gone...

ANFISA: You should call Ferapont, Olyushka, I won't be able...

OLGA: *(Calls into the hallway)* Ferapont. No one's answering... *(At the door)* Come up here, anybody!

> *Through the open door a window is visible, red from the fire's glow; the fire brigade passing near the house is heard.*

Oh, this is so horrible! And so irritating!

> *FERAPONT enters.*

Here, bring these downstairs... Give them to the Kolotilin girls. And take this...

FERAPONT: At your service, Ma'am. In 1812 Moscow burned too. My Lord God! The French were surprised.

OLGA: Go, be off...

FERAPONT: At your service, Ma'am. *(He exits)*

OLGA: *Nyanechka*, sweetheart, give everything away. We don't need anything, give it all away, *Nyanechka*... I'm so tired, I can barely stand on my feet... The Vershinins can't go home... The girls can sleep in the parlor, Aleksander Ignatyevich can stay at the Baron's... Fedotik can also stay with the Baron, or let him stay with us — in the hallway... The doctor got drunk on purpose — so horribly drunk, so no one can stay with him. And put Vershinin's wife in the parlor.

ANFISA: *(Wearily)* Dear Olyushka, don't send me away! Please don't send me away!

OLGA: What are you talking about, *Nyanya*? No one is sending you away.

ANFISA: *(She lays her head on her chest)* Mine own, my precious darling, I work so hard, so hard... Just when I'm getting weaker, people say — go! Where will I go? Where? I'm eighty years old — nearly eighty-two...

OLGA: Sit for a minute, *Nyanechka*... You're tired, poor darling... *(She helps her to sit)* Rest, my dear. How pale you are!

   NATASHA *enters.*

NATASHA: Everyone's saying we need to establish a society for the fire victims as soon as possible. Why not? It's an excellent idea. Yes, let's face it, we need to help the poor, that's the responsibility of the rich. Bobik and Sophochka are fast asleep, as if nothing was happening. There are so many people everywhere, everywhere you go, the house is full. And there's influenza spreading in town. I'm afraid the children might catch it.

OLGA: *(Not listening to her)* You can't even see the fire from here. It's so peaceful...

NATASHA: Yes... I must look a mess. *(In front of the mirror)* They say I've put on weight... but it's not true! Not at all! Oops, Masha is sleeping. She was so tired, poor... *(Coldly to ANFISA)* Don't you dare sit in my presence! Get up! Get out of here!

*ANFISA exits; pause.*

And why you still keep that old woman — I just don't get it!

OLGA: *(Struck dumb)* Excuse me, I don't think I understand...

NATASHA: She doesn't do anything. She's a peasant, she should live in the village... You are spoiling her! I like order in a house! We must get rid of everything that's unnecessary. *(She strokes OLGA's cheek)* You poor thing, you're so tired! Our headmistress is tired! And when my Sophochka grows up and enters high school, I'll be afraid of you.

OLGA: I will not be headmistress.

NATASHA: You will be, Olyechka. It's decided.

OLGA: I'll refuse. I cannot... I don't have the strength... *(She drinks water)* You treated *Nyanya* so rudely just now... Pardon me, I simply can't bear that... I feel like I'm going to faint...

NATASHA: *(Anxiously)* Oh forgive me, Olya, forgive me... I don't want to distress you.

*MASHA rises, takes the pillow and exits, angry.*

OLGA: Please understand, my dear… perhaps you can't understand this, but we have been brought up to… I cannot bear such rudeness — I'm feeling faint… I'm simply falling apart!

NATASHA: Forgive me, forgive me… *(She kisses her)*

OLGA: Even the slightest discourtesy — any indelicately uttered word — upsets me…

NATASHA: I often say the wrong thing, it's true, but you have to agree, my sweet, she should live in the village.

OLGA: She has been with us for thirty years.

NATASHA: But you must see she can't work anymore! Either you really don't get this, or you don't want to get it. She can't work. All she does is sleep or sit.

OLGA: Then let her sit.

NATASHA: *(Astonished)* Let her sit? She's a servant! *(On the verge of tears)* I don't understand you, Olya. I have a nanny and a wet-nurse, a maid, a cook… why do we still need that old woman? Why?

*Offstage alarms sound.*

OLGA: I've aged ten years tonight.

NATASHA: We need to reach an agreement, Olya. Once and for all… You're at the high school, I'm at home — you are a scholar, I take care of this house. And if I say something about the servants, then I know what I am talking about; I know what I-am-talking-about… And I want that old woman out of here tomorrow… *(She stamps her feet)* That witch!… Don't you dare make me angry! Don't you dare! *(Regaining control of herself)* It's true, if you don't move downstairs, we'll always be fighting. It's just terrible.

*KULYGIN enters.*

KULYGIN: Where's Masha? It's time to go home. They say the fire is dying down. *(Stretching)* Only one block burned, but it was so windy, you know, and at first we were afraid the whole town would burn. *(He sits)* I'm tired. My dear Olyechka... I often think — if not for Masha, then I would've married you, Olyechka. You're so good... I'm exhausted. *(He listens)*

OLGA: What?

KULYGIN: And to add to our troubles, the doctor's drunk again — completely pie-eyed! *(He rises)* Uh oh, he's coming up here... Yes... Hear him? Yes... *(He laughs)* What a character! I'll give him a scare. *(He goes to the wardrobe in the corner)* What an idiot...

OLGA: For two years he was sober, and now suddenly he goes and gets drunk... *(She moves with NATASHA upstage)*

*CHEBUTYKIN enters.*

CHEBUTYKIN: *(Morosely)* The hell with them... all of them... They think just because I'm a doctor, I can treat any illness, but of course I know absolutely nothing, I've forgotten everything I knew, I remember absolutely nothing.

*OLGA and NATASHA, unnoticed by him, exit.*

The hell with them. Last Wednesday I treated a woman in Zasyp — she died, and I'm responsible — Yes... maybe I knew something twenty-five years ago, but now I remember nothing. Nothing... My head is absolutely empty, my heart is cold as ice. Maybe I'm not even a person — I only look like a person — I have arms and legs... and a head. But maybe, I don't really exist — maybe it only seems like I exist because I walk around, eat, sleep. *(He cries)* Oh, if only I didn't exist! *(He stops crying, morosely)* What the hell... The day before yesterday at the club, they were talking about Shakespeare, Voltaire... I never read them — absolutely never — but I pretended that I had. And everyone else did too. So vulgar! So dishonorable! And all I could think about was that woman who died on Wednesday. I couldn't stop thinking... and been haunted by her, and I felt so disgusting, so vile… So I left and had a drink…

*IRINA, VERSHININ, and TUZENBAKH enter; TUZENBAKH is wearing civilian clothes, new and fashionable.*

IRINA: Let's sit here. No one's going to come in here.

VERSHININ: If it weren't for the soldiers, the whole town would have burned. Such great work! *(He rubs his hands with pleasure)* Excellent men! Akh, a job well done!

KULYGIN: *(Walking up to him)* What time is it, sir?

TUZENBAKH: It's after three already. It's getting light.

IRINA: Everyone is just sitting in the hall, no one is leaving. And your Solyony is sitting there too… *(To CHEBUTYKIN)* Doctor, you should go to sleep.

CHEBUTYKIN: It's nothing, *Madame… Merci, Madame. (He combs his beard)*

KULYGIN: You've certainly had quite a bit to drink, Ivan Romanych! *(He claps him on the shoulder) In vino veritas*, as the ancients would say.

TUZENBAKH: Everyone is asking me to organize a concert to benefit the fire victims.

IRINA: Well, who's available…

TUZENBAKH: I think we can do it. For example, Maria Sergeyevna plays the piano beautifully.

KULYGIN: Beautifully!

IRINA: But she's completely forgotten. She hasn't played in three years… maybe four.

TUZENBAKH: There's no one in this town who understands music, not one soul — but I do. I understand it so well, and I promise you, Maria Sergeyevna plays splendidly, she's gifted.

KULYGIN: You're right, Baron. I love her very much, my Masha. She's a splendid girl.

TUZENBAKH: What must it be like to play so perfectly and at the same time to know that no one — no one — understands you!

KULYGIN: *(Sighs)* Yes… But would it be proper for her to take part in a concert?

*Pause.*

Of course, Ladies and Gentlemen, I don't know anything. Perhaps it would be good. Our headmaster is a good man, a wonderful man, and highly intelligent, and he has a number of strong opinions… Of course, it's none of his business, but all the same — if you'd like — I'll talk with him.

*CHEBUTYKIN takes a China clock in his hands and examines it.*

VERSHININ: I got so filthy at the fire — disgusting!

*Pause.*

Yesterday I happened to hear that our brigade is moving somewhere far away. Some say to *Tsarskoe Polskoye* [Tsarist Poland], some say east to China.

TUZENBAKH: I heard that too. Well? Then the town will be completely empty.

IRINA: And we'll leave!

CHEBUTYKIN: *(Drops the clock, which smashes)* Bye, bye…

*Pause; everyone is distressed and confused.*

KULYGIN: *(He picks up fragments)* To break such a precious object — akh, Ivan Romanych, Ivan Romanych! F-minus for conduct! You get an F-minus for conduct!

IRINA: That was Mama's clock.

CHEBUTYKIN: Maybe… mama's — so it was mama's. Maybe I didn't break it. Maybe it only looks like I broke it. Maybe, we only think we exist, but in fact we don't. I don't know anything, no one knows anything. *(Through the door)* Has anybody noticed? Natasha is having a little romance with Protopopov, but you don't see it… You sit there and see nothing, while Natasha's having a little romance with Protopopov… *(He sings)* "Here's a fig for you…" *(He exits)*

VERSHININ: Yes… *(He laughs)* This is all so strange!

*Pause.*

When the fire started, I ran home as fast as I could. When I got closer I could see — our home was safe and out of danger, but my two daughters were standing in the doorway — in their nightgowns — their mother nowhere to be seen — and people were running around, horses everywhere — and the girls were scared to death. I don't know — my heart broke when I saw those faces. My God, I thought, what agony is still ahead for these girls — for the rest of their lives! I grabbed them, and all I could think about was the agony ahead for them!

*Alarm bell; pause.*

I rushed them over here, and their mother was here, screaming, angry…

*MASHA enters with her pillow and sits on the couch.*

And when my daughters were standing in the doorway just in their nightgowns, barefoot, the street alight with fire, with terrible noise everywhere, then I remembered something that happened many years ago, when we were besieged by the enemy — they were pillaging and setting fires everywhere… and I suddenly realized there was no difference between then and now! But with a little time, some two-three hundred years from now, they will look at our lives with horror, or maybe they'll laugh at us — they'll see our lives as ridiculous and strange. Oh, what a life that will be, what a life! *(He laughs)* Forgive me, I'm philosophizing again. But permit me to continue, ladies and gentlemen. I'm in the mood for philosophy…

*Pause.*

It's as if we're all asleep. Yes, what a life it will be! Just try to picture it… there will be people like you in this town — in about three generations — the population growing, always growing — and the time will come when it'll be just as you fervently hoped for, when people will be so much better than we are… *(He laughs)* Today I'm in such a strange mood. I feel so wild. *(He sings)* "Whether old or young, we always surrender to love…" *[Lyubvi vse vozrasty pokorny, yeyoh poryvy blagotvorny…]* *(He laughs)*

MASHA: Tram-tam-tam…

VERSHININ: Tram-tam…

MASHA: Tra-ta-ta?

VERSHININ: Tra-ta-ta. *(He laughs)*

*Enter FEDOTIK.*

FEDOTIK: *(He dances)* Gone, gone! Everything's gone — wiped clean…

*Laughter.*

IRINA: Are you joking? Is everything burned?

FEDOTIK: *(He laughs)* Everything gone. Nothing's left. My guitar's burned, my photographs burned, and all of my letters… I wanted to give you a notebook — but it burned too.

*Enter SOLYONY.*

IRINA: No, please, leave, Vasilii Vasilych. You're not allowed in here.

SOLYONY: Why is the Baron allowed and I'm not?

VERSHININ: We must leave — really. How's the fire going?

SOLYONY: They say it's dying down. No, it's positively astounding to me that that Baron is allowed and I'm not — *(He takes a flask of perfume and sprinkles himself)*

VERSHININ: Tram-tam-tam.

MASHA: Tram-tam.

VERSHININ: *(He laughs, to SOLYONY)* Let's go downstairs.

SOLYONY: Very well, sir, but I will remember this. *(Looking at TUZENBAKH)* Tysp, tysp, tysp…

   He exits with VERSHININ and FEDOTIK.

IRINA: Solyony walked in and suddenly the room was filled with smoke… *(Bewildered)* The Baron is sleeping! Baron! Baron!

TUZENBAKH: *(Waking)* I'm so tired… The brick factory… I know I sound like I'm raving, but it's true — I'm starting work soon in the brick factory, work… I've already had an interview. *(Gently to IRINA)* You are so brilliant, beautiful, charming… I can feel your brilliance brightening the dark sky, like the sun… I know you're sad, you're dissatisfied with your life… But come away with me, let's work together!

MASHA: Nikolai Lvovich, get out of here.

TUZENBAKH: *(Laughing)* Are you here too? Really? I didn't see you. *(He kisses IRINA's hand)* Goodbye, I'm leaving… I look at you now, and I remember your twentieth birthday, when you were cheerful, happy, and we were talking about the joy of labor… Oh how happy I was! Where's it gone? *(He kisses her hand)* You have tears in your eyes. Go to sleep, it's almost light outside… morning is on its way… If only I could give my life for yours!

MASHA: Nikolai Lvovich, get out! That's enough…

TUZENBAKH: I'm leaving… *(He leaves)*

MASHA: *(She lies down)* Are you asleep, Fyodor?

KULYGIN: Huh?

MASHA: You should go home.

KULYGIN: My sweet Masha, my dear Masha…

IRINA: She's tired. Let her rest, Fyodya.

KULYGIN: I'll go now… My wife is good, splendid… I love you, my one and only…

MASHA: *(Angrily)* Amo, amas, amat, amamus, amatis, amant.

KULYGIN: *(He laughs)* No, isn't she marvelous! I've been married to you for seven years, but it feels like yesterday. My word of honor. No, it's true, you are a marvelous woman. I'm happy, I am happy!

MASHA: I'm sick to death of you, sick, sick… *(She sits up)* And I can't stop thinking about — such a disgraceful situation. Can't get it out of my head and I can't keep silent anymore. It's about Andrei… He's mortgaged our house to the bank, and his wife grabbed all the money, but you realize of course, this house doesn't belong just to him — it belongs to all four of us! He should know better — if there's an ounce of decency left in him.

KULYGIN: Why are you talking about this, Masha! What's it to you? Andryusha is in debt everywhere, God bless him.

MASHA: I don't care, it's a disgrace. *(She lies down)*

KULYGIN: We aren't poor. I work, I teach at the high school, then I give private lessons... I'm an honest man. Simple... *Omnia mea mecum porto*, as they say, "Everything of mine I carry with me".

MASHA: I don't need anything, it's the injustice that gets to me.

*Pause.*

Go home, Fyodor.

KULYGIN: *(He kisses her)* You're tired, rest for a half-hour, and I'll sit downstairs and wait. Sleep... *(He walks)* I'm happy, I'm happy, I'm completely happy. *(He exits)*

IRINA: Really, Andrei's become so shallow, so boring, so old — all from being around that woman! There was a time he was studying to be a professor, and only yesterday he was bragging about his new position in the local *zemstvo* council. He's a member of the council, and Protopopov is the chairman... Everyone in town is talking, laughing, and he's the only one who doesn't get it... While everyone was running around because of the fire, he was sitting by himself in his room and paying no attention whatsoever. He sits and plays the violin. *(Nervously)* Oh, it's so awful, it's just awful, awful! *(She cries)* I can't, I can't bear it any longer!... I can't!...

*OLGA enters, tidies up around her little table.*

*(Loudly sobs)* Oh, throw me out of here, just throw me out, I can't take it anymore...

OLGA: *(Frightened)* What's wrong, what's wrong? Darling...

IRINA: *(Sobbing)* Where? Where did my life go? Where is it? Oh, my God, my God! I've forgotten everything, I've forgotten... I feel so confused... I don't remember the Italian for window — or even ceiling... I'm forgetting everything, every day I forget more — and life is racing past me — I'll never get it back, never... we'll never go to Moscow... I can see that, we'll never go...

OLGA: Sweetheart, darling...

IRINA: *(Restraining herself)* Oh, I'm so unhappy... I can't really work, I can't stand to work. Enough! Enough! I wasted my life in the telegraph office, and now I work for the town council and I detest it — I hate everything they give me to do, I hate... I'm twenty-four years old already — I've been working a long time, but my brain has dried up, there's nothing left of it, I've become stupid, old, and nothing, nothing, nothing whatsoever feels good — time keeps passing and everyday I'm moving away from the life I imagined — always moving further and further, toward some dangerous edge. I'm in despair, I'm truly in despair! And why am I still alive? Why haven't I killed myself — I don't understand...

OLGA: Don't cry, my little girl, don't cry... You're making me so upset.

IRINA: I'm not crying, no, I'm not crying... Enough... See, I've stopped crying. Enough... Enough!

OLGA: Darling, I tell you as your sister, as your friend — if you want my advice, marry the Baron!

*IRINA quietly cries.*

You know you respect him, you value him highly... It's true, he's not handsome, but he's so decent, kind... You don't have to marry for love, but just out of duty. That's what I think — I would absolutely marry without love. I would marry anyone who asked me, it makes no difference, as long as he's a decent man. I would even marry an old man...

IRINA: I always thought we'd move to Moscow, and there I would meet my true love. I dreamed about him, loved him so... But it all turned out to be nonsense, everything — nonsense...

OLGA: *(She embraces her sister)* My sweet, wonderful sister, I understand everything; when Baron Nikolai Lvovich resigned from the military and came to see us in his civilian clothes, he looked so unattractive to me — I even began to cry... He asked me, "why are you crying?" How could I tell him! But if God wants you to marry him, I would be happy. And then everything would be so different — completely different.

*NATASHA, with a candle, walks across the stage from the right door to the left silently.*

MASHA: *(She sits)* Doesn't she look like she started the fire herself!

OLGA: Oh, Masha, you're so naughty. The naughtiest person in our family — that's you! I'm sorry, forgive me, please.

*Pause.*

MASHA: I want to confess to you, my dear sisters. My heart is bursting to tell.... I'll tell you and nobody else... I'll tell you this minute. *(Quietly)* Here's my secret — I have to tell you everything... I can't be silent anymore...

*Pause.*

I love — I love — I love that man... You just saw him... Well, there's no other way to put it, I love Vershinin...

OLGA: *(She goes behind her screen)* Stop it. I can't hear you anyway.

MASHA: What can I do? *(She clasps her head)* At first I thought he was so odd — I even felt sorry for him... but then I fell in love with him... I fell in love with his voice, his words, his sadness, his two little daughters...

OLGA: *(Behind the screen)* I can't hear you, so stop it! Whatever foolishness you're talking about, I can't hear any of it.

MASHA: Oh God, you're the strange one, Olya. I love him — ah but such is my fate. Such is my destiny... He loves me... It's terrible, isn't it?

I know it's terrible — *(She pulls IRINA by the arm, draws her to herself)* Oh, my sweet girl… don't worry, we'll get through this somehow — whatever life has in store for us… When you read about falling in love in some novel, it all seems so obvious and trite, but when it happens to you, you think no one has ever experienced this before, no one can possibly understand what you feel… My dear, sweet sisters… I've said it all — now I'll be quiet… Now I'll be like Gogol's madman… shhh… shhh…

*Enter ANDREI, behind him FERAPONT.*

ANDREI: *(Angrily)* What do you want? I don't understand.

FERAPONT: *(At the doors, impatiently)* Andrei Sergeyich, I've already told you ten times.

ANDREI: In the first place, I'm not Andrei Sergeyich to you, I'm Your Honor!

FERAPONT: The firemen, Your Honor, are asking permission to drive through the garden to the river. Otherwise they have to go far, way around — they're wasting time.

ANDREI: Fine. Tell them, it's fine.

*FERAPONT exits.*

I'm so tired. Where's Olga?

*OLGA appears behind the screen.*

I came to see you, give me the key to the cupboard, I lost mine. You have the little key.

*OLGA gives him the key silently. IRINA goes behind her screen; pause.*

Such a huge fire! But it's quiet now. God knows, Ferapont makes me angry — I said something stupid… Your Honor…

*Pause.*

Why are you so quiet, Olya?

*Pause.*

It's about time you put an end to this foolishness and stop this ridiculous pouting. Ah, Masha, you're here, Irina too — good — let's have this out, once and for all. What do you have against me? What?

OLGA: Stop it, Andryusha. We'll talk about it tomorrow. *(Agitated)* It's been an excruciating night!

ANDREI: *(He is very embarrassed)* Calm down. I'm completely calm myself. I'm asking you: what do you have against me? Tell me honestly.

*VERSHININ's voice: "Tram-tam-tam!"*

MASHA: *(She rises, loudly)* Tra-ta-ta! *(To OLGA)* Goodbye Olya, God be with you. *(She goes behind the screen, kisses IRINA)* Sleep well… Bye bye, Andrei. Leave them alone, they're exhausted… you'll "have it out" tomorrow… *(She exits)*

OLGA: Can't we put this off until tomorrow?… *(She goes behind her screen)* We've got to get some sleep.

ANDREI: I have something to say and then I'll leave. Now… First of all, you seem to have something against my wife, Natasha, and I've noticed this from our wedding day. If you want to know the truth, Natasha is a wonderful, honest person, true and noble — that's my opinion. I love and respect my wife, you understand, I respect her and demand that others respect her as well. I repeat, she is an honest, noble person, and all of your minor grievances, forgive me, are simply ridiculous. Old maids never love their sisters-in-law — that's a fact.

*Pause.*

Secondly, you seem to be angry because I'm not a professor, that I'm not a famous scholar. But I have a good job, I work in the *zemstvo*, I am a member of the *zemstvo* council and I count my service as sacred and important, just as important as scholarship. I am a member of the *zemstvo* council and I'm proud of that, if you want to know...

*Pause.*

Thirdly... Yes, I have more to say... Yes, I mortgaged the house, without your permission... I am guilty of this, yes, and I ask you to forgive me. I needed to do it because of some debts... in fact, thirty-five thousand... I no longer play cards, I gave it up a long time ago, but the main reason I can justify my own behavior, is because you are girls, you receive a military pension, but I don't have... any real earnings...

*Pause.*

KULYGIN: *(At the door)* Is Masha here? *(Anxiously)* Where is she? I can't find her... *(He exits)*

ANDREI: You aren't listening. Natasha is an outstanding, honest person. *(He walks around the room silently, then comes to a stop)* When I was first married, I thought we'd be happy... all of us happy... But my God... *(He weeps)* My sweet sisters, my dear sisters, don't believe me, don't believe... *(He exits)*

KULYGIN: *(At the door anxiously)* Where's Masha? Why isn't Masha here? This is very upsetting. *(Exits)*

*Alarm bell, the stage is empty.*

IRINA: *(Behind the screen)* Olya! Who's knocking on the floor?

OLGA: It's the doctor, Ivan Romanych. He's drunk.

IRINA: What an agonizing night!

*Pause.*

Olya! *(She glances from behind the screen)* Did you hear? They're taking the brigade away, they're moving somewhere far away.

OLGA: It's only a rumor.

IRINA: We're going to be left alone… Olya!

OLGA: Yes?

IRINA: Dearest Olya, dear, I respect the Baron, I really do. He's a fine man. I will marry him, yes, I will — only let's go to Moscow! I beg you, let's go! There's no place on earth better than Moscow! Let's go, Olya! Please, let's go!

    *CURTAIN.*

# ACT IV

*The old garden at the Prozorovs' home. A long spruce-lined path, at the end of which the river is visible. On the other side of the river is a forest. On the right side is the terrace; bottles and glasses are on the table; it is apparent they were just drinking champagne. Noon. From the road to the river across the garden passersby walk from time to time; five soldiers quickly cross.*

> *CHEBUTYKIN is in a good mood, which does not desert him in the course of the entire act. He sits in the armchair, in the garden, and waits for them to call him; he is in a peak-cap and with a cane. IRINA, KULYGIN with a decoration around his neck, without his moustache, and TUZENBAKH, standing on the terrace, see off FEDOTIK and RODAY, who are walking downstairs; both officers are in field uniform.*

TUZENBAKH: *(He kisses FEDOTIK)* You're a good man. We've gotten along so well together. *(He kisses RODAY)* Once again… Farewell, my friend!

IRINA: *Do svidanya* [Goodbye].

FEDOTIK: Not goodbye but farewell, we'll never see one another again!

KULYGIN: Who knows! *(He wipes his eyes, he smiles)* Don't, I'll be crying in a minute.

IRINA: We'll meet again sometime.

FEDOTIK: In ten — fifteen years? But then we'll hardly recognize one another, we'll greet one another as strangers… *(He takes a photograph)* Hold still… One more time, just one more, for the last time.

RODAY: *(He embraces TUZENBAKH)* We'll never see each other again… *(He kisses IRINA's hand)* Thank you for everything… for everything!

FEDOTIK: *(Vexed)* Don't move!

TUZENBAKH: Yes, yes, God willing, we'll see one another again. Write to us. Be sure to write.

RODAY: *(He shouts, looking around the garden)* Farewell, trees! *(He cries)* Hup-hup!

   Pause.

Farewell, echo!

KULYGIN: Who knows, maybe you'll get married in Poland… Your Polish wife will embrace you and say: "*kokhanye!*" [in Polish, "beloved"] *(He laughs)*

FEDOTIK: *(Looking at his watch)* Just an hour to go. Solyony's the only one from our battery going on the barge. We're going with the rest of the men. Three battery divisions are leaving today, and tomorrow three more — and then finally, peace and quiet will descend upon this town.

IRINA: Aleksei Petrovich, what happened yesterday near the theater? Tell me the truth.

FEDOTIK: Nothing happened.

IRINA: Word of honor?

FEDOTIK: Nothing… honestly, nothing… It'll all blow over…

RODAY: And where's Maria Sergeyevna?

KULYGIN: Masha's in the garden.

FEDOTIK: I'll say goodbye to her.

RODAY: Farewell, we better go or I'll start crying… *(He quickly embraces*

TUZENBAKH *and* KULYGIN, *he kisses* IRINA's *hand*) We had a splendid time here...

FEDOTIK: *(To* KULYGIN*)* This is for you to remember me by... a little book with a little pencil... We'll leave by the river...

*They walk away, both looking around.*

RODAY: *(He shouts)* Hup-hup!

KULYGIN: *(He shouts)* Farewell!

*Upstage* FEDOTIK *and* RODAY *meet* MASHA *and say goodbye to her; she exits with them.*

IRINA: They're gone... *(She sits on the lowest step of the terrace)*

CHEBUTYKIN: They forgot to say goodbye to me.

IRINA: What's the matter with you?

CHEBUTYKIN: And somehow I forgot to say goodbye to them. But I'll see them soon, I'll be gone tomorrow. Yes... just one little day remains. In a year I'll be retired, then I'll return here and I'll live out the rest of my life with you. Just one little year left until I get my pension... *(He puts a paper in his pocket, takes out another)* I'll come back to you and I'll turn my life around — you'll see — I'll be so quiet, so well-well-behaved, so decent...

IRINA: Yes, you need to turn your life around, dear one — you really do.

CHEBUTYKIN: Yes. I know. *(He quietly sings)* Tarara... bumbiya... sit in the dirt I may...

KULYGIN: You're simply incorrigible, Ivan Romanych! Incorrigible!

CHEBUTYKIN:  Too bad you weren't my teacher. I'd probably have turned over a new leaf already.

IRINA:  Fyodor shaved his moustache. I can't look at him!

KULYGIN:  Shhh…

CHEBUTYKIN:  Your wife won't be able to look at you. I should tell you what you look like, but I just can't.

KULYGIN:  Well! I like it — it's the *modus vivendi* [way to live]. Our headmaster shaved his moustache, so when I got promoted, I shaved mine. No one likes it, but it doesn't matter. I'm fine about it — with a moustache or without a moustache, I'm just fine… *(He sits)*

*Upstage ANDREI pushes a carriage with a sleeping child.*

IRINA:  Ivan Romanych, my dear, I feel so nervous. Tell me what happened yesterday in town.

CHEBUTYKIN:  What happened? Nothing. Silly stuff. *(He reads the paper)* It doesn't matter…

KULYGIN:  They're saying that Solyony and the Baron met yesterday in town near the theatre…

TUZENBAKH:  Stop! Please… *(He waves his hand and exits into the house)*

KULYGIN:  Near the theatre… Solyony began to pick on the Baron, and the Baron couldn't listen anymore so he said something offensive…

CHEBUTYKIN:  I don't know. It's all nonsense.

KULYGIN: In a seminar once, the teacher wrote "nonsense" on a student's essay, but the student thought it was a Latin word *"renixa"* — which of course, doesn't exist in Latin. *(He laughs)* So funny! They say

Solyony's in love with Irina and hates the Baron... I can understand it, Irina is a lovely girl. She's a lot like Masha, thoughtful in the same way. Only you, Irina, are a little softer. Though Masha has an excellent disposition too. I love my Masha.

*From the back of the garden: "Halloo! Hup-hup!"*

IRINA: *(She shudders)* I'm just so nervous and a little frightened today.

*Pause.*

Yes, I have everything ready. After lunch I'll send off my things. Tomorrow the Baron and I will be married and we'll leave for the brick factory, and the day after tomorrow, I'll start teaching. I'll begin a new life. God help me! When I passed the examination and became a teacher, I cried for joy — such bliss...

*Pause.*

Any minute the cart will arrive for my things...

KULYGIN: Be that as it may, but somehow I don't think you're being serious — just fanciful ideas — very little reality. Well anyway, I want to wish you the best of luck — from my heart.

CHEBUTYKIN: *(With tenderness)* My splendid, good... my precious girl... You're so far ahead of me, I can't catch up. You're leaving me behind like a bird who's too old to fly. My darling, you must fly with God!

*Pause.*

It was a mistake to shave off your moustache, Fyodor Ilyich.

KULYGIN: Quiet, please! *(He sighs)* The army is leaving today, and everything will go back to what it used to be. I don't care what they say, Masha is a good, honest woman, I love her very much and I am thankful to God every day for her. God's ways are unknowable to us... There's a man who works as a tax collector. Kozyrev is his name. I went to school with him, and he got expelled because he could never work out the declension of *ut consecutivum*. Now he's so poor, he's ill, and when we meet, I always say: "Hello there, *ut consecutivum*" — "yes," he says, "exactly, *ut consecutivum*"… and then he coughs. But I've been so lucky all my life, I'm happy, I've even received the Second Order of Stanislaus and now I'm teaching others *ut consecutivum*. Of course, I'm an intelligent person, more intelligent than most, but that doesn't necessarily make for happiness.

*In the house they are playing "The Maiden's Prayer."*

IRINA: Tomorrow night I won't be here to listen to "The Maiden's Prayer," and I won't have to run into Protopopov…

*Pause.*

Yes, Protopopov is sitting right there in the parlor; he's here again today…

KULYGIN: The headmistress still hasn't arrived?

*Upstage MASHA quietly enters, strolling.*

IRINA: No. They sent for her. If you only knew how hard it is for me to live here alone, without Olya… She lives at the high school because she's headmistress. All day long she's busy with work, and I'm alone, I'm bored, nothing to do, I hate my room… All right, I see I won't ever get to Moscow, all right, so be it. It's my fate. I won't get to do anything… Everything is God's will, that's the truth. Nikolai Lvovich proposed to me. Well? I thought about it and I decided — he's a good man, I mean it's unbelievable how good he is… And when I said yes, suddenly my heart felt lighter, I became more cheerful, my heart felt easier and once again I felt that urge to work, to work… But I just know something happened yesterday — I have a terrible feeling…

CHEBUTYKIN: *Renixa.* Nonsense!

NATASHA: *(At the window)* The headmistress!

KULYGIN: The headmistress has arrived. Let's go.

*He exits with IRINA into the house.*

CHEBUTYKIN: *(He reads the paper and quietly sings)* Tara-ra... bum-biya... sit in the dirt I may...

*MASHA approaches; upstage ANDREI pushes the carriage.*

MASHA: He sits there, he'll just sit and never get up...

CHEBUTYKIN: So what?

MASHA: *(She sits)* So nothing...

*Pause.*

Were you in love with my mother?

CHEBUTYKIN: Very much.

MASHA: And she?

CHEBUTYKIN: *(After a pause)* I don't remember anymore.

MASHA: Is my man here? Once our cook Marfa called her policeman: "my man." Is my man here?

CHEBUTYKIN: Not yet.

MASHA: When you get your happiness in fits and starts, in tiny little moments and then you lose it — as I'm doing right now — then you act vulgar and start saying awful things. *(She points to her chest)* I'm raging in here... *(Glancing at her brother ANDREI, who pushes the carriage)* Look at our Andrei, our brilliant brother... Now all our hopes are lost. A thousand men may work on a church bell and finally raise it up — with all their strength — but suddenly it falls and smashes — for no rhyme or reason, it smashes. That is what happened to our Andrei...

ANDREI: When will they finally shut up in the house? It's so noisy.

CHEBUTYKIN: Soon. *(He looks at his watch, then winds it; the watch chimes)* I have an old-fashioned watch, it strikes the hour… The first, second and fifth batteries will leave precisely at one.

   *Pause.*

And tomorrow I go.

ANDREI: For good?

CHEBUTYKIN: I don't know. Maybe I'll return in a year. Who cares… it doesn't matter…

   *Somewhere far away a harp and violin play.*

ANDREI: The city is emptying out. It's as if we've been covered by a big blanket.

   *Pause.*

Something happened near the theatre yesterday; everyone's talking about it, but I don't know anything.

CHEBUTYKIN: It's nothing. Stupidity. Solyony started to tease the Baron, and the Baron suddenly got angry and insulted Solyony — and so finally, Solyony felt he had to challenge the Baron to a duel. *(He looks at his watch)* And it just might be right now, I think… At twelve-thirty, in the State forest — there — you can see it from here, beyond the river… *(He makes a disparaging noise, then laughs)* Solyony imagines he's Lermontov — he even writes poetry. Now it's all very funny, but in truth he's fought three duels already.

MASHA: Who?

CHEBUTYKIN: Solyony.

MASHA: And the Baron?

CHEBUTYKIN: What about the Baron?

*Pause.*

MASHA: I feel so confused… In any case, this shouldn't be allowed. He could injure the Baron or even kill him.

CHEBUTYKIN: The Baron is a good man, but one Baron more or less — does it really matter? Believe me, it doesn't matter!

*Beyond the garden a shout: "Halloo! Hup-hup!"*

Hold on! That's Skvortsov shouting — the second. He's out there in a boat.

*Pause.*

ANDREI: In my opinion, to participate in a duel, or even attend one — even in the capacity of a doctor — is simply immoral.

CHEBUTYKIN: It just seems that way… There's really nothing here on earth, not even us, we don't exist, it just seems as if we exist… And it doesn't mean a thing!

MASHA: Talk, talk, talk — all day long… *(She walks)* You'll still be here talking when it starts to snow… *(She comes to a stop)* I can't go in the house, I can't go in there… When Vershinin comes, let me know… *(She walks along the path)* The birds are deserting us already… *(She looks up)* Swans? Geese?… You beautiful creatures… *(She exits)*

ANDREI: Our house is finally emptying out. The officers are leaving, you're leaving, my sister is getting married, and I'm left alone.

CHEBUTYKIN: What about your wife?

*FERAPONT enters with papers.*

ANDREI: My wife — is my wife. She's honest, respectable, nice, kind, but for all that there's something inside her that reduces her to a greedy, mean animal. I can't explain it — anyway, the truth is, you're the only person I can speak to like this — I love Natasha, that's true, but sometimes I think she's unbelievably vulgar. When I see that, I get confused, and I'm not sure how I ever fell in love with her…

CHEBUTYKIN: *(He rises)* I'm leaving tomorrow, my friend, maybe we'll never see each other again, so let me give you a piece of advice. Just put on your hat, pick up your cane and walk away… just keep on walking and don't look back. The further you get, the better.

> SOLYONY *walks upstage with two officers; seeing* CHEBUTYKIN, *he turns to him; the officers walk further.*

SOLYONY: Doctor, it's time! It's twelve-thirty already. *(He greets ANDREI)*

CHEBUTYKIN: One moment, please. I'm so tired of all of you. *(To ANDREI)* If someone asks for me, Andryusha, then tell them, I'll be back in a minute… *(He sighs)* Oh my God…

SOLYONY: "Before he knew what hit him, the bear bit him." *(He goes with him)* Why are you groaning, old man?

CHEBUTYKIN: Shut up!

SOLYONY: Are you sick?

CHEBUTYKIN: *(Angrily)* Go to hell!

SOLYONY: Don't worry, *dyedushka* — I'll just have a little fun — I'll just scratch him. *(He takes out perfume and splashes it on his hands)* Look, I've used up the whole flask, and they still smell. They smell like a corpse.

> Pause.

So, sir... Do you remember the poem? "But he, restless as a storm, seeks out the storm, as though in the storm there is peace..."

CHEBUTYKIN: Yes. "Before he knew what hit him, the bear bit him." (*He exits with SOLYONY*)

*Cries can be heard: "Hup! Halloo!" ANDREI and FERAPONT enter.*

FERAPONT: Papers to sign...

ANDREI: Leave me alone! Get out! Please! (*He exits with the carriage*)

FERAPONT: But you have to sign papers, what else are they for? You have to sign papers. (*He exits upstage*)

*Enter IRINA and TUZENBAKH in a straw hat, KULYGIN crosses the stage, crying: "Halloo, Masha, halloo!"*

TUZENBAKH: There's the only man in town who's happy that the army is leaving.

IRINA: I can understand that.

*Pause.*

The whole town is emptying out.

TUZENBAKH: Sweet girl, I'll be back in a minute.

IRINA: Where are you going?

TUZENBAKH: I need to go to town to say goodbye to my comrades.

IRINA: I don't believe you... Nikolai, why are you so distracted today?

*Pause.*

What happened yesterday near the theatre?

Three Sisters ♦ 307

TUZENBAKH: *(Impatient gesture)* I'll be back in an hour. *(He kisses her hand)* My beloved... *(He peers into her face)* It's been five years since I fell in love with you and I still can't get used to it. You get more beautiful every day. What lovely, beautiful hair! What eyes! I'll carry you off with me tomorrow, we'll work, we'll be rich, my every dream will be realized. You'll be happy. There's just one thing — just one — you don't love me!

IRINA: It's not in me — I'll be your wife, I'll be faithful, and obedient, but I don't feel love — what can I do! *(She cries)* I have never been in love in my life. Oh, I've dreamed of it, yes, I've dreamed of being in love... but for ages now, my heart has been like a precious piano — locked up with the key lost.

*Pause.*

You look so anxious.

TUZENBAKH: I didn't sleep last night. You know I've never been afraid of anything in my life, but that lost key tears my heart to pieces — I can't sleep because of it. Tell me something.

*Pause.*

Tell me something...

IRINA: What? What? Everything feels so mysterious around us — the old trees are so silent... *(She puts his head on her breast)*

TUZENBAKH: Tell me something.

IRINA: What, tell you — what?

TUZENBAKH: Something...

IRINA: Enough! Enough!

*Pause.*

TUZENBAKH: It's crazy how little things suddenly seem so important — suddenly for no reason at all. You try to laugh them off — as meaningless — and yet you can't seem to stop worrying about them. Oh, let's not talk about this! I'm happy. I feel as if I'm seeing these trees for the first time in my life — these spruces, maples, birches — and they're just standing there, waiting for me... What beautiful trees, and I want everything close to them to be beautiful too!

*Shout: "Halloo! Hup-hup!"*

I have to go, it's time... Oh, that tree is dead — but look how it sways in the wind along with the others. Yes, it seems to me, if I die, I'll still be part of this life. Goodbye, my sweet girl... *(He kisses her hand)* The papers you gave me are lying on my table, under the calendar.

IRINA: I'm going with you.

TUZENBAKH: No, no! *(He quickly goes, he comes to a stop on the path)* Irina!

IRINA: What?

TUZENBAKH: *(Not knowing what to say)* I didn't have any coffee today. Tell them to have some ready for me... *(He quickly exits)*

*IRINA stands thinking, then goes upstage and sits on a bench. ANDREI enters with the carriage, FERAPONT appears.*

FERAPONT: Andrei Sergeyich, these aren't my papers — they come from the council. I didn't make them up.

ANDREI: Oh, where's it gone? — where's my past? I used to be young, happy and smart. Does anybody remember when I used to dream beautiful dreams and think brilliant thoughts? When did we start being boring, grey, dull, lazy, indifferent, useless, unhappy... This town has been here for two hundred years, it has a hundred thousand people, and there's not one who's significant, not one passionate soul — past or present — not one erudite person, not one artist, not a single notable person to look up to or admire. They only eat, drink, sleep, then they die… and others are born and they also eat, drink, sleep — and just to keep themselves from dying of boredom, they add gossip, vodka and cards to their lives. They love to sue each other and the wives cheat on their husbands, but the husbands just sit there, pretending they don't see anything, or hear anything — and this goes on generation after generation until any spark from God is extinguished and they become like corpses — just as pitiful as their mothers and fathers… *(To FERAPONT, angrily)* What do you want?

FERAPONT: Huh? Papers to sign.

ANDREI: I'm sick of you.

FERAPONT: *(Offering the papers)* I heard the porter from the state house saying… he says in Petersburg this past winter it was two hundred degrees below freezing.

ANDREI: I hate the present — but when I think about the future, something seems possible to me! — There's a light in the distance and I have hope — I see it — my children and I will rid ourselves from this great heaviness, from vodka, from too much goose with cabbage, from endless naps after lunch, from this insidious idleness…

FERAPONT: Two thousand people froze to death it seems. The people, he said, were terrified. It was either in Petersburg or Moscow — I can't remember.

ANDREI: *(Enveloped with a tender feeling)* My dear, kind sisters, my wonderful sisters! *(On the verge of tears)* Masha, my sister…

NATASHA: *(By the window)* Who's so loud out there? Is that you, Andryusha? You'll wake Sophochka. *Il ne faut pas faire du bruit, la Sophie est dormée déjà. Vous êtes un ours. (Becoming angry)* If you must talk, put the baby somewhere else. Ferapont, take the master's carriage!

FERAPONT: Yes ma'am. *(He takes the carriage)*

ANDREI: *(Confused)* I'll be quiet.

NATASHA: *(Behind the window, caressing her son)* Bobik! Naughty Bobik! Bad Bobik!

ANDREI: *(Examining the papers)* Fine, I'll look at the papers, I'll sign what needs to be signed — then take them back to the council… *(He exits into the house, reading the papers; FERAPONT pushes the carriage)*

NATASHA: *(At the window)* Bobik, what's your mama's name? Sweetheart, sweet boy! And who's that? That's Auntie Olya. Say: hi, Auntie Olya!

> *Vagabond musicians, a man and girl, play on the violin and harp; VERSHININ, OLGA and ANFISA come out of the house and they listen for a minute in silence; IRINA approaches.*

OLGA: Everyone goes through our garden like it's a public walkway. *Nyanya*, give the musicians something…

ANFISA: *(Giving the musicians money)* God bless you, sweethearts. *(The musicians bow and exit)* Poor dears. If you have enough to eat, you don't have to play. *(To IRINA)* Hello, Irisha! *(She kisses her)* Akh, sweet girl, what a life I'm living! What a life! We live in the apartment the high school gives us — it's wonderful with Olyushka — God has provided me with a good old age. Sinner that I am, I've never lived so… The apartment is so big and I have a whole room to myself and a bed. Everything belongs to the state. I wake up at night and — oh, Lord, Mother of God, there couldn't be a happier person on earth!

VERSHININ: *(Looking at his watch)* We're leaving now, Olga Sergeyevna. It's time.

> *Pause.*

I wish you everything, everything… Where is Maria Sergeyevna?

IRINA: She's in the garden somewhere. I'll go look for her.

VERSHININ: Please. I'm in a hurry.

ANFISA: I'll go and look. *(She shouts)* Mashenka, halloo!

*She exits with IRINA into the garden upstage.*

Ha-lloo, ha-lloo!

VERSHININ: Everything must end. Here we are saying goodbye. *(He looks at his watch)* The town gave us a breakfast; we drank champagne, the mayor gave a speech and I ate and listened — but my heart was here, with you… *(He looks at the garden)* I have gotten so attached to you.

OLGA: Will we see each other again?

VERSHININ: Probably, not.

*Pause.*

My wife and my daughters will live on here for another two months; please, if something happens or they need something…

OLGA: Yes, yes, of course. Don't worry.

*Pause.*

Tomorrow there won't be one soldier left in town — it will all be like it never happened… And, of course, we'll begin a new life…

*Pause.*

It never turns out as we hoped, does it…. I didn't want to be headmistress and here I am, headmistress. We'll never get to Moscow…

VERSHININ: Well… Thank you for everything. Forgive me, if everything wasn't… I'm talking too much — forgive me. Remember me kindly.

OLGA: *(She wipes her eyes)* Where's Masha…

VERSHININ: Well what else can I tell you? What shall we talk about?… *(He laughs)* Life is so hard. It seems so vague and hopeless — but you have to agree that things will get better, more clear and maybe easier… I'm sure that it won't be too long before the purpose of life is completely apparent. *(He looks at his watch)* It's late, it's late. Human beings have always been engaged with war, filling up their entire existence with marches, invasions, victories. These days — no wars — so how do we fill our existence — we're empty — with nothing to fill our days. Of course we're passionately seeking a purpose, and we'll find it. Let's hope it happens soon!

*Pause.*

If only — you know — hard work and education would come together… *(He looks at his watch)* But it's time…

OLGA: Here she comes.

*MASHA enters.*

VERSHININ: I came to say goodbye…

*OLGA walks away a bit to the side, in order not to interfere with their parting.*

MASHA: *(She looks at him)* Farewell…

*Extended kiss.*

OLGA: Please, please…

*MASHA violently sobs.*

VERSHININ: Write me... Don't forget! Let me... it's time... Olga Sergeyevna, take her, it's time...I'm late... *(Moved, he kisses OLGA's hand, then embraces MASHA again and quickly exits)*

OLGA: Please, Masha! Stop, dear...

*Enter KULYGIN.*

KULYGIN: *(Embarrassed)* It's nothing, let her cry, let her... My good Masha, my kind Masha... You're my wife, and I'm happy no matter what... I won't complain, I won't scold you at all... Olga is my witness... We'll begin to live again as we did before, and I won't say a word to you, not a hint...

MASHA: *(Restraining sobs)* "At the sea, a green oak stands with a golden chain wound round..." I'm losing my mind... "At the sea..." "a green oak..."

OLGA: Calm down, Masha... Calm down... Give her some water.

MASHA: I'll stop...

KULYGIN: See, she's stopped... she's so good...

*A shot is heard from the remote distance.*

MASHA: "At the sea, a green oak stands with a golden chain wound round..." The chain is green... the oak is round... I'm confused... *(She drinks water)* Such a sad life... I'm fine now... I'm calm... Everything's fine... What does that mean — at the sea? Why is that poem stuck in my head? I feel so confused.

*IRINA enters.*

OLGA: Calm down, Masha — that's a good girl... Let's go to our room.

MASHA: *(Angrily)* I won't go in there. *(She sobs, but instantly stops herself)* I will no longer go in that house, I will not go...

IRINA: Let's sit here together for a minute, quietly. You know I'm leaving tomorrow…

*Pause.*

KULYGIN: Yesterday in my third-year class I took away this moustache and beard from a boy… *(He puts on the moustache and beard)* I look like the German teacher. *(He laughs)* True, huh? Boys are so silly.

MASHA: Yes, you look like the German…

OLGA: *(She laughs)* Yes.

*MASHA cries.*

IRINA: Come, Masha!

KULYGIN: Just like…

*NATASHA enters.*

NATASHA: *(To the MAID)* What? Mikhail Ivanych Protopopov will sit with Sophochka, and let Andrei Sergeyich wheel Bobik around. Children are so much trouble… *(To IRINA)* You're leaving tomorrow, Irina — such a pity. Stay a while — one more week. *(Seeing KULYGIN, she screams; he laughs and removes the moustache and beard)* Well you scared me to death! *(To IRINA)* I'm used to having you around — do you think I want to lose you? Yes, I'll put Andrei and his violin in your room — let him saw away in there! — and we'll put Sophochka in his room. Amazing, wonderful child! What a sweet little girl! Today she looked at me with those eyes of hers and said — "Mama"!

KULYGIN: Yes, a wonderful child, that's true.

NATASHA: Oh dear, tomorrow I'll be all alone here. *(She sighs)* The first thing I'll do is have those fir trees cut down, then that maple. It looks so horrible — ugly… *(To IRINA)* Sweetie, that belt doesn't really suit you… It's so *gauche*. You need something brighter. Yes, I'll put flowers everywhere — flowers — and it will smell so wonderful... *(Severely)* Why is that fork lying on the bench there? *(Going to the house, to the MAID)* I want to know why a fork is lying on the bench! *(She shouts)* Shut up!

KULYGIN: She's off and running again!

*Offstage march music plays; everyone listens.*

OLGA: They're leaving.

*Enter CHEBUTYKIN.*

MASHA: Our beautiful boys are leaving. Well, then... Happy journey to them! *(To her husband)* Let's go home... where's my hat and my...

KULYGIN: I put them in the house... I'll get them. *(He exits into the house)*

OLGA: Yes, we can go home now. It's time.

CHEBUTYKIN: Olga Sergeyevna!

OLGA: What?

*Pause.*

CHEBUTYKIN: Nothing... I don't know how to tell you... *(He whispers in her ear)*

OLGA: *(In fright)* It can't be!

CHEBUTYKIN: Yes... unbelievable... I'm tired, I'm worn out, I don't want to say another word... *(Vexedly)* It doesn't mean a thing...

MASHA: What happened?

OLGA: *(She embraces IRINA)* Today is so horrible... I don't know how to tell you, my dear...

IRINA: What? Tell me quickly: what? For God's sake! *(She cries)*

CHEBUTYKIN: The Baron was just killed in a duel.

IRINA: I knew it, I knew it…

CHEBUTYKIN: *(He takes a seat on a bench upstage)* I'm so tired… *(He takes a newspaper from his pocket)* Let them weep… *(He quietly sings)* Ta-ra-ra-bumbiya… sit in the dirt I may… It doesn't matter…

*The three sisters stand, holding one another.*

MASHA: Listen to the music! They're leaving us — we're alone — they're gone forever and we're alone. We must start over again — we have to go on living… We must live… Yes, we must…

IRINA: *(She puts her head on OLGA's breast)* There'll be a time when we'll understand why we had to suffer so much — all the mysteries will be revealed — but in the meantime, we have to live… work, only work! Tomorrow I'll go alone, I'll teach in that school and I'll devote my whole life to people who need me. It's fall already — winter will come soon, and everything will be covered with snow — but I'll work, I'll work…

OLGA: *(She embraces both her sisters)* The music is so happy, cheerful. Oh yes, I want to live! Oh, my God! The day will come when we're gone forever too — and they'll have forgotten us — our faces, our voices — all forgotten — and they won't even remember there were three of us — but what we suffered will become joy for them — for all those who live after us. Happiness and peace will at last come to the earth, and they'll speak well of us and bless those of us who are living now. Oh, sweet sisters, our life is not finished yet. We'll live! The music is so happy, so joyous, and I can imagine that in just a moment more, we'll know why we're living, why we're suffering… If we only knew, if we only knew!

*The music grows more distant; KULYGIN, happy, smiling, carries MASHA's hat and wrap. ANDREI pushes another carriage, with BOBIK sitting in it.*

CHEBUTYKIN: *(He sings quietly)* Tara... ra... bumbiya... sit in the dirt I may... *(He reads the paper)* It doesn't mean a thing — not a thing...

OLGA: If we only knew — if we only knew...

*CURTAIN.*

# *The Cherry Orchard*

A Comedy in Four Acts

(1904)

# CHARACTERS

**Leonid Andreyevich Gayev (Lyonya),** owner of the cherry orchard.

**Lyubov Andreyevna Ranevskaya,** his sister and co-owner of the cherry orchard.

**Anya,** her daughter.

**Varvara Mikhailovna (Varya),** her adopted daughter.

**Yermolai Alekseyevich Lopakhin,** a rich businessman.

**Pyotr Sergeyevich Trofimov (Petya),** a student.

**Charlotta Ivanovna,** Anya's governess.

**Boris Simyonov-Pischik,** a neighbor.

**Firs,** head butler.

**Semyon Panteleyevich Yepikhodov,** a clerk.

**Yasha,** Lyubov's valet.

**Avdotya Fyodorovna (Dunyasha),** a maid.

**A Passerby.**

**A Stationmaster.**

**A Postal Clerk.**

**Guests, Servants.**

*The action takes place on L.A. Ranevskaya's estate.*

# ACT I

*A room, which has always been called the nursery. One of the doors leads to ANYA's room. It is dawn, the sun will rise soon. It is already May, the cherry trees are blossoming, but it is cold with early morning frost in the orchard. The windows in the room are closed.*

*DUNYASHA enters with a candle and LOPAKHIN is seated with a book in his hand. There is the faint sound of the train in the distance.*

LOPAKHIN: There's the train, thank God. What time is it?

DUNYASHA: It's almost two. *(She puts the candle out)* It's light already.

LOPAKHIN: How late was the train? Two hours at least. *(He yawns and stretches)* What an idiot I am! I came here just to meet them at the station and phffft — fell asleep… Asleep — sitting up! Damn it. You could have woken me up.

DUNYASHA: I thought you had gone. *(Listening)* Listen, I think I hear them coming.

LOPAKHIN: *(Listening)* No… they have to get the baggage, and so on…

*Pause.*

Lyubov Andreyevna has lived abroad for five years, I'm not sure what she's like anymore. She's a good person — no airs, easygoing — a simple person, really. I remember, when I was a kid of fifteen, my father punched me in the face with his fist — blood was running from my nose… He was drunk, as usual, and we came here to the house for something. Lyubov Andreyevna, I can just see her now, so young, so slender — she brought me up to the wash-stand, here in the nursery, in this very room. She said, "Don't cry, little peasant, it will heal in time for your wedding…"

*Pause.*

Little peasant… It's true, my father was a peasant and here I am in a white waistcoat, in fancy shoes — a pig in a parlor… Only I'm rich, I have a lot of money, but if you think about it, really look at it, who am I kidding, a peasant is always a peasant… *(He leafs through a book)* I was reading this book and I didn't understand a single word. Reading, fell asleep…

*Pause.*

DUNYASHA: The dogs didn't sleep all night, they sense their masters are coming home.

LOPAKHIN: What's the matter with you, Dunyasha…

DUNYASHA: My hands are shaking. I am going to faint.

LOPAKHIN: You are so dainty these days, Dunyasha. You dress like a grand lady, and your hair style, too. It's not right. You have to know your place.

*YEPIKHODOV enters with a bouquet; he is in a suit jacket and brightly polished boots, which squeak loudly; entering, he drops the bouquet.*

YEPIKHODOV: *(Picks up the bouquet)* Here, the gardener sent these, he says to put them in the dining room. *(He gives DUNYASHA the bouquet)*

LOPAKHIN: And bring me some *kvass*.

DUNYASHA: Yes, sir. *(She exits)*

YEPIKHODOV: Now it's dawn, it's three degrees below zero, and the cherry trees are all in bloom. I cannot approve of our climate. *(He sighs)* I cannot. Strictly speaking, our climate is not conducive to temperance. And, Yermolai Alekseyevich, permit me to add, I bought myself these boots three days ago, but, I assure you, they squeak so, that there is absolutely no possibility whatsoever — What should I grease them with?

LOPAKHIN: Leave me alone. I'm sick of you.

YEPIKHODOV: Every day some kind of terrible misfortune happens to me. I do not complain, I am accustomed to it. I even smile.

*DUNYASHA enters, hands LOPAKHIN kvass.*

I am going. *(He stumbles into a chair, which falls)* There... *(As if triumphantly)* There you see, pardon the expression, absolutely no possibility whatsoever, nothing to be done... *(He exits)*

DUNYASHA: Yermolai Alekseyevich, I must confess to you, Yepikhodov proposed to me.

LOPAKHIN: Ah!

DUNYASHA: I don't even know how... He's so shy, only sometimes he begins to talk and you can't understand a word he says. It's kind of romantic, only I just don't get what he's saying... I kind of like him. He loves me madly. But he is an unlucky person, every day there is something. We even tease him: "a disaster waiting to happen"...

LOPAKHIN: *(Listening)* Ah, I think I hear them coming.

DUNYASHA: They're coming! What is wrong with me... I'm cold all over.

LOPAKHIN: They are coming, yes sirree. Let's go meet them. Will she recognize me? We haven't seen each other in five years.

DUNYASHA: *(Agitated)* I am going to faint now... Oh, I am going to faint!

*There is a sound of two carriages driving up to the house. LOPAKHIN and DUNYASHA quickly exit. The stage is empty. Noise begins to emerge from the neighboring rooms. FIRS, having gone to meet LYUBOV ANDREYEVNA at the station, hastily crosses the stage, leaning on a cane; he is wearing antique livery and a top hat; he is muttering to himself, but it is impossible to make out a word. The noise offstage intensifies. A voice: "Let's go through here..." LYUBOV ANDREYEVNA, ANYA and CHARLOTTA IVANOVNA with a little dog on a leash. They wear traveling clothes.*

*VARYA is in an overcoat and kerchief, GAYEV, SIMYONOV-PISCHIK, LOPAKHIN, DUNYASHA with a bundle and umbrella, SERVANTS with luggage — everyone walks across the room.*

ANYA: Let's go in here. Mama, do you remember which room this is?

LYUBOV ANDREYEVNA: *(Joyfully, on the verge of tears)* The nursery!

VARYA: It is so cold, my hands are numb. *(To LYUBOV ANDREYEVNA)* Your rooms, the white one and the violet one, have remained just the same, *Mamochka.*

LYUBOV ANDREYEVNA: The nursery, my dear, wonderful room... I slept here, when I was a child... *(She cries)* And right now I am a child again... *(She kisses her brother, VARYA, then her brother again)* And Varya looks just the same — like a nun. And I recognize Dunyasha... *(She kisses DUNYASHA)*

GAYEV: The train was two hours late. Is that a way to run things?

CHARLOTTA: *(To PISCHIK)* My dog even eats nuts.

PISCHIK: *(Astonished)* What a world!

*Everyone exits, except ANYA and DUNYASHA.*

DUNYASHA: We've been waiting for you forever... *(She removes ANYA's overcoat and hat)*

ANYA: I didn't sleep on the journey for four nights... now I'm freezing.

DUNYASHA: You left during Lent. There was snow then. It was so cold. And now? My darling! *(She laughs, kisses her)* I waited for you forever, my joy, my light… I will tell you now, I can't hold it in a minute longer…

ANYA: *(Limply)* Here we go again…

DUNYASHA: The clerk Yepikhodov proposed to me after Easter.

ANYA: That's all you ever think about. *(Fixing her hair)* I've lost all of my hair-pins… *(She is so weary, she even staggers)*

DUNYASHA: I don't know what to think. He loves me, he loves me so!

ANYA: *(Glances toward her door, tenderly)* My room, my windows, it's as if I never left. I am home! Tomorrow morning I'll wake up and run to the orchard… Oh, if only I could fall asleep! I didn't sleep the whole way, I was so worried.

DUNYASHA: Pyotr Sergeyevich arrived three days ago.

ANYA: *(Joyfully)* Petya!

DUNYASHA: He is sleeping in the shed, he's living there. "I am afraid," he says, "of being in the way." *(Casting a glance at her pocket watch)* Someone needs to wake him, but Varvara Mikhailovna has forbidden it. "You," she says, "do not wake him."

*VARYA enters, she has a bunch of keys on her belt.*

VARYA: Dunyasha, coffee quickly… Mamochka is asking for coffee...

DUNYASHA: This minute. *(Exits)*

VARYA: Well, thank God, you have come. You're home again. *(Caressing her)* My darling has come back! My beauty has come home!

ANYA: I've been through so much.

VARYA: I can imagine!

ANYA: We left during Holy Week, it was cold then. Charlotta talked the whole way, doing magic tricks. Why did you stick me with Charlotta?

VARYA: You couldn't possibly travel all alone, darling. At seventeen!

ANYA: We arrived in Paris, it was cold there too, snowing. My French is terrible. Mama was living on the fifth floor. I came in and her apartment was filled with French people, ladies and an old priest with religious pamphlets, and it was smoky, so depressing. I suddenly began to feel sorry for Mama, so sorry, I held her in my arms and couldn't let go. Mama was holding me tight too, she was crying…

VARYA: *(On the verge of tears)* Don't say anything, nothing…

ANYA: She had already sold her villa near Mentone, and she had nothing left, nothing. I had no *rubles* left either, only enough to make it back home. And Mama doesn't understand! We would sit in the train station to eat lunch, and she would order the most expensive thing and give the waiter a whole *ruble*. Charlotta too. And Yasha would order something expensive for himself. It was so dreadful. You know Mama's lackey, Yasha, we brought him here…

VARYA: I've seen the scoundrel.

ANYA: Well, how is it here? Did you pay the interest?

VARYA: With what?

ANYA: Oh, my God, my God.

VARYA: The estate will be put up for sale in August…

ANYA: My God…

LOPAKHIN: *(Peeks in the door and bleats)* Baaaaaa... *(Exits)*

VARYA: *(On the verge of tears)* This is what I would like to give him... *(Shakes her fist)*

ANYA: *(Embracing VARYA, quietly)* Varya, did he propose? *(VARYA shakes her head no)* He does love you... Why don't the two of you talk it over, what are you waiting for?

VARYA: I don't think anything will come of it. He is so busy all the time, he doesn't care about me... God bless him... it's very difficult for me to see him... Everyone talks about our wedding, everyone congratulates us, but in fact, there is nothing to it. It's like my worst nightmare... *(In a different tone)* You have a brooch in the shape of a little bee.

ANYA: *(Mournfully)* Mama bought it. *(She goes toward her room and speaks happily, like a child)* And in Paris I flew in a balloon!

VARYA: My darling has arrived! My beauty has come home!

    *DUNYASHA has returned with a coffee pot and is brewing coffee.*

VARYA: *(Standing by the door)* I work all day long, darling, doing housework and I'm always daydreaming. If we could marry you to a rich man, then I wouldn't worry, I would go to a monastery, then to Kiev... to Moscow, go from one holy place to the next. I would walk and walk. The bliss!

ANYA: The birds are singing in the orchard. What time is it now?

VARYA: It must be nearly three. It's time for you to sleep, darling. *(Entering ANYA's room)* The bliss!

    *YASHA enters with a traveling rug and traveling bag.*

YASHA: *(He crosses the stage, delicately)* May I pass through here?

DUNYASHA: I didn't recognize you, Yasha. My, how you have changed since you've been abroad.

YASHA: Hm… And who are you?

DUNYASHA: When you left, I was this tall… *(She indicates a height from the floor)* Dunyasha, Fyodor Kozoyedov's daughter. Don't you remember?

YASHA: Hm… What a peach! *(He glances around and embraces her; she screams and drops a saucer. YASHA quickly exits)*

VARYA: *(In the doorway, annoyed)* What is going on in here?

DUNYASHA: *(On the verge of tears)* I broke a saucer…

VARYA: That's good luck.

ANYA: *(Entering from her room)* We must warn mama that Petya is here…

VARYA: I left instructions that he not be woken up.

ANYA: *(Pensively)* Six years ago father died, a month later my brother Grisha drowned in the river, a beautiful seven-year-old boy. Mama couldn't endure it, she left, she left without looking back… *(She shudders)* If only she knew how well I understand her!

*Pause.*

And Petya Trofimov was Grisha's tutor, he will remind her…

*FIRS enters, he is in a jacket and white waistcoat.*

FIRS: *(He goes to the coffeepot, concerned)* The mistress will have her coffee here… *(He puts on white gloves)* Is the coffee ready? *(Sternly to DUNYASHA)* You! The cream?

DUNYASHA: Oh, my God… *(She exits quickly)*

FIRS: *(He busies himself around the coffee pot)* Ekh you, nincompoop… *(He mutters to himself)* They came back from Paris… And the master used to go to Paris… in a horse and buggy… *(He laughs)*

VARYA: Firs, what are you going on about?

FIRS: What can I do for you? *(Joyfully)* My lady has come back! I was waiting! Now I can die… *(He weeps from joy)*

> LYUBOV ANDREYEVNA, GAYEV, LOPAKHIN and SIMYONOV-PISCHIK *enter.*
>
> GAYEV, *entering, moving about as though he were playing billiards.*

LYUBOV ANDREYEVNA: How does it go? Let me remember… Yellow to the corner! Bank shot to the center!

GAYEV: I cut to the corner! At one time, sweet sister, we slept in this very room, and now I am fifty-one years old. Isn't it strange…

LOPAKHIN: Yes, time flies.

GAYEV: What?

LOPAKHIN: I said, time flies.

GAYEV: It smells like patchouli in here.

ANYA: I'm going to sleep. *Bonne nuit, Maman.* *(Kisses her mother)*

LYUBOV ANDREYEVNA: My beloved baby. *(She kisses her hands)* Are you glad to be home? I just can't believe it.

ANYA: Good night, Uncle.

GAYEV: *(Kisses her face, hands)* God be with you. You look just like your mother! *(To his sister)* Lyuba, you looked the same at her age.

> ANYA *offers her hand to* LOPAKHIN *and* PISCHIK, *exits and closes her door.*

LYUBOV ANDREYEVNA: She's so exhausted.

PISCHIK: I imagine the journey must have been long.

VARYA: *(To LOPAKHIN and PISCHIK)* Well then, gentlemen, it is three o'clock in the morning, time to go.

LYUBOV ANDREYEVNA: *(Laughing)* You are just the same, Varya. *(Draws her close and kisses her)* I will finish my coffee, then we will all go to bed.

> FIRS *places a cushion under her feet.*

Thank you, my dear. I've become quite addicted to coffee. I drink it day and night. Thank you, my dear old man. *(She kisses FIRS)*

VARYA: I'll check to see whether they've brought all of the luggage… *(She exits)*

LYUBOV ANDREYEVNA: Am I really sitting here? *(She laughs)* I want to jump up and swing my arms around. *(She covers her face with her hands)* This can't be real! God knows, I love my country, I love it tenderly. I couldn't see out of the train window, I was crying the whole time. *(On the verge of tears)* But now I must drink my coffee. Thank you, Firs, thank you my dear old man. I am so happy that you are still alive.

FIRS: The day before yesterday.

GAYEV: He doesn't hear well.

LOPAKHIN: I have to go to Kharkov at five this morning. Damn it! I wanted to see you, to have a talk… You are as splendid as ever.

PISCHIK: *(He has difficulty breathing)* She's even prettier... Dresses like a Parisian... I'm simply bowled over by her.

LOPAKHIN: Your brother here, Leonid Andreyich, says to me that I am a boor, I am a *kulak*, but it doesn't matter to me. Let him talk. I only want you to trust me like before, that your sweet, kind eyes will look on me as before. Merciful God! My father was a serf who belonged to your father and your grandfather, but you have done so much for me that I have forgotten all that and I love you, like family... more than family.

LYUBOV ANDREYEVNA: I cannot sit still, not the way I feel... *(She leaps up and walks around agitatedly)* I cannot bear this joy... You ought to laugh at me, I'm ridiculous... My dear little bookcase... *(She kisses the bookcase)* My little table.

GAYEV: Nanny died while you were away.

LYUBOV ANDREYEVNA: *(She sits and drinks coffee)* Yes, God rest her soul. They wrote me.

GAYEV: And Anastasii died. Cross-eyed Petrushka left us and lives in town and works for a policeman. *(He takes a box of fruit-drops from his pocket, sucks on one)*

PISCHIK: My little daughter, Dashenka... sends her regards...

LOPAKHIN: I have something to tell you, some very good news. *(Glances at his watch)* I must go now, there's no time to talk... Well, two or three words. You all know very well your cherry orchard is going to be sold to pay your debts. The auction is scheduled for August 22. But don't worry, my dear, sleep peacefully, there is a way out... Here is my plan. Attention, Ladies and Gentlemen! Your estate is only fifteen miles from town, the railroad runs nearby, and if the cherry orchard and the land by the river were cut up into lots then rented for summer houses, you'd have at least twenty-five thousand a year income.

GAYEV: Pardon me, what nonsense!

LYUBOV ANDREYEVNA: I don't quite understand you, Yermolai Alekseyich.

LOPAKHIN: With the summer houses you would make at least twenty-five *rubles* a year per lot, and if you advertise it now, I'll bet you anything that by autumn you won't have one vacant lot left, everything will be taken. In other words, congratulations, you are saved. It's a marvelous location, the river is deep. Only, of course, it'll be necessary to clear everything out... for example, let's say, take down all the old buildings, this house here that is really no good for anything anymore, chop down the old cherry orchard...

LYUBOV ANDREYEVNA: Chop down? My sweet, forgive me, you don't understand anything. Our cherry orchard is the only interesting, even remarkable thing in this entire province.

LOPAKHIN: This orchard is only remarkable because it's very large. There's a crop of cherries once every two years, and then there's nothing to do with them, no one buys them.

GAYEV: This orchard is mentioned in the *encyclopedia*.

LOPAKHIN: *(Glancing at his watch)* If we don't think about this and come up with a solution, on August 22 the cherry orchard and all of your estate will be sold at auction. You must decide! There is no other way out, I swear to you. Absolutely none.

FIRS: In the old days, forty — fifty years ago, we used to dry the cherries, and we soaked them, marinated them, made preserves, and we used to...

GAYEV: Be quiet, Firs.

FIRS: And we used to send cartfuls of dried cherries to Moscow and Kharkov. The money came pouring in! And the cherries back then were mild, juicy, sweet, fragrant... we knew the recipe...

LYUBOV ANDREYEVNA: And where is that recipe now?

FIRS: Forgotten. No one remembers.

PISCHIK: *(To LYUBOV ANDREYEVNA)* What about Paris? How was it? Did you eat frogs?

LYUBOV ANDREYEVNA: I ate crocodiles.

PISCHIK: What a world!

LOPAKHIN: Until now in the country there've only been masters and peasants, but now summer cottages are appearing. All the towns, even the small ones, are flooded with vacationers. And I think in twenty years, they will be here in extraordinary numbers. Now they just drink tea on their balconies, but one day they may take up cultivating their own piece of land, and then your cherry orchard will be a happy, rich, prosperous…

GAYEV: *(Indignantly)* What nonsense!

   *VARYA and YASHA enter.*

VARYA: Mamochka, you have two telegrams. *(She takes out a key and unlocks the old bookcase)* Here they are.

LYUBOV ANDREYEVNA: They are from Paris. *(She tears up the telegrams, unread)* I am through with Paris…

GAYEV: Lyuba, do you know how old this bookcase is? A week ago I pulled out the bottom drawer and there were numbers branded into it. The bookcase was made exactly one hundred years ago. How about that? We could celebrate its jubilee. It is an inanimate object, but all the same, it is a bookcase.

PISCHIK: *(Amazed)* One hundred years… What a world!

GAYEV: Yes… That is something… *(Touching the bookcase)* Dear, respected bookcase! I salute your existence, the more than one hundred years in which you have been faithful to the radiant ideals of truth and justice; your unspoken appeal to fruitful labor did not weaken in the course of a hundred years, inspiring *(On the verge of tears)* optimism in generations of our family, faith in a better future and cultivating in us the ideals of goodness and social awareness.

*Pause.*

LOPAKHIN: Yes…

LYUBOV ANDREYEVNA: You are just the same, Lyonya.

GAYEV: *(A little confused)* Off the right ball to the corner! I cut to the middle!

LOPAKHIN: *(Glancing at his watch)* Well, it's time for me to go.

YASHA: *(He gives LYUBOV ANDREYEVNA medicine)* Perhaps you will take your pills now…

PISCHIK: You shouldn't take medications, dearest lady… there is neither harm nor benefit from them… hand them to me, please… much respected one. *(He takes the pills, empties them into his palm, blows on them, places them in his mouth and washes them down with kvass)* There!

LYUBOV ANDREYEVNA: *(Alarmed)* You have lost your mind!

PISCHIK: I swallowed all the pills.

LOPAKHIN: Greedy!

  *All laugh.*

FIRS: His Honor stayed with us during Holy Week, he ate half a bucket of pickles… *(He mutters)*

LYUBOV ANDREYEVNA: What is he saying?

VARYA: He's been muttering for three years now. We are used to it.

YASHA: Old age.

*CHARLOTTA IVANOVNA crosses the stage in a white dress, very thin, tightly laced, with a lorgnette strung from her waist.*

LOPAKHIN: Pardon me, Charlotta Ivanovna, I have not yet had the chance to greet you. *(He tries to kiss her hand)*

CHARLOTTA: *(Taking her hand away)* If I permit you to kiss my hand, then you will want the elbow, then the shoulder…

LOPAKHIN: I have no luck today.

*All laugh.*

Charlotta Ivanovna, show us a trick!

LYUBOV ANDREYEVNA: Yes, Charlotta, show us a trick!

CHARLOTTA: Not now. I wish to sleep. *(She exits)*

LOPAKHIN: I will see you in three weeks. *(He kisses LYUBOV ANDREYEVNA's hand)* Goodbye for now. It's time to go. *(To GAYEV)* See ya soon. *(He kisses PISCHIK, offers his hand to VARYA, then to FIRS and YASHA)* I don't want to leave. *(To LYUBOV ANDREYEVNA)* If you think about the cottages and decide, then let me know, I will lend you fifty thousand. Think about it seriously.

VARYA: *(Angrily)* Would you just leave!

LOPAKHIN: I'm leaving, I'm leaving… *(He leaves)*

GAYEV: *Kulak*. Oh, excuse me… Varya is going to marry him, he's Varya's sweetheart.

VARYA : Don't talk nonsense, Uncle.

LYUBOV ANDREYEVNA: What is wrong, Varya? I would be very happy, he is a good man.

PISCHIK: The man — to be frank — is worthy… And my Dashenka… also says, that… she says many various things. *(He starts to snore, but immediately wakes up)* But nevertheless, much respected one, lend me… a loan of two-hundred-forty *rubles*… to pay interest on my mortgage tomorrow.

VARYA: *(Alarmed)* Nothing, nothing!

LYUBOV ANDREYEVNA: I have nothing, nothing.

PISCHIK: It will turn up. *(He laughs)* I never lose hope. There I was thinking, all was *kaput*, but on the contrary — lo and behold, the railroad passed through my land, and… they paid me. Any day now, something else will turn up… Dashenka will win two hundred thousand… she bought a lottery ticket.

LYUBOV ANDREYEVNA: The coffee is finished, we can go to bed.

FIRS: *(Brushes GAYEV, instructively)* You put on the wrong trousers again. What am I going to do with you!

VARYA: *(Quietly)* Anya is sleeping. *(Quietly opens the window)* The sun is coming up, it's not cold. Look Mamochka: what wonderful trees! My God, the air! The starlings are singing!

GAYEV: *(Opens the other window)* The orchard is all white. You have not forgotten, Lyuba? There is that long path that runs straight, straight, just like a silver ribbon. It shines on moonlit nights. Do you remember? You haven't forgotten?

LYUBOV ANDREYEVNA: *(Gazes out the window at the orchard)* Oh, my childhood, my innocence! I used to sleep in this nursery, I would look out at the orchard, feeling happy every morning, and it is exactly the same, nothing has changed. *(She laughs from joy)* All, all white! Oh, my orchard! After every dark, foul autumn and cold winter, you are young, full of happiness, the heavenly angels have not abandoned you… If only I could let go of this heavy burden from my heart, if only I could let go of my past!

GAYEV: Yes, and now they want to sell the orchard to pay our debts. It is so strange.

LYUBOV ANDREYEVNA: Look, it's mama — walking in the orchard… in a white dress! *(She laughs from joy)* It's mama.

GAYEV: Where?

VARYA: God be with you, Mamochka.

LYUBOV ANDREYEVNA: There is no one, it was just my imagination. To the right, on the path to the shed, a white sapling is bent down, it looks like a woman…

*TROFIMOV enters in a threadbare student's full dress uniform, wearing glasses.*

What a marvelous orchard! The masses of white blossoms, the deep blue sky…

TROFIMOV: Lyubov Andreyevna! *(She turns to look at him)* I only came to pay my respects and I will go at once. *(He feverishly kisses her hand)* I was told to wait until morning, but I couldn't stand it.

*LYUBOV ANDREYEVNA looks at him with bewilderment.*

VARYA: *(On the verge of tears)* It is Petya Trofimov…

TROFIMOV: Petya Trofimov, the former tutor of your Grisha… Have I changed so much?

*LYUBOV ANDREYEVNA embraces him and cries quietly.*

GAYEV: *(Embarrassed)* That's enough, that's enough, Lyuba.

VARYA: *(Cries)* Petya, I told you to wait a little until tomorrow.

LYUBOV ANDREYEVNA: My Grisha… my little boy… Grisha… my son…

VARYA: What can we do, Mama. It is God's will.

TROFIMOV: *(Softly, on the verge of tears)* Don't cry, don't cry…

LYUBOV ANDREYEVNA: *(Cries quietly)* My boy was lost, drowned… Why? What for? *(Quietly)* Anya is sleeping there, but I am talking so loudly… so noisy… Why, Petya? Why have you grown so ugly? So old?

TROFIMOV: On the train a peasant girl called me "Professor Fleabag."

LYUBOV ANDREYEVNA: You were just a boy then, a sweet student, but now your hair is thin, you have glasses. Is it possible you're still a student? *(She walks to the door)*

TROFIMOV: I will probably be a perpetual student.

LYUBOV ANDREYEVNA: *(She kisses her brother, then VARYA)* Well, go to bed… You have grown old too, Leonid.

PISCHIK: *(Goes to her)* Yes, to bed now… Oh, my gout. I will stay here tonight. Lyubov Andreyevna, my soul, tomorrow morning, if you would… two hundred forty *rubles*…

GAYEV: Always the same story with him.

PISCHIK: Two hundred forty *rubles*… to pay the interest on my mortgage.

LYUBOV ANDREYEVNA: I don't have any money, dear friend.

PISCHIK: I'll pay it back, my dear… It's a tiny sum.

LYUBOV ANDREYEVNA: Well, fine, Leonid will give it to you… Give it to him, Leonid.

GAYEV: I will give it to him. Hold out your pocket.

LYUBOV ANDREYEVNA: What are you doing, give it to him… He needs it… He'll pay it back.

*LYUBOV ANDREYEVNA, TROFIMOV, PISCHIK, and FIRS exit.*

*GAYEV, VARYA, and YASHA remain.*

GAYEV: My sister is still throwing money away. *(To YASHA)* Move away, my good man, you smell like the chicken coop.

YASHA: *(With a grin)* And you, Leonid Andreyich, you are just the same as ever.

GAYEV: What? *(To VARYA)* What did he say?

VARYA: *(To YASHA)* Your mother came from the village. She has been sitting in the servants' quarters since yesterday, she wants to see you —

YASHA: Good for her!

VARYA: You should be ashamed.

YASHA: She could have come tomorrow. *(He exits)*

VARYA: Mamochka is exactly the same, she hasn't changed at all. If she had her way, she would give away everything.

GAYEV: Yes…

*Pause.*

If you prescribe too many remedies for a disease, it means the disease is incurable. I have racked my brain, and I have many remedies, a great many, but in truth, there's not a single cure. It would be grand to receive an inheritance from someone, it would be grand to marry our Anya to a very rich man, it would be grand to go to Yaroslavl and try our luck with our aunt the countess. She is very, very rich, you know.

VARYA: *(She cries)* If only God would help us!

GAYEV: Don't howl. Our aunt is very rich, but she doesn't like us. In the first place, my sister married a lawyer, not an aristocrat…

*ANYA appears in the doorway.*

She married beneath her, and I can't say she has conducted herself very virtuously. She is good, kind, sweet, and I love her very much, but whatever excuses you invent, it must be confessed, she is *louche*. You can see it in her smallest movement.

VARYA: *(With a whisper)* Anya is standing in the doorway.

GAYEV: What?

*Pause.*

What on earth — something has gotten in my right eye. I can hardly see out of it. And on Thursday, when I was at the circuit court…

*ANYA enters.*

VARYA: Why aren't you asleep, Anya?

ANYA: I can't sleep. I can't.

GAYEV: My little one. *(He kisses ANYA's face, hands)* My baby… *(On the verge of tears)* You are not just my niece, you are an angel, you are everything to me. Believe me, believe…

ANYA: I believe you, Uncle. Everyone loves you, respects you… but dear Uncle, you must keep quiet, just keep quiet. What did you just say about mama, about your own sister? Why did you say that?

GAYEV: Yes, yes... *(He covers his face with her hands)* Yes, it's horrible! My God! God, save me! And today I made a speech to the bookcase... how stupid! And it was only when I finished that I understood how stupid it was.

VARYA: It is true, Uncle dear, you must be quiet. Just keep quiet, that's all.

ANYA: If you would keep quiet, things would be easier for you.

GAYEV: I will be quiet. *(He kisses ANYA's and VARYA's hands)* I will be quiet. Only this is about business. On Thursday I was at the circuit court. Well, a group of us got together, and started talking about this and that, and, it seems, it may be possible to arrange a loan on a promissory note, to pay the interest to the bank.

VARYA: If only God would help us!

GAYEV: On Tuesday I'll go and have another talk. *(To VARYA)* Don't howl. *(To ANYA)* Your mother will have a talk with Lopakhin; he will not refuse her, of course... And you, when you're rested, will go to Yaroslavl to the old countess, your great-aunt. So then we will operate on three fronts — and we're sure to win. We will pay the interest, I am convinced... *(He places a fruit-drop in his mouth)* On my honor, on whatever you want, I swear the estate will not be sold! *(Excitedly)* I swear on my happiness! Here is my hand, call me worthless, a dishonorable man, if I let it go to auction! I swear with all my being!

ANYA: *(She is suddenly happy)* How good you are, Uncle, how smart! *(Embraces her uncle)* I am calm now! I'm calm! I'm happy!

    FIRS enters.

FIRS: *(Reproachfully)* Leonid Andreyich, have you no fear of God? When are you going to bed?

GAYEV: I'm going, I'm going. *(To FIRS)* Shoo! I am going. All right, don't worry, I will undress myself. Well, children, nightie-night... Details tomorrow, but now I'm going to sleep. *(He kisses ANYA and VARYA)* I am a man of the Eighties... People look down on those times these days, but I always say, in my life I have suffered a great deal as a result of my convictions. It is no wonder the peasants love me. You should know the peasant! You should know with what...

ANYA: You are doing it again, Uncle!

VARYA: Uncle dear, be quiet.

FIRS: *(Angrily)* Leonid Andreyich!

GAYEV: I'm coming, I'm coming... Go to bed. From two sides to the middle. I make a clean shot! *(He exits, FIRS doddering behind him)*

ANYA: I'm calm now. I don't want to go to Yaroslavl, I don't like my great-aunt, but still I feel calm. Thanks to uncle. *(She sits)*

VARYA: We should go to sleep. I'm going. While you were gone, there was some unpleasantness. As you know, only the old servants still live in the servant quarters: Yefimyushka, Polya, Yevstignyey, and, of course, Karp. They began to let all kinds of drifters spend the night — I didn't say anything. Only then I heard the servants were spreading rumors that I ordered them to be fed only peas. From stinginess, you see... And it was Yevstignyey the whole time... All right, I think to myself, if that is how it is, then just stay calm. I call for Yevstignyey... *(She yawns)* He comes in... "How could you be such an idiot, Yevstignyey," I said... *(Looking at ANYA)* Anyechka!

   Pause.

She's asleep! *(She puts her arm around ANYA)* Come to bed... Come! *(She leads her)* My darling has fallen asleep! Come...

*They are going.*

*Far beyond the orchard a shepherd plays a reed-pipe. TROFIMOV crosses the stage and, seeing VARYA and ANYA, stops.*

VARYA: Shh... She's sleeping... sleeping... Let's go, my dear.

ANYA: *(Quietly, half-asleep)* I'm so tired... all the little bells... Uncle... dear... Mama and Uncle...

VARYA: Let's go, my dear, let's go... *(They exit into ANYA's room)*

TROFIMOV: *(With emotion)* My sunshine! My spring!

CURTAIN.

# ACT II

*A field. An old, crooked, long-deserted chapel, near a well, large stones that to all appearances were tombstones sometime in the past, and an old bench. The road to GAYEV's estate is visible. On one side are dark poplars: the cherry orchard begins there. In the distance is a row of telegraph poles, and even further on the horizon a large city appears, which is only glimpsed in very good, clear weather. The sun will set soon. YASHA and DUNYASHA sit on the bench; YEPIKHODOV stands nearby and plays a guitar; all sit pensively.*

YEPIKHODOV: (*Plays on the guitar and sings*) "What is the busy world to me, who is my friend and who is my enemy…" How pleasant it is to play a mandolin!

DUNYASHA: That's a guitar, not a mandolin. (*She looks in a mirror and powders her face*)

YEPIKHODOV: For a man who is madly in love, this is a mandolin… (*He croons*) "If only my heart could be warmed…"

    *YASHA joins in singing.*

YEPIKHODOV and YASHA: "If only my heart could be warmed by the one I love, love, love, love."

    *CHARLOTTA enters. She is wearing an old military peak-cap. She takes a rifle from her shoulder and adjusts the buckle on the strap.*

CHARLOTTA: These people sing horribly… fooey! Like hyenas. I'd like to talk to someone but there's no one to talk to — no one.

DUNYASHA: (*To YASHA*) Nevertheless, how lucky you are to have been abroad.

YASHA: Yes, that's true. I can't disagree with you there. (*He yawns, then lights up a cigar*)

YEPIKHODOV: Naturally. Abroad everything has been fully developed for a long time now.

YASHA: Obviously.

YEPIKHODOV: I am a culturally developed man. I read various remarkable books, but in no way can I understand my own path, strictly speaking, whether I want to live or blow my brains out. But nevertheless I always carry a revolver. Here it is… (*He shows a revolver*)

CHARLOTTA: I'm finished. I am going now. (*She takes up the rifle*) You, Yepikhodov, are a very intelligent person and very scary; women must love you madly. Grrr! (*She starts to go*) These "culturally developed" people are all so stupid, I can't talk to them… I'm always alone, alone, I have no one… who I am, why I am — unknown… (*She exits, taking her time*)

YEPIKHODOV: Strictly speaking, not touching on other subjects, I must express myself, absolutely, no possibility whatsoever, that fate treats me without pity, like a storm to a small ship. If, let us suppose, I am mistaken, then why did I wake up this morning, say for example, and see a spider of a terrifying size on my chest… Like this. (*He demonstrates with both hands*) Or I take some *kvass* to drink, and I see something in it that is absolutely disgusting, like a cockroach.

   *Pause.*

Have you read Henry Thomas Buckle's *History of Civilization in England*?

   *Pause.*

Avdotya Fyodorovna, may I trouble you with a few words.

DUNYASHA: Speak.

YEPIKHODOV: It would be preferable to speak with you in private… (*He sighs*)

DUNYASHA: (*Embarrassed*) All right… only first bring me my wrap… It is by the bookcase… it's a little damp here…

YEPIKHODOV: Certainly… I will deliver it… Now I know what to do with my revolver… (*He takes the guitar and exits playing*)

YASHA: A "disaster waiting to happen." A stupid man, if you ask me. (*He yawns*)

DUNYASHA: Please God, don't let him shoot himself.

    Pause.

I've become so anxious, I worry about everything. I was just a little girl when the masters took me in, now I'm no longer used to a peasant's life. Look, my hands are white-white, like a grand lady. I've become so sensitive, so delicate, refined, I am afraid of everything… It's all so terrifying. And if you deceive me, Yasha, I don't know what will happen with my nerves.

YASHA: (*Kisses her*) Little peach! Of course, every girl must remember her place, and what I hate most of all, is when a girl goes too far.

DUNYASHA: I have fallen madly in love with you. You are educated. You can talk about anything.

    Pause.

YASHA: (*Yawns*) Yes… In my opinion, if a girl tells me she loves me, it means she's immoral.

    Pause.

It is nice to smoke a cigar in the fresh air… (*He listens*) Someone's coming… It's them.

    *DUNYASHA impetuously embraces him.*

Go home, take the path that goes along the river, like you went out for a swim. I don't want them to think I've been with you. I can't have that happen.

DUNYASHA: (*She coughs quietly*) I have a headache from that cigar...

*She exits.*

*YASHA remains, sits by the chapel. LYUBOV ANDREYEVNA, GAYEV and LOPAKHIN enter.*

LOPAKHIN: Ladies and gentlemen, you must finally decide — time won't wait. The question is so simple. Do you agree to use the land for cottages or not? Answer one word: yes or no? Just one word!

LYUBOV ANDREYEVNA: Who has been smoking those disgusting cigars here... (*She sits*)

GAYEV: It's very convenient now that they've built the railroad. (*He sits*) We went into town and had breakfast today... yellow to the center. Now, I would like to go back home, play a game...

LYUBOV ANDREYEVNA: Let's wait a little.

LOPAKHIN: Just one word! (*Imploring*) Give me an answer!

GAYEV: (*Yawning*) What?

LYUBOV ANDREYEVNA: (*She looks in her purse*) Yesterday I had a lot of money, but today there is very little. My poor Varya is feeding everyone milk soup to save *kopeks*. In the kitchen she gives the old ones one pea, and yet somehow I keep spending... (*She drops her purse, spilling gold coins*) There, it's raining *kopeks*. (*She is annoyed*)

YASHA: Allow me, I'll pick them up. (*He gathers the money*)

LYUBOV ANDREYEVNA: Yes, please, Yasha. And why did I go with you to have breakfast... your silly restaurant with that silly music, and tablecloths that smell of soap… Why drink so much, Lyonya? Why eat so much? Why talk so much? Today in the restaurant you were talking a lot again and it was all so silly. About the seventies, about the Symbolists. And to whom? Talking to the waiter about the Symbolists!

LOPAKHIN: Yes.

GAYEV: (*He waves his hand*) I am incorrigible, that's obvious… (*Irritated, to YASHA*) What's the matter with you, you are constantly under foot.

YASHA: (*He laughs*) I can't hear your voice without laughing.

GAYEV: (*To his sister*) It is either he or I…

LYUBOV ANDREYEVNA: Leave, Yasha, be off…

YASHA: (*He gives LYUBOV ANDREYEVNA the purse*) I'm going now. (*He can barely restrain himself from laughter*) Right away… (*He leaves*)

LOPAKHIN: That rich tycoon Deriganov intends to buy your estate. They say he's coming to the auction himself.

LYUBOV ANDREYEVNA: And where did you hear that?

LOPAKHIN: They're talking about it in town.

GAYEV: Our aunt in Yaroslavl promised to send something, but when and how much she will send, we don't know.

LOPAKHIN: How much? One hundred thousand? Two hundred?

LYUBOV ANDREYEVNA: Well… ten thousand — maybe fifteen. We must be thankful for small mercies.

LOPAKHIN: Forgive me, I have never encountered such frivolous, un-businesslike people as you, ladies and gentlemen. You've been told in plain language that your estate will be sold, but you just don't understand.

LYUBOV ANDREYEVNA: What are we to do? Instruct us.

LOPAKHIN: I instruct you every day. Every day I say the same thing. The cherry orchard and the land have to be leased for summer houses. Do this now, hurry — the auction is around the corner! Understand! If you finally decide on those houses, they will give you as much money as you like, and then you'll be saved.

LYUBOV ANDREYEVNA: Summer houses and summer people — it is so vulgar, forgive me.

GAYEV: I completely agree with you.

LOPAKHIN: I don't know whether to sob, or shout, or swoon. I can't stand it! You have worn me out! (*To GAYEV*) You are an old woman.

GAYEV: What?

LOPAKHIN: A *babushka*! (*He starts to leave*)

LYUBOV ANDREYEVNA: (*Frightened*) No, don't go, stop, my friend. I beg you. Maybe we will think of something!

LOPAKHIN: What is there to think about!

LYUBOV ANDREYEVNA: Don't go, I beg you. I feel better with you here…

   Pause.

I feel something terrible is going to happen, like the sky will suddenly fall.

GAYEV: (*Deep in thought*) Bank shot to the corner… curve to the center.

LYUBOV ANDREYEVNA: Oh, so many sins...

LOPAKHIN: You? What sins...

GAYEV: (*He places a fruit-drop in his mouth*) They say that I've eaten up my entire fortune in fruit-drops... (*He laughs*)

LYUBOV ANDREYEVNA: Oh, my sins... I have always thrown money away without any restraint, like a madwoman. I got married to a man who never earned a *kopek* in his whole life — only spent them. My husband died from champagne — he drank constantly. So I fell in love with another man. I had an affair with him, and exactly at that time — this was my first punishment, a knife straight to the heart — here in the river... my little boy drowned. I went abroad, left forever, never to return, never to see this river again... I closed my eyes, ran, as far as I could get, but he came after me... desperately, ruthlessly. I bought a villa near Mentone, because he fell ill there, and for three years I didn't have a moment's rest day or night. His constant demands exhausted me, my soul dried up. And last year, when the villa was sold for debts, I left for Paris, but he followed me there and took everything I had, left me, ran off with another woman. I tried to poison myself... It was so stupid, so shameful... And suddenly I was drawn back to Russia, to my country, to my little girl... (*She wipes away tears*) Lord, Lord, be gracious, forgive me my sins! Do not punish me anymore! (*Takes a telegram from her pocket*) I received this today from Paris... He asks my forgiveness, begs me to return... (*She tears the telegram*) Do I hear music somewhere? (*She listens*)

GAYEV: That is our celebrated Jewish orchestra. Do you remember, four fiddles, a flute and double-bass.

LYUBOV ANDREYEVNA: It still exists? We should invite them over for something, have a party.

LOPAKHIN: (*Listening*) I can't hear them... (*He quietly sings*) "And for money Germans will Frenchify a *kulak*." (*He laughs*) What a play I saw yesterday at the theatre, very funny.

LYUBOV ANDREYEVNA: And it probably wasn't funny at all. Don't go to plays, instead look at yourselves more often. How boring your lives are, how much nonsense you talk.

LOPAKHIN: That's true. I admit it, our life is stupid…

*Pause.*

My papa was a peasant, an idiot, he didn't understand anything, didn't teach me anything, only beat me when he was drunk — always with a stick. And in truth, I'm the same — a blockhead and an idiot. I didn't learn anything, my handwriting is bad, I write so poorly that I'm ashamed for people to see it — like a pig.

LYUBOV ANDREYEVNA: You should get married, my friend.

LOPAKHIN: Yes… that is true.

LYUBOV ANDREYEVNA: Perhaps to our Varya. She's a good girl.

LOPAKHIN: Yes.

LYUBOV ANDREYEVNA: She comes from simple people, she works all day, but the important thing is, she loves you. And what's more, you've liked her for a long time.

LOPAKHIN: Well then? I'm not against it… She is a good girl.

*Pause.*

GAYEV: They offered me a job at the bank. Six thousand a year… Did you hear?

LYUBOV ANDREYEVNA: You can't be serious. You stay put!

*FIRS enters; he is carrying a topcoat.*

FIRS: (*To GAYEV*) Allow me, sir. Put this on, it is damp.

GAYEV: *(He puts the coat on)* I am sick of you, old man.

FIRS: No matter... This morning you left without telling me. *(Inspecting him)*

LYUBOV ANDREYEVNA: How old you've become, Firs!

FIRS: What can I do for you, Madam?

LOPAKHIN: She says, you've grown very old!

FIRS: I have been living a long time. They were planning my wedding before your papa was on this earth... *(He laughs)* When the freedom came, I was already a senior butler. I never agreed to freedom then, I stayed with the masters...

   Pause.

And I remember, everyone thought they were so happy, they didn't even know why, they were just happy.

LOPAKHIN: Oh yes, those were the good old days. It was wonderful how they beat everyone.

FIRS: *(Not catching what LOPAKHIN said)* And how! Peasants with masters, masters with peasants, but now it's all mixed up, you can't understand anything.

GAYEV: Be quiet, Firs. Tomorrow I need to go to town. They promised to introduce me to a general who may give me a promissory note.

LOPAKHIN: Nothing will come of it. And you will not pay the interest. Be quiet.

LYUBOV ANDREYEVNA: There he goes again. There is no general.

   TROFIMOV, ANYA and VARYA *enter.*

GAYEV: Here come our darlings.

ANYA: Here's mama.

LYUBOV ANDREYEVNA: *(Tenderly)* Come, come... My dears... *(Embracing ANYA and VARYA)* If you only knew how much I love you both. Sit close to me, here.

*Everyone takes a seat.*

LOPAKHIN: Our perpetual student is always with the young ladies.

TROFIMOV: It's none of your business.

LOPAKHIN: He will be fifty soon, and he's still a student.

TROFIMOV: Stop your idiotic jokes.

LOPAKHIN: Are you angry again, you crackpot?

TROFIMOV: Leave me alone.

LOPAKHIN: *(Laughs)* Let me ask you a question, how do you see me?

TROFIMOV: Yermolai Alekseyevich, this is how I see you: you are a rich man, soon you will be a millionaire. You are a necessary part of the evolutionary process. You are the wild beast that eats up everything in his path.

*Everyone laughs.*

VARYA: Petya, better stick to talking about the planets.

LYUBOV ANDREYEVNA: No, let's continue yesterday's conversation.

TROFIMOV: What were we talking about?

GAYEV: About the proud man.

TROFIMOV: We talked for a long time yesterday, but we didn't arrive at any conclusion. To your way of thinking, there is something exalted about a proud man. From your point of view you may be right, but to speak objectively, what is there to be proud of? Physiologically, we are nothing to brag about. Temperamentally, the vast majority of us are crude, inept, profoundly unhappy. We have to stop being so impressed with ourselves. We should just work.

GAYEV: And then we die.

TROFIMOV: Who knows? And what does that mean — die? It may be that a person has a hundred senses and when we die only the five we know go with us, but the remaining ninety-five stay alive.

LYUBOV ANDREYEVNA: How smart you are, Petya!

LOPAKHIN: *(Ironically)* Oh, sure!

TROFIMOV: Humanity is progressing forward, perfecting its strengths. Everything that is unattainable for us now, some day will be closer, will be more clear to us. Only we must work. We must support those who strive for a higher truth. But in Russia, very few people are on that quest. The vast majority of intellectuals — and believe me, I know a lot of them — aren't striving for anything, they don't do anything, they're not capable of working. They call themselves the "intelligentsia," they think they are above everyone else. They treat the peasants like animals. They're terrible students, they read nothing serious, they do exactly nothing about anything. They only talk about science and art. But they don't understand a single thing about either one. They pretend to be so serious, they walk around with grave faces, and they are always talking about "important" things. They philosophize, and meanwhile right before their eyes the workers are starving, they sleep without beds, thirty or forty in one room, bedbugs everywhere, stench, dampness, moral filth... And obviously, all of this talk, talk, talk is only meant to keep them from looking at the reality of the situation. Show me, where is the child welfare they talk so much about, where are the libraries to teach people to read? They only write about them in novels, in fact they do not exist. Only filth exists, vulgarity, barbarism…. I am frightened and I hate grave faces and serious talk. Better we should just shut up!

LOPAKHIN: You know, I wake up at five o'clock every morning, and I work from morning until evening. I deal with a lot of money — my own and other people's, and I get to see what people are really like. It doesn't take much to see how few honest, decent people there are. Sometimes, when I can't sleep, I think, Lord, you gave us vast forests, immense fields, the deepest horizons, and, by rights, we who live here should be giants —

LYUBOV ANDREYEVNA: Giants! Giants are good only in stories. In real life, they are frightening.

*At the back of the stage YEPIKHODOV passes through playing a guitar.*

(*Pensively*) There goes Yepikhodov…

ANYA: (*Pensively*) There goes Yepikhodov…

VARYA: Why is Yepikhodov living with us? All he does is eat and drink tea all day long.

LOPAKHIN: And he intends to shoot himself.

LYUBOV ANDREYEVNA: But I like Yepikhodov. When he talks about his "misfortunes," it's funny. Don't dismiss him, Varya.

VARYA: He must be dismissed, Mamochka — it's impossible.

GAYEV: The sun has set, Ladies and Gentlemen.

TROFIMOV: Yes.

GAYEV: (*Low, as if reciting*) O nature, marvelous, you shine with eternal radiance, beautiful and indifferent. You, whom we call mother, combine in yourself living and dying. You give life and you destroy it…

VARYA: *(Imploring)* Uncle, dear!

ANYA: Uncle, you're doing it again!

TROFIMOV: You'd better put the yellow ball in the side pocket.

GAYEV: I will be quiet, I will be quiet.

> *Everyone sits, pensive. Silence. One can only hear FIRS quietly muttering. Suddenly a distant sound is heard, as if from the sky. The sound of a breaking string, dying away, mournfully.*

LYUBOV ANDREYEVNA: What was that?

LOPAKHIN: I don't know. Somewhere far away a cable wire broke in the mines. But somewhere very far away.

GAYEV: Or maybe a bird of some kind… like a heron.

TROFIMOV: Or an owl…

LYUBOV ANDREYEVNA: *(She shudders)* It makes me feel uneasy.

> *Pause.*

FIRS: Before the catastrophe it was the same: the owl cried, the samovar droned endlessly.

GAYEV: Before what catastrophe?

FIRS: Before the freedom.

*Pause.*

LYUBOV ANDREYEVNA: You know, friends, let's go, it's evening already. *(To ANYA)* You have tears in your eyes… What's wrong, little girl? *(Embraces her)*

ANYA: Nothing, Mama. It's nothing.

TROFIMOV: Someone is coming.

*A PASSERBY appears in a worn white peak-cap and topcoat; he is slightly drunk.*

PASSERBY: Permit me to ask you, can I get to the station from here?

GAYEV: You can. Take that path.

PASSERBY: I humbly thank you. *(Coughing)* Superb weather we're having... *(Recites)* "My brother, suffering brother... come down to the Volga, whose groans..." *(To VARYA)* Mademoiselle, grant a hungry Russian thirty *kopeks*...

*VARYA is frightened, she cries out.*

LOPAKHIN: *(Angrily)* Have you no sense of decency!

LYUBOV ANDREYEVNA: *(Struck dumb)* Here, take... this... *(She looks in her purse)* No silver... oh, it's all the same, here is a gold coin...

PASSERBY: I humbly thank you! *(He leaves)*

*(Laughter)*

VARYA: *(Frightened)* I am leaving... I am leaving... Oh, Mama, our servants have nothing to eat, but you give him gold.

LYUBOV ANDREYEVNA: What's wrong with me, it was so stupid! I will give you everything I have at home. Yermolai Alekseyevich, may I have another loan!

LOPAKHIN: At your service.

LYUBOV ANDREYEVNA: Let's go, ladies and gentlemen, it's time. And, Varya, we've just promised you in marriage, congratulations.

VARYA: *(On the verge of tears)* You should not joke like that, Mamochka.

LOPAKHIN: Ordealya… get thee to a nunnery…

GAYEV: My hands are trembling: it has been too long since I played billiards.

LOPAKHIN: Ordealya, o nymph, remember me in your prayers!

LYUBOV ANDREYEVNA: Let's go, Ladies and Gentlemen. We'll have supper soon.

VARYA: He frightened me. My heart is pounding.

LOPAKHIN: Please remember, Ladies and Gentlemen: on August 22 the cherry orchard goes up for sale. Think about this! Think!

*Everyone leaves, except TROFIMOV and ANYA.*

ANYA: *(Laughing)* Thank you, Mr. Passerby, you frightened Varya, and now we can be alone.

TROFIMOV: Varya is afraid that we will suddenly fall in love with one another, so she won't leave us alone. With her narrow mind, she cannot understand that we are above love. We must avoid those petty and illusory things that hinder us from being free and happy. This is our goal. Forward! We are moving ineluctably to the bright stars that burn in the distance! Forward! Do not fall behind, friends!

ANYA: *(Clasping her hands)* How well you speak!

*Pause.*

It is wonderful here today!

TROFIMOV: Yes, the weather is amazing.

ANYA: What have you done to me, Petya, why don't I love the cherry orchard anymore? I loved it so tenderly, it seemed to me there was no better place on earth than our orchard.

TROFIMOV: All of Russia is our orchard. The earth is great and wonderful, there are many miraculous places on it.

*Pause.*

Just think, Anya: your grandfather, great-grandfather and all of your ancestors owned serfs, they were in possession of living souls, and don't you see how those souls gaze at us from behind every blossom in the orchard, every leaf, every tree. Can't you hear their voices… To *own* living souls — that has changed all of you, your whole family. Your mother, you, your uncle don't even notice that you are living on the credit of all those centuries of people. We're behind the times by at least two hundred years. We still have exactly nothing, no real relationship to the past. We only philosophize, complain about boredom and drink vodka. But you see, it's so clear — to begin to live in the present, it is necessary to first atone for the past. The only way we can atone is with true suffering, and with uninterrupted, hard work. Do you understand that, Anya?

ANYA: The house we live in hasn't been our home for a long time, and I will leave, I give you my word.

TROFIMOV: Throw away the keys and run as fast as you can. Be as free as the wind.

ANYA: *(In rapture)* How well you speak!

TROFIMOV: Believe me, Anya! I am not yet thirty. I am young, I am still a student, but I have already suffered so much. When winter comes, I am hungry, ill, anxious, as poor as the most wretched, and I've seen everything. But inside my soul, I have an unquenchable feeling. I have a feeling that happiness is coming, Anya. I can already see it…

ANYA: *(Pensively)* The moon is rising.

*YEPIKHODOV is heard playing the same sad song on the guitar. The moon is rising. Among the poplars VARYA is looking for ANYA and calls: "Anya! Where are you?"*

TROFIMOV: Yes, the moon is rising.

*Pause.*

Here it is, happiness, here it comes, it is always getting closer and closer, I already hear its footsteps. And if we don't recognize it, what does it matter, others will!

*The voice of VARYA: "Anya! Where are you?"*

It's Varya again! *(Angrily)* Disgusting!

ANYA: Well? Let's go to the river. It's so nice there.

TROFIMOV: Yes, let's go.

*They go.*

*The voice of VARYA: "Anya! Anya!"*

*Enter FIRS, then CHARLOTTA IVANOVNA. FIRS is muttering, looking for something on the ground near the bench. He lights a match.*

FIRS: *(Mutters)* Ekh, you nincompoop!

CHARLOTTA: *(She takes a seat on the bench and takes off her cap)* Is that you, Firs? What are you looking for here?

FIRS: The mistress lost her purse.

CHARLOTTA: *(She looks)* Here is a fan… And here is a handkerchief… it smells like expensive perfume.

*Pause.*

There is nothing else. Lyubov Andreyevna is perpetually losing something. She even loses her own life. *(She quietly sings a song)* I don't have a current passport, Grandpa. I don't even know how old I am, but it always seems to me that I am quite young. *(She puts her cap on Firs; he sits motionless)* Oh, I love you, my sweet old dear. *(She laughs)* Einz, zwei, drei! *(She takes the cap off FIRS and puts it on herself)* When I was a little girl, my father and mother were circus performers at fairs. They were very good. And I did the *salto-mortale* and other grand tricks. When Papa and Mama died, a German lady took me in and she began to teach me. *Gut.* I grew up, then I became a governess. But where I'm from, who I am — I don't know... Who my parents were, if they were even married... I don't know... *(She takes a cucumber from a pocket and eats)* I don't know anything.

FIRS: When I was twenty or twenty-five, I was out for a walk with the deacon's son, and the cook Vasilii, and we saw someone sitting on a stone by the side of the road — someone strange, a nobody really. I got scared and after I left, they killed the man. He had some money on him.

CHARLOTTA: Well? *Weiter.*

FIRS: Later, well, they arrested them and questioned them. Then the trial came. They got me too. I was in jail for two years... It was a long time ago.

*Pause*

I don't remember all of it...

CHARLOTTA: You will die soon, Grandpa.

*We hear YEPIKHODOV's guitar... The moon is rising... Somewhere by the poplars VARYA looks for ANYA and calls: "Anya! Where are you!"*

*CURTAIN.*

# ACT III

*The drawing room, separated from the ballroom by an arch. There is a chandelier. We can hear the same Jewish orchestra that was mentioned in the second act playing in the entry hall. It is evening. In the ballroom they are dancing the grand-ronde. The voice of SIMYONOV-PISCHIK: "Promenade à une paire!" They enter the drawing room: in the first pair are PISCHIK and CHARLOTTA IVANOVNA, in the second — TROFIMOV and LYUBOV ANDREYEVNA, in the third — ANYA and the POSTAL CLERK, in the fourth — VARYA and the STATIONMASTER and so forth. VARYA quietly weeps and, dancing, wipes her tears. In the last pair is DUNYASHA. They cross the drawing room, PISCHIK cries out: "Grand-ronde, balancez!" and "Les cavaliers à genoux et remerciez vos dames!"*

*FIRS in a tailcoat carries seltzer water on a tray.*

*PISCHIK and TROFIMOV enter the drawing room.*

PISCHIK: I have high blood pressure. I've already had two strokes, it's difficult to dance, but, as they say, when in Rome… I'm healthy as a horse. My late father, the joker, God rest him, used to say that our ancient Simyonov-Pischik clan is descended from the very horse that Caligula made a senator… *(He takes a seat)* But the calamity is: no money! A hungry dog thinks only about meat… *(Begins to snore and immediately wakes up)* So I… I can think only about money…

TROFIMOV: Come to think of it, you do look something like a horse.

PISCHIK: Well… a horse is a good beast… you can sell a horse…

*They are playing billiards in the neighboring room. VARYA appears in the ballroom under the arch.*

TROFIMOV: *(Teasing)* Madame Lopakhina! Madame Lopakhina!

VARYA: *(Angrily)* Professor Fleabag!

TROFIMOV: Yes, I am Professor Fleabag and I'm proud of it!

VARYA: *(In bitter thought)* Here we hired musicians, but how do we pay them? *(She exits)*

TROFIMOV: *(To PISCHIK)* All the time and energy you spend looking for money to pay your debts, you could turn the world upside down.

PISCHIK: Nietzsche... the philosopher... the greatest, most celebrated... a man of colossal intellect, he says that it is all right to make counterfeit money.

TROFIMOV: You've read Nietzsche?

PISCHIK: Well... My Dashenka told me. But now I am in such a terrible spot, that I would gladly counterfeit money... the day after tomorrow I have to pay three hundred and ten *rubles*... I already have one hundred thirty... *(He feels his pockets, anxiously)* The money is gone! I lost the money! *(On the verge of tears)* Where is the money? *(Joyfully)* Here it is, behind the lining... Phew, I broke out in a sweat...

*LYUBOV ANDREYEVNA and CHARLOTTA IVANOVNA enter.*

LYUBOV ANDREYEVNA: *(She hums a lezginka)* Why has Leonid been gone so long? What's he doing in town? *(To DUNYASHA)* Dunyasha, offer the musicians tea...

TROFIMOV: In all probability, the auction didn't take place.

LYUBOV ANDREYEVNA: This is the wrong time to have a party... Well, never mind... *(She takes a seat and hums quietly)*

CHARLOTTA: *(Gives PISCHIK a pack of cards)* *Voila!* Here is a pack of cards. Think of a card.

PISCHIK: I'm thinking of one.

CHARLOTTA: Now shuffle the pack. Very good. Give it here, o my sweet *Herr* Pischik. Tell us your card.

PISCHIK: The eight of spades.

CHARLOTTA: *Einz, zwei, drei!* Now look for it, it is in your side pocket...

PISCHIK: *(Takes the card from his side pocket)* The eight of spades, absolutely correct! *(Astonished)* What a world!

CHARLOTTA: *(Holds the pack of cards in her palm, to TROFIMOV)* Say, quickly, what card is on top?

TROFIMOV: All right, the ace of spades.

CHARLOTTA: Indeed! *(To PISCHIK)* Well? What card is on top?

PISCHIK: Queen of hearts.

CHARLOTTA: Indeed! *(She claps her hands, the pack of cards vanishes)* What nice weather we are having today!

*A mysterious female voice answers her, seemingly from under the floor: "Oh, yes, splendid weather, Madame."*

You are absolutely my ideal.

*Voice: "I like you very much as well, Madame."*

STATIONMASTER: *(Applauds)* Bravo, Madam ventriloquist!

PISCHIK: *(Astonished)* What a world! You are most charming Charlotta Ivanovna... I am simply in love...

CHARLOTTA: In love? *(She shrugs her shoulders)* Are you capable of love? *Guter Mensch, aber schlechter Musikant.* ("A good man, but a bad musician.")

TROFIMOV: *(He slaps PISCHIK on the shoulder)* What a horse you are...

CHARLOTTA: I beg your attention, there is still one more trick. *(She takes the blanket from a chair)* Here is a very good shawl that I wish to sell… *(She shakes it)* Does anyone wish to buy it?

PISCHIK: *(Astonished)* Marvelous!

CHARLOTTA: *Einz, zwei, drei!* (*She quickly lifts up the fallen blanket*)

*ANYA stands under the blanket; she curtsies, runs to her mother, hugs her, and runs back to the ballroom amid general delight.*

LYUBOV ANDREYEVNA: *(Applauds)* Bravo, bravo!

CHARLOTTA: Now another! *Einz, zwei, drei.* (*Lifts blanket*)

*VARYA stands under the blanket and she bows.*

PISCHIK: *(Astonished)* What a world!

CHARLOTTA: The end! *(She throws the blanket on PISCHIK, curtsies and runs into the ballroom)*

PISCHIK: *(Hurriedly to her)* What a naughty woman! So naughty! *(He exits)*

LYUBOV ANDREYEVNA: And Leonid still isn't back. I don't understand what he is doing in town for so long! I'm sure it is over already, either the estate is sold or the auction didn't take place, but why must we be kept in the dark for so long!

VARYA: *(Trying to comfort her)* Uncle bought it, I'm sure of that.

TROFIMOV: *(Sarcastically)* Oh, yes.

VARYA: Great Aunt sent him money to transfer the estate to her name. She did it for Anya. And I'm certain, God willing, uncle is buying it.

LYUBOV ANDREYEVNA: Your great aunt in Yaroslavl sent fifteen-thousand to buy the estate in her name — she doesn't trust us — but that money wouldn't even cover the interest. *(She covers her face with her hands)* Today my fate is being decided, my fate…

TROFIMOV: *(Teases VARYA) Madame* Lopakhina!

VARYA: *(Angrily)* Perpetual student! You have already been thrown out of the university twice!

LYUBOV ANDREYEVNA: Why are you angry, Varya? He is teasing you about Lopakhin. Well, if you want to — marry Lopakhin. He is a good man — interesting. If you don't want to, don't marry him, no one is forcing you, darling…

VARYA: Honestly Mamochka, I take these things seriously. He is a good man, I like him.

LYUBOV ANDREYEVNA: Then marry him. I don't understand what you're waiting for.

VARYA: Mamochka, I can't propose to him myself. For two years now everyone has talked to me about him. Everyone talks about it, but when he is with me, he is either silent or he makes jokes. I understand. He's preoccupied with his business. He is busy getting rich, and he's not concerned with me. If I had money, even a little, even a hundred *rubles*, I would leave everything, I would go far away. I would go to a convent.

TROFIMOV: The bliss!

VARYA: *(To TROFIMOV)* A student is supposed to be smart! *(In a gentle tone, with tears)* How ugly you've become, Petya, how old! *(To LYUBOV ANDREYEVNA, no longer crying)* I can't be without something to do, Mamochka. I must do something every minute.

*YASHA enters.*

YASHA: *(Barely restraining himself from laughter)* Yepikhodov broke a billiard cue! *(He exits)*

VARYA: Why is Yepikhodov here? And who let him play billiards? I do not understand these people… *(She exits)*

LYUBOV ANDREYEVNA: Don't tease her, Petya. You see that she's suffering.

TROFIMOV: She's such a busybody. She pokes her nose into business that isn't hers. The whole summer she hasn't given me or Anya any peace. She was afraid that we would have a romance. What business is it of hers? Anyway, it never even crossed my mind. I am so far from that vulgarity. We are above love!

LYUBOV ANDREYEVNA: And I, therefore, must be below love. *(In strong agitation)* Why isn't Leonid here? I just need to know — was the estate sold or not? This is so terrible for me, I don't know what to think. I am losing my self-control… I could scream now… I could do something very foolish. Save me, Petya. Say something, speak…

TROFIMOV: Whether the estate was sold today or not — what difference does it make? We've been down this path before, now there is no turning back. Calm down, dear. There's no need to fool yourself. For once in your life you need to look at the truth.

LYUBOV ANDREYEVNA: What truth? You see so clearly what truth is, but it's as though I've gone blind, I see nothing. You fervently solve all these important problems, but tell me, my friend, isn't it because you're young, and you've never really known life? Yes, you look boldly into the future and see a brave new world out there, but have you ever had to live with your idealistic visions? You are braver, more honest, more profound than we, but think about it, be a little generous, have mercy on me. You see I was born here, my father and mother lived here, my grandfather. I love this house. Without the cherry orchard I don't understand my own life, and if it's really necessary to sell it, then sell me along with it. *(She embraces TROFIMOV, kisses him on the forehead)* You know my son drowned here... *(She weeps)* Pity me, good, kind man.

TROFIMOV: You know I deeply sympathize with you.

LYUBOV ANDREYEVNA: Yes, but you should have said that differently, very differently. *(She takes out a handkerchief, a telegram falls onto the floor)* Today my soul is so heavy, you can't imagine. It's so noisy here tonight and my soul trembles at every sound, I am trembling all over, but I can't be left alone, I'm terrified of my own thoughts. Don't condemn me, Petya... I love you as I do my own family. I swear to you I would gladly have you marry Anya, only, my friend, you must finish your studies. You don't do anything, you let fate toss you from one place to another. It's so strange... Isn't it true? Yes? And you ought to do something about that beard, let it grow out somehow... *(She laughs)* You are so funny!

TROFIMOV: *(Picks up the telegram)* I do not wish to be handsome.

LYUBOV ANDREYEVNA: That telegram is from Paris. I receive one every day. That ridiculous man is sick again, things aren't going well with him... He asks forgiveness, he begs me to come, and I really should go to Paris to be with him. Don't look at me that way, Petya — what can I do? He's sick, he's alone, unhappy, and who will look after him, who will keep him from making mistakes, who will give him his medicine? And the truth is, I love him. Yes, I love him, I love him... He's a stone around my neck, I will sink to the bottom with him, but I love that stone and I cannot live without it. *(She presses TROFIMOV's hand)* Don't think badly of me, Petya, don't say anything, don't speak...

TROFIMOV: *(On the verge of tears)* Forgive my bluntness, but for God's sake he robbed you!

LYUBOV ANDREYEVNA: No, no, no, don't talk like that... *(She covers her ears)*

TROFIMOV: He's a parasite. You are the only one who doesn't see this! He is a rotten parasite, a nonentity...

LYUBOV ANDREYEVNA: *(Angry, but restrained)* You are twenty-eight or twenty-nine, but you're still a little school boy.

TROFIMOV: Very well!

LYUBOV ANDREYEVNA: You should be a man. At your age, you should have someone who loves you. And you should love... you yourself should fall in love! *(Angrily)* Yes, yes! You have no true purity. You're just a prig, a ridiculous eccentric, a freak, a virgin...

TROFIMOV: *(In horror)* What is she saying!

LYUBOV ANDREYEVNA: "I am above love!" You're not above love, but as Firs would say, you are a nincompoop! Not to have a lover at your age!

TROFIMOV: *(In horror)* This is horrible! What is she saying?! *(He quickly goes into the ballroom, clutching his head)* It is horrible... I cannot... I am leaving... *(He exits, but immediately returns)* Everything is over between us! *(He goes into the entry hall)*

LYUBOV ANDREYEVNA: *(She cries after)* Petya, wait a moment! Silly man, I was joking! Petya!

> *We hear a crash, as if someone has fallen down the stairs. ANYA and VARYA cry out, followed by an immediate burst of laughter.*

What happened?

> *ANYA runs in.*

ANYA: *(Laughing)* Petya fell down the stairs! *(She runs out)*

LYUBOV ANDREYEVNA: What a crackpot Petya is...

> *The STATIONMASTER comes to a stop in the middle of the ballroom and reads "To the Sinner" by A. Tolstoy:*

STATIONMASTER:
"The crowd gushes, gaiety, laughter abound;
The ballroom, richly adorned, rings with their sound.
Everywhere the glitter of crystal and gold.
Beyond the long ballroom, she reigns;
Her immodest dress reveals what must not be told,
Her dang'rous charm lures men in,
Gazing upon her they all fall to sin."

> *They listen to him, but he has barely read a few lines when the sound of a waltz carries in from the ballroom and the reading comes abruptly to an end. Everyone dances. TROFIMOV, ANYA, VARYA, and LYUBOV ANDREYEVNA cross into the ballroom.*

LYUBOV ANDREYEVNA: Well, "Professor Purity"… well, Petya… I beg your forgiveness… Come dance… *(She dances with PETYA)*

> *ANYA and VARYA dance.*

> *FIRS enters, stands his cane near the side of the door. YASHA also has come in from the drawing room, he watches the dances.*

YASHA: What is it, Grandpa?

FIRS: Don't feel well. In the old days we had generals, Barons, admirals dancing at our balls, but now we send for the postal clerk and the station master, and they do not come willingly. I feel weak. The late master, the grandfather, cured all our illnesses with sealing-wax. I have been taking sealing-wax every day for over twenty years — maybe I'm alive because of it.

YASHA: I am sick of you, Grandpa. *(He yawns)* If only you'd shrivel up and die soon.

FIRS: Ekh, you… nincompoop! *(Mutters)*

> *TROFIMOV and LYUBOV ANDREYEVNA dance in the ballroom, then in the drawing room.*

LYUBOV ANDREYEVNA: *Merci.* I need to sit for a bit... *(She sits)* I'm tired.

   *ANYA enters.*

ANYA: *(Anxiously)* In the kitchen just now, some man said that the cherry orchard has been sold.

LYUBOV ANDREYEVNA: To whom was it sold?

ANYA: He didn't say. He left. *(She dances with TROFIMOV, they both exit into the ballroom)*

YASHA: That was just some old man jabbering. A stranger.

FIRS: And Leonid Andreyich is still gone, he hasn't come back. The top-coat he's wearing is light, I'm afraid he will catch a cold. Ekh, youngsters!

LYUBOV ANDREYEVNA: I can't stand it. Yasha, go find out to whom it was sold.

YASHA: He left a long time ago, that old man. *(He laughs)*

YEPIKHODOV: *(Offstage)* Off the right ball to the corner, I cut to the middle.

LYUBOV ANDREYEVNA: *(Slightly irritated)* Well, what are you laughing at? What are you so happy about?

YASHA: Yepikhodov sure is a riot. What a waste! "A disaster waiting to happen."

LYUBOV ANDREYEVNA: Firs, if the orchard is sold, where will you go?

FIRS: Where you order me to go, I will go.

LYUBOV ANDREYEVNA: Why are you so pale? Are you ill? You should sleep...

FIRS: Yes… *(With a smile)* I should sleep, and who will serve? Who will see to things? Only me in the whole house.

YASHA: *(To LYUBOV ANDREYEVNA)* Lyubov Andreyevna! Permit me to make a request, be so kind! If you go to Paris again, take me with you, do me that favor. It is positively impossible for me to stay here. *(He looks around, in an undertone)* You can see for yourself, the whole country is uneducated, the people are immoral, and the boredom — in the kitchen they feed us disgracefully, and Firs goes around mumbling all kinds of ridiculous things all the time. Take me with you, for the love of God!

*PISCHIK enters.*

PISCHIK: Allow me to invite you… to a waltz, most beautiful… *(LYUBOV ANDREYEVNA goes to him)* Charming, but all the same I must have one hundred eighty *rubles* from you… I need it… *(They dance)* One hundred eighty *rubles*…

*They cross into the ballroom.*

YASHA: *(Quietly sings)* "Can't you see my heart is breaking?"

*In the ballroom a figure in a grey top hat and in checked trousers waves her arms and jumps. There are shouts: "Bravo, Charlotta Ivanovna!"*

DUNYASHA: *(Stopping to powder her nose)* The mistress ordered me to dance — there are many gentlemen, but very few ladies, — and my head is spinning from dancing, my heart is pounding. Firs Nikolayevich, just now the official from the post office said something to me that simply took my breath away.

*The music stops.*

FIRS: What did he say?

DUNYASHA: "You," he said, "are like a flower."

YASHA: *(Yawns)* As if he knows anything — *(He exits)*

DUNYASHA: "Like a flower"... I am such a delicate girl, I love tender words so very much.

FIRS: They'll be the death of you.

　*YEPIKHODOV enters.*

YEPIKHODOV: Avdotya Fyodorovna, you run away from me... as though I am some kind of insect. *(Sighs)* Ekh, life!

DUNYASHA: Are you speaking to me?

YEPIKHODOV: Undoubtedly, perhaps, you are right. *(Sighs)* But, strictly speaking, if I look at it from another point of view, I will permit myself to express myself like this: pardon my bluntness, you have completely reduced me to an utter state of mind. I know my *fortuna*, every day some sort of new misfortune happens to me, and I have been accustomed to this for a long time, so that with a smile I gaze at my own lot in life. You gave me your word, and although I...

DUNYASHA: I beg you, we can talk later on, but leave me in peace. Now I am dreaming. *(She plays with her fan)*

YEPIKHODOV: A new misfortune every day, and I, strictly speaking, I just smile, I even laugh.

　*VARYA enters from the ballroom.*

VARYA: You haven't left yet, Semyon? What an ill-bred man you are! *(To DUNYASHA)* Off with you, Dunyasha. *(To YEPIKHODOV)* You play billiards and break a cue, then you walk around the drawing room like a guest.

YEPIKHODOV: Permit me to express to you, I am not accountable to you.

VARYA: Accountable! You just keep your mouth shut! All you do is wander around this house, never doing anything helpful. Someone please tell me, why do we employ a bookkeeper?

YEPIKHODOV: *(Hurt)* If I work, if I wander around, if I eat, if I play billiards, only people of proper understanding and maturity can discuss that with me.

VARYA: You dare say that to me! *(Flaring up)* You dare? So, I don't understand anything? Get out of here! This minute!

YEPIKHODOV: *(Cowering)* I beg you to express yourself in a more delicate fashion.

VARYA: *(Losing her temper)* Get out of here this minute! Out!

*He goes to the door, she after him.*

"Disaster waiting to happen!" Don't ever darken this door again! I don't ever want to see you here again!

*YEPIKHODOV has exited; from the other side of the door his voice: "I will lodge a complaint about you."*

Oh, are you coming back? *(She takes the cane FIRS stood by the door)* Come… Come… Come, I have something to show you… Oh, are you coming? Are you coming? This is for you… (*She raises it threateningly, at the same time LOPAKHIN enters*)

LOPAKHIN: Damn — thanks a lot.

VARYA: *(Angrily and sarcastically)* It's my fault!

LOPAKHIN: Please, it's nothing. I give you my most humble thanks for the lovely welcome.

VARYA: Don't mention it. *(She moves away, then looks around and asks softly)* Did I hurt you?

LOPAKHIN: No, it's nothing. The lump coming up, however, is humongous.

*A voice in the ballroom: "Lopakhin is here! Yermolai Alekseyevich!"*

PISCHIK: Here he is, in the flesh! *(He and LOPAKHIN kiss one another)* You smell slightly of cognac, my dear, my soul. And we're enjoying ourselves here too.

*LYUBOV ANDREYEVNA enters.*

LYUBOV ANDREYEVNA: Is that you, Yermolai Alekseyevich? What took so long? Where's Leonid?

LOPAKHIN: Leonid Andreyevich came with me, he is coming…

LYUBOV ANDREYEVNA: *(Agitatedly)* Well, what? Was there an auction? Say something!

LOPAKHIN: *(Confused, afraid to reveal his joy)* The auction was over by four o'clock… We got to the train station late, we had to wait until nine-thirty. *(Sighing heavily)* Oof! My head is spinning a little…

*GAYEV enters; in his right hand is a package, with his left he wipes tears.*

LYUBOV ANDREYEVNA: Lyonya, what? Lyonya, well? *(Impatiently, with tears)* Quickly, for God's sake…

GAYEV: *(He doesn't speak to her, he only waves his hand; to FIRS, weeping)* Take these… They're anchovies, Kerch herrings… I ate nothing today… You can't imagine what I have been through —

*The door to the billiard room is open; one can hear the tap of balls and YASHA's voice: "Yellow ball to the corner, cut to the center." GAYEV's expression changes, he is no longer crying.*

I am terribly tired. Firs, help me change clothes. *(He exits to his room across the hall, FIRS after him)*

PISCHIK: What about the auction? Tell us!

LYUBOV ANDREYEVNA: Was the cherry orchard sold?

LOPAKHIN: It was sold.

LYUBOV ANDREYEVNA: Who bought it?

LOPAKHIN: I bought it.

*Pause.*

*LYUBOV ANDREYEVNA feels faint. She sits. VARYA takes the keys from her belt, throws them onto the floor in the middle of the drawing room, and exits.*

LOPAKHIN: I bought it! Wait a minute, Ladies and Gentlemen, be so kind, my head is spinning, I can't speak... *(He laughs)* We arrived at the auction, Deriganov was already there. Leonid Andreyich had only fifteen thousand, but right away Deriganov bid thirty more than the mortgage. I see, so that's how it's going, I leap in with him, offer forty. He forty-five. Me fifty-five. He then increases it by five, I by ten... five, ten, five, ten... well, it ended. I bid ninety thousand over the debt, and it was mine. The cherry orchard is now mine! Mine! *(He guffaws)* My God, Lord, the cherry orchard is mine! Tell me, am I drunk, am I crazy, am I dreaming... *(He stamps his feet)* Don't laugh at me! If my father and grandfather were to get up from their graves and see this moment, how their Yermolai, beaten, barely-literate Yermolai, who ran barefoot in the winter, how that same Yermolai bought the estate — the most beautiful estate in the world. I bought the estate, where my grandfather and father were serfs, where they weren't even permitted in the kitchen. I'm dreaming. I must be crazy, it can't be true... *(He picks up the keys, affectionately smiling)* She threw the keys down, she wants to show that she is no longer the mistress of the house — *(He jingles the keys)* Well, it makes no difference.

*One can hear the orchestra tuning up.*

Hey, musicians, play, I want music! Everyone come and see how Yermolai Lopakhin chops down every tree in the cherry orchard — every damn one of them. We'll build summer houses, and our grandchildren and great-grandchildren will see a new life here... Music, play!

*Music plays. LYUBOV ANDREYEVNA lowers herself onto a chair and cries bitterly.*

*(With reproach)* Why, why didn't you listen to me? My poor, good friend, we can't go back now. *(With tears)* Oh, if only all of this would pass, if somehow our absurd, unhappy lives would pass.

PISCHIK: *(He takes him by the arm, quietly)* She is crying. Let's go into the ballroom. Leave her alone... Come... *(He takes him by the arm and leads him to the ballroom)*

LOPAKHIN: What's wrong? Music, play louder! Let's have it the way I want it! *(With irony)* A new landowner is coming, a new master of the cherry orchard! *(He accidentally pushes the little table, almost toppling the candelabra)* I can pay for everything! *(He leaves with PISCHIK)*

*In the ballroom and drawing room there is no one except LYUBOV ANDREYEVNA, who is sitting, bitterly crying, her entire body contracted. The music plays quietly. ANYA and TROFIMOV enter quickly. ANYA crosses to her mother and kneels in front of her. TROFIMOV remains in the entrance to the ballroom.*

ANYA: Mama! Mama, are you crying? My sweet, kind, good mama, my beautiful, I love you... I bless you. The cherry orchard was sold, it is already gone, it is true, true, but don't cry, Mama, your life is still ahead of you, your good, pure soul remains... Come with me, come away from here, come! We'll plant a new orchard, more splendid than this, you'll see, you'll understand, and joy, quiet, true joy will fill your soul, like the sun at twilight, and you'll smile, Mama! Come, sweet! Come!

*CURTAIN.*

# ACT IV

*The Nursery. There are neither curtains on the windows, nor pictures. The little furniture that remains is piled in one corner, as if for sale. A feeling of emptiness. Near the front door and at back of the stage suitcases and trunks are piled up. On the left a door is open, VARYA and ANYA's voices are heard. LOPAKHIN stands, waiting. YASHA holds a tray with little glasses, filled with champagne. In the entry hall YEPIKHODOV packs a suitcase. Offstage there are voices of the peasants who have come to say goodbye. The voice of GAYEV: "Thank you, brothers, thank you."*

YASHA: The peasants came to say goodbye. It is my opinion, Yermolai Alekseyich, the people of this country are good-hearted, but they really comprehend nothing.

*The noise dies down. LYUBOV ANDREYEVNA and GAYEV enter through the entry hall; she is not crying, but is pale, her face trembles, she is unable to speak.*

GAYEV: You gave all your money away, Lyuba. You can't do that! You cannot do that!

LYUBOV ANDREYEVNA: I couldn't help it! I couldn't help it!

*They both exit.*

LOPAKHIN: *(Through the door, after them)* Please, I most humbly beg you! Have a farewell glass of champagne. I forgot to bring any from town, but I found a bottle at the train station. Please!

*Pause.*

Well, Ladies and Gentlemen, don't you want any? *(He moves away from the door)* If I had known, I wouldn't have bought it. Well then, I won't have any.

*YASHA carefully rests the tray on a chair.*

At least you have a drink, Yasha.

YASHA: To those departing! Good fortune to those who remain! *(He drinks)* This champagne is not the good stuff, I can assure you.

LOPAKHIN: Eight *rubles* a bottle.

   *Pause.*

It is damned cold in here.

YASHA: They didn't light the stove today. It doesn't matter since we are leaving. *(He laughs)*

LOPAKHIN: Why are you laughing?

YASHA: Because I'm so happy.

LOPAKHIN: It's October but it's sunny and quiet, like in the summer. Good weather for building. *(Glancing at his watch, through the door)* Ladies and Gentlemen, please remember you have forty-six minutes remaining until the train departs! It means we leave for the station in twenty minutes. Hurry.

   *TROFIMOV enters from outside in a topcoat.*

TROFIMOV: I think it's time to go. The horses are here. Where the hell are my galoshes? I've lost them. *(Through the door)* Anya, my galoshes aren't here! I can't find them!

LOPAKHIN: And I have to go to Kharkov. I'm taking the same train as you. I'll spend the whole winter in Kharkov. I stood around all summer yammering with you and I did nothing. I can't be without work, I don't know what to do with my hands; they just hang there, like they were somebody else's.

TROFIMOV: We're leaving soon, and you can once again go back to your useful work.

LOPAKHIN: Have a little champagne.

TROFIMOV: No thanks.

LOPAKHIN: So, now Moscow?

TROFIMOV: Yes, I'll take them to town, and tomorrow I'll go to Moscow.

LOPAKHIN: Yes… Well, the professors must have stopped giving lectures. They must be waiting for you to arrive!

TROFIMOV: Cut it out.

LOPAKHIN: How many years have you been studying at the university?

TROFIMOV: Think up something new, we've heard it all before. *(He looks for the galoshes)* You know, very likely, we won't see one another again, so permit me to give you a piece of advice before we all leave: Stop waving your arms all around! Break yourself of the habit — of… *(He gestures waving his arms)* And building summer cottages here, counting on vacationers becoming individual "agriculturists," relying on that — that's waving your arms around too… Well, what the hell, I like you anyway. You have fine, beautiful hands, like an artist, you have a fine, beautiful soul…

LOPAKHIN: *(Embraces him)* Farewell, my friend. Thank you for everything. Here, take some money for the trip.

TROFIMOV: Why? I don't need it.

LOPAKHIN: But you don't have any.

TROFIMOV: I have. Thank you. I received some for a translation. It's here in my pocket. *(Anxiously)* But where are my galoshes!

VARYA: *(From the other room)* Take your filth! *(She throws a pair of rubber galoshes onstage)*

TROFIMOV: Why are you angry, Varya? Hm... These aren't even my galoshes!

LOPAKHIN: In the spring I planted poppy seeds on twenty-seven hundred acres and now I've earned a clean forty thousand — and when my poppies were in bloom, what a picture it was!— So here I am telling you, I earned forty thousand and it means I can give you a loan. Why turn your nose up? I am just a peasant... no ceremony.

TROFIMOV: Your father was a peasant, mine, a pharmacist — and from this follows absolutely nothing.

*LOPAKHIN takes out his wallet and stuffs the money into TROFIMOV's pocket.*

Take it back, take it back. Even if you offered me two hundred thousand, I wouldn't take it. I'm a free person. And the things that all of you value so much don't have the slightest power over me. It's like a puff of smoke in the wind. I can manage without you, I don't need your money. I am strong and proud. Humanity is moving toward a higher truth, to the greatest happiness possible on earth, and I am in the front ranks!

LOPAKHIN: Will you reach it?

TROFIMOV: I will reach it.

*Pause.*

I will reach it or I will show others the way to reach it.

*In the distance one can hear an axe tapping on a tree.*

LOPAKHIN: Well then, farewell, my friend. It is time to go. We've been turning up our noses at one another, but you know, life is short. When I am hard at work, without stopping, without resting, then my thoughts become a little more clear, and I start to understand why I am here on this earth. But tell me brother, how many people are there in Russia who have any idea why they exist? Well, the world keeps spinning all the same. They say Leonid Andreyich took a position at the bank, six thousand a year... but you know he won't hold down the job, he's very lazy...

ANYA: *(In the doorway)* Mama asks, please don't start chopping down the orchard until she has left.

TROFIMOV: Can't you show some respect? *(He exits through the entry hall)*

LOPAKHIN: Yes, of course... Damn it, how could I let that happen — *(He exits after him)*

ANYA: Did they send Firs to the hospital?

YASHA: I told them to this morning. I'm sure they sent him.

ANYA: *(To YEPIKHODOV, who is crossing through the hall)* Semyon Panteleyich, please ask someone if they took Firs to the hospital.

YASHA: *(Offended)* I've already done that. Why ask for the tenth time!

YEPIKHODOV: The aged Firs, in my personal opinion, is not fit for mending, he should join his forefathers. And I can only envy him. *(He has laid his suitcase on a hatbox and crushed it)* Well, there, of course. I should have known. *(He exits)*

YASHA: *(Derisively)* "A disaster waiting to happen..."

VARYA: *(From the other side of the door)* Did they take Firs to the hospital?

ANYA: They took him.

VARYA: Why didn't they take the letter to the doctor?

ANYA: We need to send it after him... *(She exits)*

VARYA: *(From the neighboring room)* Where is Yasha? Tell him his mother has come and wants to say goodbye to him.

YASHA: *(Waving his arm)* She's driving me crazy.

*DUNYASHA all of this time is busying herself about the luggage. Now, when YASHA is left alone, she goes to him.*

DUNYASHA: Look at me once, Yasha. You are leaving… abandoning me… *(She weeps and throws her arms around his neck)*

YASHA: What's there to cry about? *(He drinks champagne)* In six days I'll be in Paris again. Tomorrow I'll be sitting on the express and whoosh! *(Makes a noise like a speeding train)* I just can't believe it. *Vive la France!* This place is not for me, I can't live here… that's the truth. Enough of this ignorance and ill breeding! *(He drinks champagne)* What is there to cry about? Learn to behave yourself, then you won't need to cry.

DUNYASHA: *(She powders her face, looking in the mirror)* Send me a letter from Paris. I loved you, Yasha, loved you so! I am a delicate creature, Yasha!

YASHA: They're coming. *(He busies himself near the suitcases, quietly humming)*

*LYUBOV ANDREYEVNA, GAYEV, ANYA and CHARLOTTA IVANOVNA enter.*

GAYEV: We must go. There's not much time left. *(Looking at YASHA)* Who smells like herring?

LYUBOV ANDREYEVNA: We must be seated in the carriage in ten minutes. *(She glances over the room)* Farewell, sweet home, old friend. Winter will go by, spring will come, and you won't be here anymore, they are going to tear you down. These walls have seen so much! *(She feverishly kisses her daughter)* My treasure, you are radiant, your eyes are sparkling like two diamonds. Are you happy? Very?

ANYA:  Very! A new life is beginning, Mama!

GAYEV:  *(Cheerfully)* Indeed, everything is good now. Until the sale of the cherry orchard we were in such a state, but once the matter was finally decided, irrevocably, everyone calmed down, even became cheerful… I am a banker… now I am a financier… yellow ball to the center. And you, Lyuba, you look so much better.

LYUBOV ANDREYEVNA:  Yes. My nerves are better, that's true.

*They give her her hat and coat.*

I'm sleeping well. Carry my things, Yasha. It's time. *(To ANYA)* My little girl, we will see one another soon… I will go to Paris, I'll live there on the money your great aunt sent to buy the estate — long live your great aunt! — but the money won't last long, I'm afraid.

ANYA:  Mama, you will return soon, soon… won't you? I'll study hard and get my degree and then I'll go to work so I can help you. Mama, we'll read books together… won't we? *(She kisses her mother's hand)* We'll read in the autumn evenings, read many books and a new, miraculous world will open before us… *(She dreams)* Mama, do come back…

LYUBOV ANDREYEVNA:  I will, my treasure. *(She embraces her daughter)*

*LOPAKHIN enters. CHARLOTTA quietly hums a song.*

GAYEV:  Charlotta is happy, she is singing!

CHARLOTTA:  *(She carries a bundle resembling a wrapped baby)* My little baby, bye, bye…

*The crying of a baby can be heard: "Wa, wa!"*

Hush, my good, my sweet child.

*"Wa! wa!"*

I feel so sorry for you! *(She throws the bundle on a piece of luggage)* Please find me a job. I can't go on like this.

LOPAKHIN: We will find you something, Charlotta Ivanovna, don't worry.

GAYEV: Everyone is leaving us, Varya is going away… we have suddenly become superfluous.

CHARLOTTA: I can't live in this town. I must leave… *(She hums)* It doesn't matter…

*PISCHIK enters.*

LOPAKHIN: The miracle of nature!

PISCHIK: *(Out of breath)* Oh, let me recover my breath… I am worn out… My most honorable… Give me water…

GAYEV: Ah, you're here for money? Your obedient servant, I will remove myself from sin… *(He exits)*

PISCHIK: It's been ages since I've been here. Most beautiful… *(To LOPAKHIN)* You're here… I am happy to see you… a man of most colossal intellect… take… receive… *(He gives LOPAKHIN money)* Four hundred *rubles*… I still owe you eight hundred forty…

LOPAKHIN: *(Shrugs his shoulders in bewilderment)* It's like a dream… Where did you get it?

PISCHIK: Hold on… it's so hot in here… a most extraordinary thing happened. Some Englishmen came to my place and found some kind of white clay on my land… *(To LYUBOV ANDREYEVNA)* And four hundred for you… beautiful, astonishing… *(He gives her money)* The rest later. *(He drinks water)* Just now a young man was saying on the train, he thought he was some kind of philosopher, he started telling people,

"Jump. Just jump off the roof." As if this was his whole philosophy. What a world! Water!

LOPAKHIN: Who were these Englishmen?

PISCHIK: I leased them the lot with the clay for twenty-four years... What a world! But now, forgive me, there is no time... I must ride much farther... I am going to Znoikov's... to Kardamonov's...I owe everyone... *(He drinks)* I wish you well... I will come back on Thursday...

LYUBOV ANDREYEVNA: We're leaving for town now, and tomorrow I'm going abroad...

PISCHIK: What? *(Anxiously)* Where? Oh I see the furniture... suitcases... Well, never mind... *(On the verge of tears)* Never mind... People of supreme intellect... these Englishmen... Never mind... Be happy... God help you... Never mind... Everything on this earth comes to an end... *(He kisses LYUBOV ANDREYEVNA's hand)* And if you should hear that my end has finally come, remember this old... horse and say: "On earth there was such and such a man... as Simyonov-Pischik... God rest his soul"... Most splendid weather... Yes... *(He exits strongly embarrassed, but immediately returns and says in the doorway)* Dashenka sends her regards! *(He exits)*

LYUBOV ANDREYEVNA: Now we can go. I'm leaving with two things on my mind. First — Firs is ill. *(Glancing at her watch)* Maybe five minutes more...

ANYA: Mama, they've already sent Firs to the hospital. Yasha sent him this morning.

LYUBOV ANDREYEVNA: My second problem — Varya. She is used to getting up early and working, and now without work she'll be like a fish out of water. She has grown thin, she has grown quiet and the poor little thing cries...

*Pause.*

Yermolai Alekseyich, you know very well that I was hoping… you would marry her, and everything looked as though it was going that way. *(She whispers to ANYA, who nods to CHARLOTTA, and they both exit)* She loves you, and I think she is to your liking, and I don't know, I don't know why you two just avoid one another. I don't understand!

LOPAKHIN: To tell you the truth, neither do I. Everything is so strange… If there's still time, then I am ready now… Let's get it over with — *basta*. But without you still here, I don't think I can do it.

LYUBOV ANDREYEVNA: Superb. You'll only need a minute. I'll call her now…

LOPAKHIN: Luckily we have champagne.

LYUBOV ANDREYEVNA: *(Animatedly)* Wonderful. We'll leave —

LOPAKHIN: *(He casts a glance at the bottle)* It's empty, somebody already drank it.

*YASHA coughs.*

That's what they call lapping it up…

LYUBOV ANDREYEVNA: Yasha, *allez*! I'll call her… *(Through the door)* Varya, leave everything, come here. Come! *(She exits with YASHA)*

LOPAKHIN: *(Looking at his watch)* Yes…

*Pause.*

*Behind the door is restrained laughter, whispering, finally VARYA enters.*

VARYA: *(She inspects the luggage for a long time)* It's strange, somehow I can't find…

LOPAKHIN: What are you looking for?

VARYA: I packed it myself and I can't remember.

*Pause.*

LOPAKHIN: Where are you going now, Varvara Mikhailovna?

VARYA: I? To the Ragulins… I agreed to take care of their home… as a… housekeeper.

LOPAKHIN: Is that in Yashnevo? That's fifty miles.

*Pause.*

Looks like life in this house has come to an end…

VARYA: *(Looking around at the luggage)* Where is it… Or, maybe, I packed it in the trunk… Yes, life in this house is coming to an end… it will be no more…

LOPAKHIN: And I am leaving for Kharkov now… on the same train. A lot to do. And I'll leave Yepikhodov in charge of the estate… I hired him.

VARYA: *(She gasps)* Who…?

LOPAKHIN: Last year at this time, if you recall, it was snowing already, but now it's quiet, sunny. Only it's cold… Three degrees below zero.

VARYA: I didn't notice.

*Pause.*

Besides our thermometer is broken…

*Pause. A voice in the door from the courtyard: "Yermolai Alekseyevich!"*

LOPAKHIN: *(As though he has long been waiting for this summons)* I'm coming. *(He quickly exits)*

*VARYA, sitting on the floor, lays her head on a bundle, quietly sobs. The door opens, LYUBOV ANDREYEVNA carefully enters.*

LYUBOV ANDREYEVNA: Well?

*Pause.*

We must go.

VARYA: *(No longer crying, she rubs her eyes)* Yes, it's time, Mamochka. I have just enough time to get to the Ragulins' today. Hopefully we won't be late for the train.

LYUBOV ANDREYEVNA: *(Through the door)* Anya, get ready!

*ANYA enters, then GAYEV, CHARLOTTA IVANOVNA. GAYEV wears a warm topcoat with a hood. The servants come in. YEPIKHODOV busies himself with the luggage.*

Now we can start our journey.

ANYA: *(Joyfully)* Our journey!

GAYEV: My friends, my sweet, dear friends! Abandoning this home forever, can I be silent, can I hold myself back and not express those feelings that fill my being…

ANYA: *(Imploringly)* Uncle!

VARYA: Uncle dear, you shouldn't!

GAYEV: *(Dejectedly)* Yellow ball to the center with a bank shot… I will be quiet…

*TROFIMOV enters, then LOPAKHIN.*

TROFIMOV: Well, Ladies and Gentlemen, it is time to go!

LOPAKHIN: Yepikhodov, my coat!

LYUBOV ANDREYEVNA: I'll sit for one more minute. This feels good, so good… It's as though I've never seen these walls before, these ceilings, and now I look upon them so greedily, with such tender love…

GAYEV: I remember, when I was six years old, on Trinity Sunday I stood at this window and watched my father go to church…

LYUBOV ANDREYEVNA: Did they take all of our things?

LOPAKHIN: It looks like it. *(To YEPIKHODOV)* Yepikhodov, will you see that everything is in order.

YEPIKHODOV: *(He speaks in a hoarse voice)* Don't you worry, Yermolai Alekseyich!

LOPAKHIN: What's wrong with your voice?

YEPIKHODOV: Just now when I drank some water, I swallowed something.

YASHA: *(With contempt)* Disaster…

LYUBOV ANDREYEVNA: We will leave — and not a soul will remain here…

LOPAKHIN: Until spring.

VARYA: *(She takes an umbrella from a bundle, it looks as if she is raising it threateningly; LOPAKHIN pretends he is frightened)* You don't really— you don't actually… I wasn't even thinking of that…

TROFIMOV: Ladies and gentlemen, please take a seat in the carriage… It's time! The train will arrive momentarily.

VARYA: Petya, here they are — your galoshes, by the suitcase. *(With tears)* And they're so dirty, so old…

TROFIMOV: *(Putting on the galoshes)* Let's go, ladies and gentlemen!

GAYEV: *(Strongly embarrassed, afraid he will begin to cry)* The train... the station... curve to the center, white with a bank shot to the corner...

LYUBOV ANDREYEVNA: Let's go!

LOPAKHIN: Is everybody here? No one in there? *(He locks the side door on the left)* Okay, locked. I've got some things piled up in there. Let's go!

ANYA: Farewell, house! Farewell, old life!

TROFIMOV: Hello, new life! *(He exits with ANYA)*

*VARYA takes a look around the room and takes her time exiting. YASHA and CHARLOTTA exit with a dog.*

LOPAKHIN: Well, then, until spring. Let's go, Ladies and Gentlemen... See ya soon! *(He exits)*

*LYUBOV ANDREYEVNA and GAYEV remain, the two together. As if they had been waiting for this, throw their arms around one another and sob restrainedly, quietly, frightened they will be heard.*

GAYEV: *(In desperation)* My sister, my sister...

LYUBOV ANDREYEVNA: Oh, my sweet, my delicate, beautiful orchard! My life, my youth, my happiness, farewell! Farewell!

*ANYA's voice happily calling: "Mama!" TROFIMOV's voice, excitedly: "Halloo!"*

LYUBOV ANDREYEVNA: *(She cries)* Shh, we must cry quietly... Listen... Last time to look at the walls, at the windows... Our dear mother loved to walk in this room...

GAYEV: My sister, my sister!

*ANYA's voice: "Mama!" TROFIMOV's voice: "Hello!"*

LYUBOV ANDREYEVNA: We're coming!

*They exit.*

*The stage is empty. We can hear a key lock the main door, then the carriages departing. It becomes quiet. Amid the silence we hear the muffled tap of an axe on a tree, it sounds solitary and sad. Footsteps are heard. FIRS appears from the right door. He is dressed, as always, in a jacket and white waistcoat, slippers on his feet. He is ill.*

FIRS: *(He goes to the door, tries the handle)* Locked. They left... *(He sits on the couch)* They forgot about me... Never mind... I'll sit here for a little while... oh, it's so good... I'm sure Leonid Andreyevich didn't put on his fur coat, he went in a topcoat... *(He sighs, preoccupied)* I didn't look after him... Youngsters! *(He mutters something, which cannot be understood)* Life just slipped by, as if I wasn't there at all. I need to lie down for a bit... No strength, nothing left, nothing... Ekh, you... nincompoop! *(He sits motionless)*

*A distant sound can be heard, as if from the sky, the sound of a breaking string, dying away, mournfully. Silence sets in, and we can only hear, far away in the orchard, an axe tapping on a tree.*

CURTAIN.

# *About Libby Appel*

In twenty seasons at OSF: Artistic director, 1995-2007. Director: thirty productions including *Seagull* (also adapter); *Pride and Prejudice*; *Paradise Lost*; *A View from the Bridge*; *The Cherry Orchard* (also adapter); *The Tempest*; *The Winter's Tale* (2006, 1990); *Bus Stop*; *Richard III*; *Richard II*; *Macbeth*; *Saturday, Sunday, Monday*; *The Trip to Bountiful*; *Three Sisters*; *Henry V*; *Hamlet*; *Measure for Measure*; *Uncle Vanya*; *King Lear*; *The Magic Fire* (also at the Kennedy Center); *The Merchant of Venice*; *Enrico IV* (The Emperor); *The Seagull* (OSF Portland)

**Other theatres**: Intiman Theatre, Guthrie Theater, Indiana Repertory Theatre, Seattle Repertory Theatre, South Coast Repertory, PlayMakers Repertory Company, Arizona Theatre Company, Alliance Theatre, Milwaukee Repertory Theater, New Mexico Repertory, Goodman Theatre, Court Theatre, Syracuse Stage, Repertory Theatre of St. Louis, San Jose Repertory Theatre, Utah Shakespearean Festival, and the Alabama, Colorado and Kern Shakespeare Festivals.

**Other credits**: Artistic Director, Indiana Repertory Theatre 1992-1996; Dean and Artistic Director, School of Theatre at the California Institute of the Arts; Head of the Acting Program at California State University, Long Beach; wrote *Mask Characterization: An Acting Process*; created and produced *Inter/Face: The Actor and the Mask* (video); co-author of two plays, *Shakespeare's Women and Shakespeare's Lovers*; OSF-commissioned new adaptations of Chekhov's *The Cherry Orchard*, *Seagull*, *Uncle Vanya*, *Three Sisters*, and *Ivanov*.

**Education**: Honorary doctorates from Southern Oregon University, University of Portland and Willamette University; M.A., Northwestern University; B.A., University of Michigan (Phi Beta Kappa).

**Awards**: Kennedy Center 2010 Stephen and Christine Schwarzman Legacy Award for Lifetime Achievement and Excellence in Theatre.

# *About Allison Horsley*

Allison Horsley has worked as a dramaturg on plays and musicals for the O'Neill National Music Theater Conference, Denver Center Theatre Company, Oregon Shakespeare Festival, Kitchen Dog Theater, La Jolla Playhouse, Yale Repertory Theatre, Baltimore's Centerstage, and Dallas Theater Center. Since its La Jolla premiere in 2004, she has been the dramaturg for the Tony-winning musical *Jersey Boys*. Other Broadway developmental or research contributions include *Chaplin* and *Dracula, the Musical*. She is a frequent collaborator with writer/performer Luciann Lajoie, whose multi-media production *Date\** premiered at Off-Center @ The Jones (Denver Center Theatre Company) and is now touring. Allison holds an MFA from the Yale School of Drama and is an associate professor at University of Denver.